Rich
Tradition

*How **Rich Brooks** revived the football
fortunes of the Kentucky Wildcats*

Tom Leach
Voice of the Wildcats

Presenting Sponsor

Central Bank | UK

OFFICIAL BANK OF UK ATHLETICS

The
Clark
Group

Lexington, Kentucky

"Touchdown
Kentucky"
Tom Leach

Clark Publishing
dba The Clark Group
250 East Short Street
Lexington, KY 40507
800 944 3995
info@theclarkgroupinfo.com

Visit our Web site at www.TheClarkGroupInfo.com

First Edition: August 2009

Printed in the United States of America by
Welch Printing, Louisville, Ky.
www.welchprinting.com

10 9 8 7 6 5 4 3 2 1

ISBN: 978-0-9822201-5-3 Softcover Edition
ISBN: 978-0-9822201-6-0 Hardcover Edition

Cover photo by David Coyle
Cover design by Sid Webb
Book design by Kelly Elliott

Table of Contents

Rich Tradition

Introduction

"I HAVE TRIED TO TEACH THEM to show class, have pride and display character. I think winning games takes care of itself if you do that."

That quote comes from Paul "Bear" Bryant, the most successful football coach ever at the University of Kentucky. It's a statement that could have easily come from Rich Brooks, who could conceivably be the school's second-winningest coach—if he stays on the job long enough.

At the end of Brooks' third season at UK in 2005, it is safe to assume that no one outside the Wildcat football family thought that kind of accomplishment was even remotely possible.

In his first three seasons at Kentucky, Brooks' teams won nine games. Since Bryant left the program for Texas A&M in the 1950's, John Ray (with seven victories) was the only coach to win as infrequently as Brooks in the first three years at the helm. And seven games into the '06 campaign, a 49-0 loss at LSU dropped the Wildcats to 3-4.

Two-and-a-half years later, Brooks' teams have won 20 of their last 32 games, including an upset of a number one team and three consecutive bowl wins, a feat unprecedented at Kentucky. At a school without a winning tradition in football, with a coach who many felt was over the hill, a turnaround that dramatic is unheard-of. And Brooks did not accomplish this by deploying some revolutionary piece of new strategy. He just believed in his players and more importantly, they believed in him. That's what made this story so interesting that I thought a book that explores it in more depth might find a very receptive audience in Kentucky.

It's refreshing that values like honesty, loyalty, integrity and consistency still resonate with young people and cut across generational and cultural divides. Every current or former player I sought out, even the ones from a disappointing first season under Brooks, was eager to talk about his respect and admiration for this coach and what he has done for the Kentucky program.

So how did this coach who was almost eligible for Social Security when he took the job make such a strong connection with a group of mostly 18-to-22 year old football players? I think former Kentucky free safety Marcus McClinton put it best when I asked him for one word to describe Brooks. "Real," he replied. A 2008 sciencedaily.com story cited a study on narcissism in today's youth as compared to three decades earlier. It found no difference in the levels of "arrogance, exhibitionism and a sense of entitlement." So despite all the technological advances and new ways of communicating, young people have remained consistent. Perhaps the reason Brooks has connected with his young men so strongly is that he, too, is consistent in his interaction with those players.

We've seen it before at Kentucky in the person of Jerry Claiborne, who earned the respect of his players more for his substance than his style. Claiborne came as close as any coach before Brooks to getting Kentucky football on an upward track. Ask Brooks why the Cats have enjoyed this run of success, and he will point back to the players. He's right, of course, but it is the head coach and his staff who made the recruiting evaluations and sales pitches to get those players into UK uniforms.

I came across the Bear Bryant quote the same day former Wildcat star Jeremy Jarmon had to announce to the world that he had inadvertently taken an NCAA banned substance, costing him his final season of eligibility at UK. To see him break down in tears as he completed his statement was heartbreaking, but the class he showed in that moment of incredible disappointment spoke well of his character. And it also speaks well of the kinds of players Brooks and his staff have recruited—players with the mental toughness to keep working when others might have given up and waited for the next coach to take his shot at transforming Kentucky football.

That resiliency has been the hallmark of the Kentucky football fan. Despite limited success since Bryant left town, Cat fans keep coming back in large numbers to support their team. They've been rewarded with success in short spurts, but nothing has been sustained. At long last, the UK program is in a position to make that happen and Rich Brooks is the one who has led that resurgence.

My first memory of Kentucky football is one of those flashes of brilliance. It was the opening game of the 1971 season, and I was listening on my parents' old tabletop radio as Cawood Ledford called Doug Kotar returning the opening kickoff for a touchdown at Clemson. The Cats won that game, but as was the case in those days, it was not a harbinger of success, as Kentucky won only twice more that season.

When Commonwealth Stadium opened, my dad purchased two season tickets for the first time (section 125, row 29, seats 1 and 2), and I think I have only missed one UK home game since then. The tradition of a college football Saturday is a special experience. I can remember sitting with my dad in the car in the parking lot, listening to Leonard's Losers before going inside the stadium, as clearly as I can remember yesterday.

Gathering the material for this book has been an enjoyable experience, from the extended conversations with Brooks to the visits with his family, friends, coaching associates and current and former players. There are many people who have supported me in this first literary project. Here's the list (and I know I have missed someone and for that I am profoundly sorry):

Thank you to Rich Brooks for having the confidence in my abilities to work with me as a first-time author on this project. Rich is the consummate professional and it has been my pleasure to work with him week in and week out each fall. Rich is donating all of his royalties from the sales of this book to the Rich Brooks Foundation;

RICH TRADITION

My family (my wife, Robyn and our kids, Connor and Caroline); their encouragement kept me focused through several cases of writer's block and no one means more to me than them;

Jim Host and J.C. Faulkner, my business partners in Tom Leach Productions (tomleachky.com); any businessperson should be so fortunate to have two friends as supportive and wise as advisors;

Bobby Clark, President of The Clark Group, for guiding me through the process of writing my first book;

Trice Glass, my former marketing director at TLP, for her hard work in various pre-production tasks;

Van Florence, for his assistance in securing our title sponsor, Central Bank, thus enabling this project to make a greater contribution to the Rich Brooks Foundation and the Kentucky charities it supports;

Justin Keehne and Paul Mattingly, our interns at TLP whose work in transcribing a plethora of interviews was invaluable;

Shane Bowman, UK fan, for suggesting the title for this book;

Tony Neely and Susan Lax in the UK media relations department, for assistance in securing stats, rosters, etc.;

Lisa Ellis, Sandy Griffin and Quaintance Clark in the UK football office for answering an untold number of questions and requests; and a big thank you to everyone in the football offices for always being so cooperative and helpful;

Will Southerland, Craig Welch and everyone associated with the Rich Brooks Foundation;

Ralph Hacker, who has always been a wonderful mentor for me since I joined his staff at WVLK in 1984; and

My mom, Louise, and my late father, Alvin, for inspiring me to pursue my dreams.

—*Tom Leach, author "Rich Tradition"*

To learn more about Tom, and to read his daily coverage of University of Kentucky sports, go to: **tomleachky.com**.

Chapter One

21 Days in October that Changed Kentucky Football

IT WAS THE KIND OF GAME too many Kentucky football teams had lost too many times in too many excruciating ways.

The Wildcats took the lead against mighty Georgia but just enough time remained for the opponent to spoil the upset bid. It had happened so many times that UK fans half-jokingly called it a curse. Rich Brooks didn't like those jokes. They represented the kind of mindset he had to change if he was going to beat the odds, turn this program around and keep it there—the same thing he had done at Oregon. This day represented the opportunity for a defining moment—to stop Georgia, seal the upset win and give Kentucky football the signature victory the Brooks era desperately needed.

Brooks' wife, Karen, was watching from a box between the decks of Commonwealth Stadium, alongside one of their daughters, Kerri Brooks Robinson. Brooks' son, Denny, was standing on the sidelines, a few feet from his dad. Over 2,400 miles away from Lexington, in Eugene, Oregon, another daughter, Kasey Brooks Holwerda, was watching her son play soccer as she listened to the game on her satellite radio. Another son, Brady, was listening, too, as he was pulling into his driveway in Sacramento, California. Here is what they heard in the game's final minute:

(On the radio...

"Stafford retreats. Now the protection breaks down. He slides right, he throws...intercepted! Trevard Lindley at the 41- yard line.")

Lindley's interception enabled Kentucky to claim this unexpected victory, 24-20. It was the school's first win over traditional SEC power Georgia in nine years, and it set off a wildly joyous celebration at Commonwealth Stadium.

Out in Oregon, Kasey started to cry. So did Brady. On the sidelines, Denny saw the unbridled jubilation of a group of young men who never stopped believing in a coach many said was too old to connect with them. And up in the coaches' wives' box, Kerri was watching her father's glory unfold amid a sea of delirious Kentucky fans pouring onto to the field to tear down the goalposts. Kerri stood up on a chair and ripped off her sweatshirt. Underneath, she wore a blue T-shirt emblazoned with the words "we believe." As she began shouting that phrase, a group of fans in front of her joined in the chorus. Meanwhile, thousands of others poured over the stadium walls, to bask in the jubilation over the kind of victory Brooks needed to solidify his turnaround of the long-suffering Kentucky program.

Photo provided by Kerri Brooks Robinson

Kerri Brooks Robinson sports the t-shirt she wore the day her father's Kentucky team upset Georgia at Commonwealth Stadium.

It was a scene few could have envisioned three weeks earlier. Kentucky had been drubbed 49-0 at LSU, dropping Brooks' record in three-plus seasons to 12-29. Who would have imagined that the Wildcats would win 11 of their next 13 games, including the first bowl triumph since Apple introduced the Mac

(1984) and the first upset of a number one-ranked team since the Beatles' first US album (1967). And it was all orchestrated by a veteran coach who personified resiliency but also walked off the field in Baton Rouge thinking he might get fired if his team didn't win its next game.

Tiger Stadium at LSU on a sultry Saturday night is one of college football's legendary settings. It is not the place to go with a banged-up team and a roster still being rebuilt from probation. To say LSU dominated the game would be an understatement. The Bayou Bengals outgained Kentucky 546-277 on the way to a 49-0 rout. It was Brooks' most lopsided loss in three-and-a-half years in Lexington and it dropped the Wildcats' record to 3-4, 1-3 in the SEC.

Photo by Victoria Graff

Brooks questions a call in the 49-0 loss at LSU in 2006.

"I was embarrassed. I knew that we were at a very major crossroads for going forward. If I was going to complete what I had come here to do, I knew that we had to win quite a few more games in the remaining part of the season," Brooks recalled. "I knew that if we didn't get to a bowl or didn't beat somebody we weren't supposed to beat, that I would have a very difficult time going into the next year. It probably would end and somebody would be coming in here and starting all over again."

Oscar Combs, founder of *The Cats Pause*, the weekly publication and website that chronicles UK sports, remembers a prediction he made on the pregame radio show on the Big Blue Sports Network. He believed LSU would win handily but also felt that the schedule that followed provided the Cats with a chance to bounce back.

"But I didn't think it was going to be THAT bad," he said of the way LSU

3

The disappointment of the UK players in their poor play at LSU was reflected in the faces of Jacob Tamme (left) and Dicky Lyons, Jr.

Photo by Victoria Graff

manhandled Kentucky.

A circle of close friends could tell that Brooks believed he was on thin ice as coach of the Wildcats.

Brett Setzer befriended the coach shortly after Rich and Karen settled into their new home, just down the road from Setzer's family in Jessamine County. Setzer says he and Brooks talk every Sunday, usually as the coach heads home after reviewing the film of the previous day's game. But on the Sunday after the LSU loss, Brooks didn't call.

"Sunday came and went and I didn't hear from him, so I called him on Monday and he doesn't call me back. He is the type of person that if you call him, he will call you back but I didn't hear from him. Then on Tuesday, he surfaces," Setzer remembered. "I said 'I thought you disappeared. I thought I was going to have to put you on a milk carton or something.'"

Setzer was a little surprised when Brooks talked about finding a potential buyer for his house, in case things didn't turn around. "He said, 'I think I am going to be out of here (if we don't win this next game). This is it'. That was a pretty depressing moment," Setzer said.

"The LSU game, I think that was the lowest I had seen him," observed Dr. Grady Stephens, who developed a friendship with Brooks through a golf outing in the coach's second year. "I think he felt, and he said to us, that 'if we don't get this thing turned around, I won't be here next year.'"

Larry Vaught has covered Kentucky football for almost 40 years for the *Danville Advocate-Messenger*. He remembers thinking that Brooks sounded and looked like a coach who knew he was close to being counted out.

"I can remember thinking in the Sunday teleconference and even the Monday press conference (at the stadium) that for the first time Rich Brooks looked to me a little down," Vaught said. "Then, I went to practice on Wednesday and talked to some of the players, and I got to thinking 'this guy is going to be able to make it' because his players believed in him. You could tell they were very sincere. I had always been a Rich Brooks backer because I thought he was doing things the right way and he had inherited a program that was in a little worse shape than people thought. But I'll have to admit that on that Saturday night after the LSU game, I didn't think he was going to make it. But by Wednesday, I thought he was. The players gave me the pep talk and I think somewhere along the way, they got him (Brooks) re-energized."

No one in UK's administration told Brooks that his job was in jeopardy, but he could see the storm clouds forming.

"I don't know if I was worried about it that week (after LSU), but I knew that if we didn't win the next game at Mississippi State, then it was a distinct possibility before the end of the season," Brooks admitted. "It does happen in football. Athletic directors in today's age want to clear the table so they don't get criticized for going behind the coach's back and talking to potential replacements before there is a job open. It usually always gets out and certainly then, they can expedite the process and not lose too much ground in recruiting. I think that was a distinct possibility that year, and there was no question it was a possibility before the end of the season."

Kentucky athletics director Mitch Barnhart wouldn't say he was close to pulling the plug on Brooks. But Barnhart was catching as much heat for hiring Brooks as the coach was for losing games. Still, Barnhart knew from the players themselves that they believed firmly in their coach.

"He (Rich) was down and came over and shook my hand and told me how sorry he was that we lost in that fashion. As he always did, he took responsibility for it. He didn't blame anyone and it was on his shoulders," Barnhart said of the scene at Tiger Stadium. "He is a man's man about those sorts of things. He has never pointed the finger to anybody but himself and gives credit when things go well to others. That is what makes him great as a coach and it makes him a good guy to work with, and I am appreciative of that. But, that night was brutal. The flight home was rough and there was a lot of soul searching going on by a lot of people, me included. People started questioning where we are and what we are doing. There were people calling for Rich's head and my head. We are fortunate that we had a president who was supportive and would listen. (And) we had players who were committed."

When Brooks was hired, some wondered how he would relate to the young men he would coach. After all, Brooks had been away from the college game for nine years—seven in the NFL and two in retirement. That fact, combined with his age, prompted the doubts. But the way Brooks balances honesty with a genuine love and concern for his players produces a connection that is not affected by any generation gap. Brooks may have lost a lot of Kentucky fans on that dismal night in Baton Rouge, but he never lost his team. It was evident in the locker room that night when the usually reserved quarterback Andre Woodson stood up and addressed his teammates, challenging them to respond the right way and save their season—and their coaches.

"It's time we start really taking practice serious. Just go out there and start performing because our coaches' jobs are on the line. We're embarrassing our university," Woodson remembers telling his teammates. A leadership role falls to the person manning the quarterback position almost by default but Woodson had never embraced that job in this fashion before.

"I think a lot of guys responded really well. We had a wonderful practice (the next week). We knew what we were capable of doing, and we started showing we could play in this conference. When we finally beat Georgia that said a lot about how we responded to that LSU game," Woodson said. "We all came there for our coaches. You have to fight for what you really want. With us winning those games, it paid off and that's why now, things are looking so bright for the University of Kentucky."

"That was, I would think in my memory, the first time he took it upon himself to talk to the whole offense," Brooks said, "and basically be a leader and do the things that a quarterback needs to do sometimes. He stepped to the front and spoke up and obviously his play the rest of that year was outstanding. Everything got better."

Tight end Jacob Tamme saw a transformation in Woodson that night.

"He wasn't always like that, but after that game you knew he was going to be different," Tamme said. "I think coach kept to the task and kept us positive and doing things the right way. We knew we had to keep in stride to compete with the best teams in the country, and LSU was one of the best teams in the country that year. And when we played them again a year after, I think we proved that we had made some of those strides."

"It was unlike Andre at that time. But he stepped up and became a different kind of leader than he had been," said Joker Phillips, the former Wildcat (1981-84) who in early 2008 was designated as Brooks' successor as UK's head coach. "That became a positive, when your quarterback, who has been the guy that everybody's been looking for leadership, hadn't really stepped up (finally answers the call)."

Quarterbacks coach Randy Sanders says Woodson's speech that night was the product of a transformation the signal-caller made in the months leading up to that moment.

"One of the things I tried to work with Andre on when I first got here was being more of a leader, being more out front of the team and the offense. That's not always by being vocal but by the way you approach your business on the practice field and in the off season," he said. "I think it was building, so when he stepped up and did say something, it had more impact, because he had been preparing himself for that situation for several months. That's one of the big reasons he won the job to begin with."

Brooks coaches up Woodson during a 2004 game at Mississippi State.

When Brooks took his turn to talk to his team that night, he told his players their season was at a crossroads. They still had time to achieve their goal of making it to a bowl game, but they had no margin for error.

"I think he challenged them," said Brooks' son, Denny, who witnessed the debacle at LSU firsthand. "He challenged their character, their manhood, and whether they really wanted to be there and really wanted to compete. It was almost like a parent talking to his children. He was scolding them, but not too hard because you don't want to lose them."

"He put it in their laps," added Mike Archer, who served as Brooks' defensive coordinator from 2003-06. "He said, 'it's up to you.'"

It would be two weeks before the Cats would take the field again—at Mississippi State. And Archer says the team needed some time off.

"The players needed a break. We all needed a break. I remember that week, going recruiting, I couldn't wait to get out of town. Everybody needed to get away and refocus and reenergize," he said, adding that when it came to start preparing for the game, everybody was back on the same page." There was no after-effect of what happened (at LSU). The kids were different," Archer noted. "There was some pep and some excitement and enthusiasm. I credited the senior class—Durrell White and Lamar Mills. And a lot of it was the junior class—Wesley (Woodyard) and Andre (Woodson), Keenan Burton and those guys. They all made a commitment that they weren't going to stand by and let that thing roll over again."

And Brooks decided that he needed to refocus on his core coaching values if he was going to get his team back on track.

Photo by Victoria Graff

Mike Archer (left) says the leaders on the 2006 team asserted themselves at the team's darkest hour.

Chapter Two

An
Old-School
Solution

"IT'S A ONE-GAME SEASON."

Brooks says that's the message he continually preached to his team in the two weeks that followed the LSU beatdown. Longtime UK football equipment manager, Tom Kalinowski, took the words to heart and removed every opponent's name but Mississippi State from the schedule board in the Nutter Training Center.

Brooks is old school in many ways but he is not inflexible. He knows style of play is important in recruiting the kind of offensive talent needed to succeed in the Southeastern Conference, so he allowed his staff to open things up and build their scheme around a strong-armed quarterback and a group of big-play receivers. For Brooks, though, the pendulum had swung too far to the finesse side. If the Wildcats were going to reverse their fortunes, he knew they needed to make a renewed commitment to be more physical.

"We had to get back to the basics. I talked to my staff the next day (after the LSU loss) and told them that I thought we were getting away from some of the things I believed in—as far as being more physical—and part of that was what we were doing offensively," Brooks explained. "We were spending too much time in the (shot) gun (formation). We needed to get back under center a bigger percentage of the time. We needed to run the football, even if we didn't run it successfully, because we needed to set up the play-action passing game off the run fake and take some pressure off the offensive line."

One method Brooks utilized to send this message to his players was something called "The Wildcat Drill." It's one offensive player against one defensive player and when the whistle blows, it's a man-on-man battle. It's nothing abusive—just a drill designed to build toughness and accountability.

This is the kind of drill Brooks would use in the spring or fall training camp but it was taken out of the practice routine once the season started to reduce the risk of injury. But for the first time in his tenure at Kentucky, Brooks opted to put "The Wildcat Drill" back into their routine for the rest of that season.

"We were physically beaten badly in the LSU game. It was like we didn't compete. One thing about football is that every play you are faced with a physical challenge. You need to be winning a lot of those battles rather than lose every one. And we lost nearly every one in the LSU game. That was why the score was so lopsided," said Brooks. "Although someone is bigger and stronger than you are, you can still compete and win a lot of those battles. That is what we went back to, the mentality that I don't care if it's Rich Brooks lining up against (310-pound former defensive tackle) Myron Pryor and he outweighs me by 100 pounds and he is much stronger, I am going to get him one of these times. And I am going to get him and keep fighting and battling until I do get him. It is a physical drill. The only reason you do that drill is if you are not doing

Photo by Victoria Graff

Brooks committed his team to a more physical brand of football in an effort to save their season.

those three things well—blocking, moving your feet and moving your hips. Shedding the blocks, using your hands, keeping pad level down and the physical part of it are the keys"

Joker Phillips, named UK's head coach of the offense before the 2008 season, says the staff wanted to make sure their best players avoided injuries in practice. But after the LSU debacle, he says they realized that this approach was taking away too much of the team's aggressiveness.

"We had made them soft in trying to protect them and get everybody to the games. We got 'em there but we didn't get 'em there with the right mindset. We were not a physical football team—especially that night," he said. "He (Brooks) knew what was missing. He gave us a plan of how we were going to get our football team more physical and in that two-week span, (we did)."

Players get into a routine with their week-to-week preparation and this kind of physically draining practice was a major change. Sometimes, especially when a season has taken a turn for the worse, a team will resist that approach. Players may not voice it to the head man or the assistants, but the grousing will be evident in the locker room or when players get together away from the field.

The Wildcats' response testified to the faith this group had in its coaches.

"I think that, because of the way the players responded to more difficult practices, challenging drills and more physical contact—which unless you are doing it in a game is never what you would call fun in practice—(was encouraging)," Brooks said. "I think that they didn't complain and anyone that did, some of the other players and leaders on the team straightened them out. The Jacob Tammes, Andre Woodsons, Keenan Burtons, and Wesley Woodyards—those people stepped up and shut it off, if there was any of that. I am sure there was some but I don't think there was a lot. But I also know that during that two-week period is when a lot of the leadership on this team stepped forward."

"If we wanted to change it and wanted to get things turned around and make it to a bowl, we had to do something. We had too many good players on our team," said center Matt McCutchan, now a graduate assistant on the UK staff. "Luckily, it wasn't on national television or anything and our fans didn't see it. The plane ride wasn't fun, but when we got back in town, it was like a switch had flipped. The second we got back, we went to the drawing board. Coach said 'we can change our season and do some things that haven't been done at UK'. That was always a big thing (with him), to turn around history and re-write history. For two weeks, I remember he came up to me personally to talk about the season and let me know he was disappointed with how I was playing. I was upset and that was not how I wanted things to go. I just went out there and went after it everyday. With Coach Brooks, hard work is always going to solve the problem. There are no shortcuts."

Brooks says the response he got from his team during the two weeks leading up to the Mississippi State game was very encouraging.

Photo by Victoria Graff

Brooks cuts up with then center Matt McCutchan at the 2006 team photo day.

"They got me going because of the way they were responding and working. They helped pick me up," he said. "I never thought it was over. I knew that things were bleak. I just think the way they responded to what we had talked about after the game, the energy was there, the attitude was there and the willingness to work was there. There wasn't anybody hanging their heads."

"We knew what kind of hot seat he was on," added punter Tim Mastay, "and the adversity that he had gone through. The fact that he still believed it could be done and he was pouring as much into it sort of fired all of us up to do the same thing."

But the positive response on the practice field wasn't doing anything to reduce the pressure on the players and coaches off the field, when they made recruiting calls and visits.

"We felt it. We went out on the road and I called him and said, 'hey coach there are a lot of people saying we're done'," said Phillips. "We had two weeks to prepare for a one game season against Mississippi State. Everyday we prepared for Mississippi State and the kids showed up to work and it was only Mississippi State. It wasn't Georgia, it wasn't the next one; it was Mississippi State. We worked during the week to get our kids tougher and did blocking drills because we felt we had gotten away from that. So we made our team tougher and that was one of the smartest things he has done since he has been here. He had gotten back to the basics in the middle of the season."

When it comes to game week, Monday is an off day from practice but a few players are asked to attend Brooks' news conference and answer questions from reporters. The sports information staff tries to vary the list of players each week, depending on who can fit it into their class schedule. When your team is coming off a 49-0 drubbing and fans are talking about the need for a coaching change, this event is not exactly a cherished assignment. But Dicky Lyons, Jr. is not the kind of young man who shrinks from adversity.

His father, Dicky, Sr., was one of the most versatile players in Kentucky and SEC football history but even his considerable talents could not help the Wildcats to win more than eight games in his three varsity seasons.

When Phillips went to recruit the younger Lyons and saw a room filled with Kentucky blue, he knew it would to be an easy sell. Dicky, Jr. wanted desperately to follow in the footsteps of his father and once there, he was determined to leave a mark. But it was that passion that got Lyons in Brooks' doghouse at that Monday news conference.

With the Cats facing what Brooks viewed as a true must-win game at Mississippi State, Lyons proclaimed to the media that "I really feel like we're better. I feel like we can get our backups in....I want to do to them what LSU did to us."

Lyons says he sensed his teammates' confidence was shaken after that LSU game, so he wanted to challenge them.

"That's why I went and made those statements, just trying to get the team fired up and it got Coach Brooks fired up, and I think the whole team rallied around that game. I think that, you could put that whole turnaround on that week alone," he said. "I think that's when we really found a spark as a team and with our coach."

Brooks was furious. With so much on the line, the last thing he needed was one of his players giving the opponent some bulletin board material to use as motivation.

"He didn't guarantee a win. What he said was that he wants to go down and beat Mississippi State like LSU beat us. He wants to beat them bad, beat them up physically and that is what we are going to do. I don't remember the word 'guarantee'—it might have been in there—but I have always been a believer in not putting the cart before the horse, if you will. And you give the opponent the respect you should going up to a game and after a game, and also, (brash talkers are) putting their teammates in a bad situation by running their mouth," Brooks said.

Brooks made Lyons off-limits to the media for the rest of the week, and he ordered him to do extra running after practice. A reporter friend of mine wondered if Brooks was perhaps using Lyons as a way to test his team's unity, but Brooks insists that this was not on his mind. He says his anger was genuine because he saw it was Lyons disrespecting an opponent. Nevertheless, the

Photo by Victoria Graff

DeMoreo Ford (8), Wesley Woodyard (16) and Dicky Lyons, Jr. (12) goofing off at the 2006 Media Day at Commonwealth Stadium.

team did rally around Lyons, with some of his teammates joining him for the extra running drills, and the coach noticed.

"That's just me being me. Like Dicky being Dicky, that's just me, being me. I am never going to tolerate that. I guess I am an old-fashioned guy. I think some of the new-age antics in athletics are uncalled for, and I think that is one of the things that are uncalled for. (But) I liked that," Brooks said of the support Lyons got. "I thought that was a positive thing that there were some players that did the extra running and not leave Dicky hanging by himself."

"I think that's what was needed," teammate Keenan Burton said of Lyons' proclamation. "You know, sometimes you do negative things, but those negative things kind of help you build your identity and Coach Brooks gave us opportunity to build our own identity."

Mike Archer thinks the media buzz created by Lyons' comments did serve to alleviate some of the pressure the team might have felt if the reporters were focusing more on Brooks' job security. But he also scolded Lyons for giving the opponent motivational fuel and challenged him to let his play support his brashness.

"I said 'the thing you have to do is back it up' and he said, 'I will'. And he backed it up," said Archer. "He played like a warrior. In hindsight, that might have loosened our guys and taken all of the other things that could have been written and said—'this is a must game or it could be over'—it dealt more with what Dicky said."

Lyons had seen Andre Woodson emerge as more of a vocal leader in the locker room that night at LSU and on game day, the quarterback challenged Lyons to walk the walk after his bold comments earlier in the week.

"Andre knew I wanted the ball that game, and he made sure I got it. He's like, 'you want to win, let's see what you can do'. And he started trusting me, and I think that's when we began to get some trust, as a quarterback and a receiver, where he can know he can come to me in clutch situations," Lyons said.

Late in the first quarter, with UK at the MSU 18-yard line and leading 7-0, Lyons made a leaping, one-handed grab of a Woodson pass but the officials on the field ruled that he was out of bounds along the back line of the end zone. Woodson was shaken up on a hit as he released the pass and backup signal-caller Curtis Pulley was inserted into the game. There was enough confusion that Kentucky had to call a timeout, giving the replay official in the press box some extra time to review Lyons' catch. After several minutes passed, the referee on the field changed the initial ruling and signaled a touchdown for the Wildcats.

"Thank goodness, I think it was Andre that got hurt. We took a timeout

Photo by George Green/TeamCoyle

Lyons' incredible one-handed grab for a TD gave the Cats an early spark in a must-have win at Mississippi State.

and Curtis came in when they were reviewing. Well, then they had time to review it, if that hadn't happened I didn't think they would have reviewed it for it to be overturned," said Brooks. "He made the great one-handed catch, one foot down, one of the greatest catches I'd ever seen and he made many more. It showed that he knew after shooting his mouth off, that he had to step up and walk the walk. And he walked the walk— (and) people walked the walk with him."

Lyons finished that game with career highs for receptions (eight) and yards (117).

The leadership Woodson vocalized in the locker room at

Photo by Victoria Graff

Lyons backed up his brash talk with career highs in receptions and yards.

LSU was evolving. Randy Sanders, whose protégés at Tennessee included Peyton Manning, recalls seeing his quarterback starting to grow up that day in Starkville, Miss.

"I remember talking to him on the sidelines that 'being a leader doesn't mean you have to make every play. Being a leader sometimes means you put other guys in position to make plays'. There were a few checks he made during that game that took some of the pressure off him and put it on the other 10 guys. They responded and I think it bred a lot of confidence throughout the whole team," Sanders said.

Brooks' renewed emphasis on a more physical brand of football also paid dividends. State was limited to 24 rushing yards while the Cats amassed 106, led by third-string tailback Alfonso Smith. He bulled his way to a

Photo by Victoria Graff

Wesley Woodyard salutes the UK fans who made the trip to Starkville for that crucial 2006 game at Mississippi State.

personal-best of 92 yards on a day when the Cats' top two runners were sidelined with injuries. The defense gave up some big plays with its aggressive blitzing packages, but Woodson and his crew countered with enough big plays of their own to enable Kentucky to escape with a 34-31 win.

"We had our best run defense game of the year, in the past few years. We held Mississippi State to 24 yards rushing (71 yards below State's season average) when they had been running the football on everyone pretty well," the coach noted. "We also ran the football better than we had been running, even though it wasn't great. We overcame (some) things to move forward."

"I look back at that as the turning point of my tenure here," Brooks said of the victory at MSU. "If that game (at Mississippi State) would not have happened, I don't think I would have had the opportunity for the next week, the Georgia game at home. I think if we would have followed up the 49-0 embarrassment (at LSU) with a loss at Mississippi State, there might have been an interim coach the next week."

Chapter Three

Signature Win

"HERE WE ARE AGAIN," Rich Brooks proclaimed in his opening remarks at the 2006 Kentucky football Media Day. "I know some of you may be surprised. I hope I can surprise you again this year."

Few, if any, of the reporters in Commonwealth Stadium's Wildcat Den that day believed it would happen. But on November 4, with traditional SEC power Georgia in town, Brooks' players were presented with an opportunity to justify his unwavering confidence in their potential.

In those days, the pregame "Cat Walk" attracted mostly just family and friends to form the gauntlet through which the team would enter the stadium. And with overcast skies and a 4-4 record combining to dampen optimism in the Big Blue nation, the attendance that day was some 8,000 below capacity. But, in perhaps the defining moment of the Brooks era, that was a big enough crowd to bring down the goalposts at Commonwealth for just the second time in school history.

"Players always have to buy in first. The problem in the process is part of the players buy in and the perception of the fans, media, what is written, what is talked about, what they see on TV, what they hear on campus, all of that is part of trying to get everyone to believe that you can do this, that you can win," said Brooks. "When parts of that are missing it becomes hard for other parts to happen. Players don't believe, if no one believes around them. It's hard for them to be convinced that they can do it when everyone around them is thinking they can't."

Brooks doesn't remember feeling any more confident that week about the chances for an upset, but he did think the way his team battled through setbacks at Mississippi State the week prior was a significant breakthrough for his team. It had to do with a mindset of finishing strong that Brooks had been working to instill in his players for almost four years.

Burton thinks the turnaround began on the practice field. In an interview in 2008, the St. Louis Rams' wideout was asked what he missed most about his days at Kentucky. "Girls," he laughed, then adding that it was "the Thursday practice sessions." That's the final major workout before a game and it always ends with the first-string offense against the number one defense in a series

of two-minute drills. Burton says he was trash talking for the offense while his buddy, Wesley Woodyard, would counter for the defense and their teammates fed off that competitiveness.

"That was one thing he (Brooks) preached—finishing," Woodyard recalled. "That was something that our program never did and was something that had to change and fortunately for us, we were able to change it and were able to win."

"It was a competition," Joker Phillips said of those Thursday practice sessions. "For every player, it was the last play of the game for him. It was the

Keenan Burton says the rivalries that came alive on the practice field fueled the Wildcats' passion on game days.

Photo by Victoria Graff

competitions on Thursdays that taught us how to win on Saturdays. It was a great competition. When we got to the game, we knew what we had to do. We became better finishers because of what we did on Thursdays."

The 2006 Georgia game was full of twists and turns. The Bulldogs threw an interception inside their own five-yard line, but Kentucky responded with a turnover of its own. Then, just before halftime, Trevard Lindley thwarted a potential UGA touchdown with an interception in the end zone.

UK took its first lead of the game, 17-14, on Burton's second TD catch of the day. It came with 8:29 remaining in the fourth quarter, but Georgia responded with an 83-yard drive to retake the lead with just under five minutes to play. That set the stage for the drive that defined the Brooks era at Kentucky.

Taking over at their own 31-yard line, the Wildcats moved methodically down the field, covering 69 yards in 11 plays for the go-ahead touchdown.

"I remember there was 4:50 on the clock when we got the ball back for that last drive," said Joker Phillips. "We still had time to run the ball and we did in that drive. I think those two weeks (before the Mississippi State game) that we prepared to get our team more physical gave us a chance to run the football at Georgia. I'm not sure we would have done that if we had not practiced that way. We figured they were going to be playing us for the pass."

The game-winning march relied on key elements that would fuel the Cats' reversal of fortune that followed—physical toughness, Andre Woodson's emerging leadership and an attitude of believing in their capabilities rather than giving in to the doubts.

"Andre was always calm," Brooks said. "I thought the look (in his eyes) was confidence, no problem. We just did it the series before. I think there was total confidence by our players."

"I remember the whole team being calm," Sanders added. "I think that goes back to the way Coach Brooks was approaching it. There wasn't any panic among the coaches and that came across to Andre. Being able to respond and score in that situation was not only huge in that game but in the next couple of years."

The Atlanta Journal-Constitution's Tony Barnhart is one sportswriter who believes in the axiom that teams take on the personality of their coach. And that's what played out as the Wildcats repeatedly executed key plays during that decisive trip down the field.

"He (Brooks) doesn't panic. One of the things coaches have to learn (in this league) is within the course of a game, there are going to be good things that happen and disastrous things, and somehow you've got to convince your guys to keep playing," he said. "I think he's a guy that brings a certain amount of calm to the sidelines and the players feed off that confidence."

Sophomore tailback Tony Dixon, playing with a sore hamstring, had five carries for 32 yards and two catches for 12 on the drive. And when he slammed over the goal line from three yards, Kentucky was back in front, 24-20.

(On the radio...

"Senior center Matt McCutchan leads them up to the line. Three wideouts right, Burton split back to the left. Dixon the setback— straight behind Woodson. Georgia with four down linemen, not showing blitz. Let's see if they come. They come late. Handoff to Dixon, up the middle. Touchdown, Kentucky! The Wildcats take the lead with 1:21 to play.")

"I think we had actually called a pass play, but Andre got to the line and checked to a run. It was just an inside zone play and Tony bent it back. One of the good things about Tony is that he is so short that from behind the line he popped out the back side and found the way to the end zone," Brooks explained.

"I think that the thing that salvaged our season, after the Mississippi State game, is the players really started to believe. And the Georgia game convinced them totally. Although the fans were still skeptical, the players were no longer skeptical. So, the combination of beating Mississippi State on the road and upsetting Georgia, to me, sold our players and particularly, the players that had the ability to make plays."

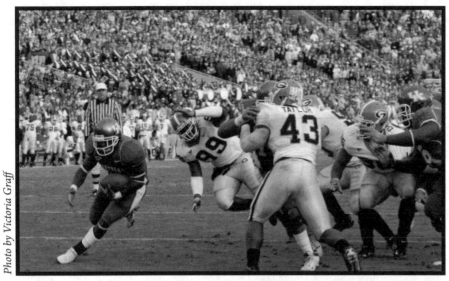

Tony Dixon scores the game-winning touchdown in a dramatic 24-20 upset of Georgia in 2006.

"I saw the defense they were in and I knew the play would work," said Dixon, "so I was just hoping he checked to it. I was already in my head knowing where to go. Andre made the right check, out of the pass play, and I scored."

"I think that's what was needed for the Kentucky program," he said of the win, "to have the confidence that we could beat teams like LSU (the next year)."

Brooks says having to rally twice in the fourth quarter to get the signature win his Kentucky resume was lacking was a key ingredient in speeding up the turnaround for the program.

"They came back and scored again with four or five minutes left in the game, and you could hear that almost all the air had been sucked out of Commonwealth Stadium. (Fans) are thinking, 'here we go again. Another close—but'..." Brooks said. "(Then) the offense takes the field and goes down the field. We are converting when we needed to on third down; we are not stumble and fumble. It's execution, poise, it's SEC football and we go down and take the lead back. And again, the fans get really excited again but they think Georgia is going to come back and do it. Then, a redshirt freshman, Lindley, steps up and makes the interception."

At last, Brooks saw his players put into practice the lessons he tried to teach them about combating self-doubt when the game was on the line. It was a message he articulated to his teams at Oregon starting in the 1970's from a book called "The Inner Game of Tennis."

Author Tim Gallway was captain of his tennis team at Harvard, and his

Photo by Ken Weaver/TeamCoyle

best-selling book tells the athlete how to control the mind to keep it from affecting his or her performance. The Amazon.com review of the book says it is "built on a foundation of Zen thinking and humanistic psychology" and "was really a primer on how to get out of your own way to let your best game emerge. It was sports psychology before the two words were pressed against each other and codified into an accepted discipline."

For Brooks, the book provided him with a vehicle to drive home the message that players can be masters of their own fate.

Brooks says he was taught that the "depth of learning is directly related to the volume of the lesson."

"It was about how each point in a tennis match goes and the points early in a match shouldn't be any different than match point but in some people's minds, they become different. All of a sudden you get thoughts in your mind about not doing it right or 'God, I hope I don't screw it up'. Negative thoughts that impact your mind affect how your body functions at the match point level," Brooks explained.

"I took those lessons and talked to my team about them at Oregon. I had quotes out of the book and used them. You can't be out there in the fourth quarter and thinking negative things or your body isn't going to function like it did the first three quarters. Here, I didn't use (that book) but I used that same analogy. You need to finish games and you can't panic in the fourth quarter and you can't get negative in the fourth quarter."

Brooks says the mindset was no more of an issue at Kentucky than it had been at Oregon, but make no mistake, it was something he had to confront at UK.

"I don't think it was more prevalent (at UK) but it was just as prevalent. It was prevalent in the fan base, it was prevalent in the media and it was prevalent in our players' heads," he said.

"A lot of the guys on the team, and it was passed down from Coach Brooks—wanted nothing more than to change that way of thinking," Jacob Tamme noted. "That has to end for a program to be where we felt we should be. People, fans, players—nobody can think like that and be pessimistic in those situations. What Coach Brooks saw us doing was going out on the field and actually doing some things that can change it. That is the only way you can change things is by going out and doing it on the field. Coaches kind of instilled that in everybody, that we were no different that any other team. We had as good of a chance as anyone else to make a fourth quarter comeback. We had as good of a chance as anyone to hang on to a lead. We just had to play football. We had guys that believed in that and really cared about changing things."

When the fourth quarter drama was playing out against Georgia, Brooks sensed the uneasy feeling that hung over the Kentucky crowd at Commonwealth Stadium. The coach found himself waving his arms to request more noise when Georgia had the ball because he could tell the UK fans had grown quiet out of fear the upset win would somehow be snatched from the Wildcats' grasp.

"They're into the game but they're so apprehensive that they're not making noise at the right time. They feel like something ominous is about to happen because of the past history. You could almost feel like the air is getting sucked out of the stadium," he said. "From the fans' standpoint, it was almost disbelief when Trevard Lindley intercepted that ball. It was like 'Oh my god. We did do it.'"

Defensive coordinator Mike Archer had talked with his players about wanting to have the chance to be the unit on the field when victory would be determined. Back in 1993, when Bill Curry was the head coach trying to turn the UK program around, Archer was in charge of the defense and watched as Florida snatched an upset from Kentucky's grasp with a touchdown pass on the last play of the game. It was one of the myriad of examples of heartbreaking defeats that some Big Blue fans lumped under the heading of the "Commonwealth Curse." Archer understood the fan apprehension Brooks was sensing in the stadium, but those folks weren't privy to a new mindset that was taking hold among the Kentucky football players.

Photo by Bill Patterson/TeamCoyle

"I'll never forget (what happened) on the sidelines," said Archer. "Wesley (Woodyard) was adamant and Lamar Mills, who really never said much, was adamant. (They said) 'this is our chance. It's our time to do our part for this program, to win a game we're not supposed to.' And they did. I'll never forget walking off the field. That's when I think they began to expect to win. Up to that point, we hoped to win. We finally learned how to win. And I think that's what

Woodson and company celebrate Kentucky's first win over Georgia in 10 years.

has set that program apart now. That's a mental thing and it's something that took a long time."

When Lindley made his game-clinching interception of future NFL overall number one draft pick Matthew Stafford, it set off a frenzy on the Kentucky sideline.

"I am going to relate Trevard Lindley to my days back at Oregon," Brooks said. "Steve Brown, as a redshirt freshman, intercepted a ball against Cal-Berkeley at Autzen Stadium to ensure us to get a 19-14 win, which was a huge upset at that time. Steve Brown, the next year as a sophomore, because he didn't know the history of losing and screwing everything up, (intercepted another pass) and ran it back for a touchdown at Huskie Stadium for us to beat the Washington Huskies for the first time in umpteen years. So, sometimes the key play is made by young players with talent who don't have the same beaten down mentality of 'oh my god, let's not screw this up. Don't throw it my way, don't call my number'. It's interesting."

The win over Georgia sold the players on the potential Brooks continually preached about. And while some pundits initially dismissed it as a victory over a subpar Bulldog squad, it is worth noting that Georgia came back to beat three straight ranked opponents, including West Virginia in the Chick-Fil-A Bowl.

Keenan Burton says Kentucky's triumph provided validation for all of the hard work and faith that sustained the team through all of the bad times.

"It was a signature win. I mean we hadn't beat Georgia in so many years, and I think that us doing that kind of got our mentality different, got our swagger different, and it kind of swung everything and let us believe that we could do what we said we could do, beat these upper echelon teams," Burton noted.

"I think it is just a testament to the type of person he is," said Dr. Stephens, who watched the upset unfold from a spot on the Kentucky sideline.

"I think they believe in him. I don't think he let them see that he was in a state of, not despair, but just down. I don't think he let them see that or know that. The coaches just stuck with their plan and didn't veer from that plan. I think the kids sensed that and they kept fighting for him. I think that showed how much they thought of him that they didn't just lay over."

Was November 4, 2006 the defining moment for Kentucky football? Maybe—or maybe it just the day that a large enough number of players were finally fully converted to Brooks' side to finally push the program out of its Sisyphusian mode of pushing the rock to the top of the hill, only to have it roll back over top of them.

"I think it goes to the toughness of Rich Brooks. He would not let our kids quit. He would not let his coaching staff quit. He stayed in the fight and continued to believe that with a

Athletics Director Mitch Barnhart says UK's resurgence is a testament to the toughness of Rich Brooks.

few breaks and effort we could get to a spot that looked different than we were before," observed Mitch Barnhart. "Our kids believed they could get there and never quit on the dream to get there. But it was remarkable to be celebrating the win against Georgia three weeks after the biggest loss I have been a part of. Everything was edgy. We have seen it a hundred of times. At Kentucky we have had a lot of chances to get over the top but just couldn't. This game, Tony Dixon ran the heck out of it that day and carried the offense for a stretch and ran the ball like a champion and the offensive line did a really nice job. There was energy with our crowd and we had some people make plays."

University of Kentucky president Dr. Lee Todd remembers wondering why the school had scheduled an opponent the caliber of Georgia for the Homecoming game. But it turned out to be a wise decision.

Before he was president of his alma mater, Todd was a Big Blue fan and he was right in the middle of the post-game party.

"I went down on the field and I recall that there were two girls and a boy—students—laying there with the goal post and they motioned me over to take a picture with them, so I did," he said. "I thought this will be an interesting picture, the president helped take the goal post down. But I was willing to undergo that because I would have done it anyway. It was such a great moment to see the rush of the field. It cost us some money, but I told the SEC commissioner (Mike Slive) that what you need to understand is that this isn't 18-to-20-year old kids running out there but 60-to-70-year old people who have never had this chance before. It was quite a moment."

And despite what Brooks had been thinking three weeks earlier, Todd says there was no talk of a midseason coaching change.

"We weren't going to make a decision that early anyway. And he was able to turn it around. I think he used that defeat (at LSU) to his advantage with the players and the players hung in there with him," said Todd. "I don't remember all the details, but I never had a phone call from Mitch saying we needed to make a change."

Photo by Kerri Brooks Robinson

When the Cats upset Georgia, fans tore down the goal posts at Commonwealth Stadium for the second time ever.

While the fans rushed the field to tear down the goalposts, Brooks' wife and daughter were celebrating in the box where they watched the game.

"My mom and I were balling and crying," said Kerri. "I think the whole fourth quarter, in between the game, there were tears—happy, scared, tears. It was very emotional."

I'm tired of losing
I wanna win
I'm tired of being close
I wanna finish
Forget the naysayers and all the haters
Forget the reporters and all the newspapers,
Cause we can do
Cause we believe in Mitch
We believe in Rich, man
We believe in this
So catch an attitude
And poke your chest out
Protect the Commonwealth
'Cause this is our house
And that Kentucky blue
How that jersey feel
This is our state
It's not Louisville's,
So jump around
Get crunk
And knock some heads off
Winter time workouts
We have paid the cost
And we believe

— Marcus McClinton
We Believe

"I left him a blabbering message and then I talked to him later that day," said son Brady. "You could sense the relief (in his voice). It was a special day."

The 'we believe' mantra adopted by the 2006 Wildcats had its genesis in a rap song penned by free safety Marcus McClinton. He says the idea came out of a meeting with Leslie Phillips (Joker's wife) and others about ways to energize the Kentucky home crowd. McClinton says it took about 45 minutes to write the song.

From there, McClinton set about producing a video, with teammates Burton, Rafael Little, Woodyard and Braxton Kelly serving as backup singers and dancers. They pitched their idea to athletics director Mitch Barnhart, who liked it and approved having it played in the stadium prior to the games.

Rich Brooks had some reservations about his players going public with the song, because he felt it would open them to some harsh criticism if the team failed to live up to the expectations only the players and coaching staff had for them.

"I thought it was a pretty creative thing by Marcus McClinton, but I got a little concerned because, to me, those players on that video, they were kinda sticking their neck out to be criticized or ridiculed if we didn't do something that year. I felt I had to sit down and talk to them and find out if they were willing to risk that," said Brooks. "They were personalizing their position and their support and that would have left them open to individual criticism. (But) they were good with it. I did think it was risky, but it obviously became (a rallying cry)."

McClinton says he and his teammates had no doubts.

"We were at rock bottom. It couldn't get no worse. And we believed we were going to be a better team. We wanted to be SEC champions. No doubts. Either they (the fans) were gonna accept or they're not," McClinton said.

"We wanted to get the crowd into what we were believing and I think that's what that song did," said tailback Tony Dixon, adding that when the Cats heard the "boo" sound from their home crowd the previous year, it was something that surprised him. "And I think that's going to be a slogan for a long time. It gave the fans the perspective of the players—that we weren't just out there playing to lose. We

Photo by Victoria Graff

Marcus McClinton (2) penned the lyrics to "Believe," the song that became the anthem for the 2006 Wildcats.

believed in ourselves, and we wanted the fans to believe in us as well."

"The way that crowd reacted after that game was unlike anything I'd ever seen, even at any basketball game at Kentucky," Larry Vaught observed, who had left the press box to watch the final minutes unfold from field level. "It was like the whole Big Blue family suddenly bought into Rich Brooks—and his players. It certainly helped that he had a group of guys that was very lovable. I remember seeing Jacob Tamme cry and look up to the skies and Wesley Woodyard hugging anybody in sight. It was a pretty emotional moment. You finally thought 'Rich Brooks is going to get it done.'"

"I guess there were more on the field than there were in the stands. They just kept coming from everywhere," he continued. "And a lot of them were actually crying and cutting up the sod and ripping sweatbands off the guys, just to have some kind of memento. And I'd never seen so many flashes of people taking pictures. Four hours after the game, when I went out into

Photo by TeamCoyle

Big Blue fans took the mantra "believe" to heart as the Wildcats got the program turned around under Rich Brooks.

the parking lot, there were still thousands of people out there cheering and clapping."

Kentucky parlayed the euphoria over the upset of Georgia into a 38-26 win over Vanderbilt a week later, clinching bowl eligibility for the first time in seven years. The emerging Woodson had his best day as a Wildcat to that point, passing for 450 yards and four touchdowns. And an often-maligned defense forced four Vandy turnovers.

The high of the achievement of qualifying for postseason play may have contributed to a letdown the next week. Kentucky found itself in a shootout with unheralded Louisiana-Monroe. For the third game in a row, the Cats found themselves trailing in the fourth quarter. ULM was actually in position to tie the game in the final minutes but redshirt freshman defensive end Jeremy Jarmon single-handedly thwarted an option play on a two-point conversion try and the Cats escaped with a 42-40 win.

"I think anytime you have a team that hasn't had much success, lost to a certain team many times, or hasn't had a signature win, once you get those wins, it now becomes a problem to get them back on track and focused to play the games you are supposed to win and go out and win rather than having a letdown. So you don't get into the highs and lows emotionally, thinking you are something special when you have beaten someone really good and then throw it away by losing to someone you shouldn't lose to," Brooks said.

With a seventh win in the bag, the Wildcats knew they had played themselves into a better bowl game and they set their sights on ending a losing streak against the Tennessee Volunteers that stretched back to 1984. The underappreciated UK defense produced its best performance of the season, with a physical style of play that set a tone that said the Wildcats were not going to be pushed around any longer by the Vols.

"That game and the Clemson game, that's when I think our defense really grew up," said Mike Archer. "I had never been with a group of kids that played as hard as they did in Knoxville. We still got beat but our kids laid it on the line. They (Tennessee) carted their two tailbacks off the field twice." Archer believes a good number of previously skeptical Wildcat fans fully bought into

Photo by Victoria Graff

Brooks' fighting spirit kept his players believing in his leadership even when many others were jumping off the UK bandwagon.

the turnaround Brooks was orchestrating when they saw the way their team beat up the heavily favored Vols that day.

A few breakdowns on offense and special teams left some points on the table. When a last-ditch drive deep into Tennessee territory came up short, a dejected Kentucky walked off the field at Neyland Stadium on the short end of a 17-12 score.

"That was one of the more frustrating losses that I know of. At least three of them have been against Tennessee, where I felt we were in position to win, could have won and didn't," Brooks said. "That is very frustrating because everyone wants to beat Tennessee. And no one wants to more than I do, or our players do. To be so close, and on that day I think we outplayed Tennessee and that always hurts more than when you go out and don't play that well. I have had about five or six of those games in the last four years where I thought it was a great college football game but the wrong team ended up winning. That was one of those."

Still, even in defeat, it was clear that a breakthrough had occurred for the Kentucky football program. Matt McCutchan says it was the payoff for a coach who never lost faith in his players.

"You are not going to believe in someone if they don't believe in you. He always believed that we had some great things going but we had to weed out players from the past. Going into that '06 summer and '06 year, we had weeded out some of those guys. It was that 'we believe we can do this' and 'we believe in Coach Brooks'," McCutchan said. "The whole time we knew we could do it here and had a good group of guys who had that mentality and dedication."

Chapter Four

Nashville Turns Big Blue

FROM THE ASHES OF AN EMBARRASSING PERFORMANCE at LSU, the Wildcats had won four of their last five games. It earned them a spot in the Music City Bowl in Nashville, opposite ACC power Clemson. Outside of the Big Blue family, though, there weren't many believers and Clemson was installed as a 10-point favorite by the oddsmakers. That made Kentucky the biggest underdog of any bowl team that season.

For UK fans, the fact that this team came from behind in the fourth quarter in three of those four victories marked a distinct reversal of form. They had seen their Cats come out on the short end of far too many of those late-game swings.

"I go back to (defensive back) Marcus McClinton, who sung that 'we believe' song that he wrote. They never stopped believing that they were going to get there to postseason play (even though) no one else did," noted Mitch Barnhart. "When people gave up on them, they never stopped believing and the beauty of that is that they believed in their head coach, their coaching staff and never threw it in anyone's face saying you all quit on us. They didn't do that. They handled it in such a classy fashion and were so good about the way they represented the University of Kentucky and the fans. I really admired that for 18-20 year old kids to handle it well."

Photo by Victoria Graff

Brooks and Keenan Burton (center) savor the announcement of Kentucky's upcoming bowl trip during a 2006 ceremony at Rupp Arena.

Despite the disappointment at Tennessee in the regular season finale, Brooks had noticed a transformation in his team. The squad that was embarrassed at LSU five weeks earlier was now a more physically and mentally tougher group that had confidence it could play with anybody. And that mindset carried over into the practices for the upcoming matchup with Clemson.

"I think they handled everything that we threw out at them, they handled it well. It is always scary getting ready for a bowl game because you don't want to leave your game on the practice field. You don't want to lose your best players in practice when you are preparing but you also don't want to prepare like you are playing a powder puff game," Brooks said, noting that he also liked the fact that his players won every single competition—from rib eating to karaoke—during the various bowl week events.

Game day brought an invasion of Kentucky fans into Nashville and thousands of them turned out for "The Cat Walk," a pregame tradition in which UK fans form a gauntlet of cheering supporters through which the players and coaches enter the stadium. When the team buses rolled into the LP Field parking lot and the players saw that turnout, they were overwhelmed.

"I think the fan base was reluctant to buy into this team. The LSU game stuck out in people's minds as well as the uncertainty of our staff was certainly being discussed. I think there was no question that our team was very pleasantly surprised and almost in awe of the Cat Walk going into that Music City Bowl," said Brooks. "To me, it was one of the most remarkable things I have seen since I had been here because it followed, I would say, a less than enthusiastic home season.

Photo by Victoria Graff

Brooks does his best Chet Atkins impersonation with the commemorative guitar from the Music City Bowl.

So I think it was in my mind, a little unexpected to see (the turnout) in that volume. I think our players were inspired by that. And then more impressive was when we got in the stadium and before the kickoff, you look up and see at least three quarters of the stadium was blue-and-white."

"I thought it would never end, because I mean, it was really so long," Dicky Lyons said of the Cat Walk. "That's when you knew that we had the fan base and that we had all the fans behind us, and they believed in us, and it's crazy, you know, how much things changed in just a four week period, just four games, and how the whole (state) rallied around us, and started believing in us, and just gave us an extra edge to want to win that much more. I credit everything to the fans as well, you know, because if they hadn't believed in us year in, year out when things were going bad, they were really our only motivation to keep trying to win at one point."

Mike Archer felt his confidence in Kentucky's chances for victory growing as he watched the reaction of the players to the unexpectedly large turnout of supporters.

"The fans were lined the entire length of the field, and we walked that hundred yards and that's one of the neatest things I've ever seen. I think our kids expected the normal 200 or 300 fans. I always waited till everybody got off the bus, and I saw our kids' eyes as they saw that mass of humanity and I knew our kids would be ready to play. I remember walking that walk and I'll never forget it," he said.

"I get goose bumps with the mention of the bowl game," McCutchan added. "There was no doubt we were going to win that game. We stepped onto the field and see 50,000 fans screaming for Kentucky. My parents called me before the game and said that it was all blue, like a caravan (on interstate 65) down to Nashville. Then the Cat Walk was just amazing and brought back some special memories. We stopped and were like, 'what is going on?' So we had our minds right after that."

With more than a month of prep time, a team playing in a bowl game uses the first few weeks to take a look at players that failed to make it into the

A UK fan outside LP Field sends his message to the Cats at the 2006 Music City Bowl.

rotation during the regular season.   Occasionally, one of them will emerge as a significant contributor in the postseason and that's what happened with wideout Stevie Johnson, a highly touted junior college transfer.   Anyone attending those early December practices soon heard the buzz about how, for Johnson, the light had come on. With veterans Burton and Lyons resting from scrimmage action during that time, they were able to serve as coaches on the field for Johnson, constantly telling him what he needed to do better or differently.   In the bowl game, Johnson had three catches for 67 yards.

"Stevie, wherever he got the help from, most of it came from his own mind. We had been talking to Stevie all along. Telling him he had big-time ability and needed to be making more plays and it showed up big in that game," said Brooks. "It also showed up with Andre, as he became more confident in looking to Stevie and throwing it to him to allow him to make some plays."

For all of the focus on fundamentals on the practice field, Brooks also recognized that the psychological component of preparing his players for

Photo by Kerri Brooks Robinson

Thousands of UK fans showed up for the Cat Walk, to welcome the team to the Music City Bowl in 2006.

their first bowl game was crucial to their success as well. He wanted to make sure his team wasn't satisfied to merely achieve its goal of playing in a postseason game. Brooks delivered that message frequently, but he also wanted to back it up with action.

That's part of the reason he installed a new play for goal-line situations, designed to let true freshman middle linebacker, Micah Johnson, to carry the football. Every time they ran the play in practice, it failed. But when Kentucky moved inside Clemson's five-yard line on its opening drive, Brooks called Johnson's number and the Cats took a lead they would never relinquish.

Photo by Victoria Graff

Stevie Johnson had a breakout performance in the win over Clemson, foreshadowing the big year to come in 2007.

"I think just to show that we did have confidence in him and to do something different," Brooks said of his gamble. "To make players aware that this wasn't just another game, this was a bowl game and that we wanted to try some different things to make sure we were not just going to a bowl game to be there, but that we were going to win it. That is the way we went in and approached that game. Going to a bowl game is memorable—winning a bowl game makes it a different experience. If you go and lose, those memories fade. Then, when you go back to a reunion or when you get 10 or 20 years down the road, when you win those bowl games, it makes things a lot more fun going forward. It also certainly makes for a much better offseason going into the next year."

While he felt good about his team's readiness, Brooks had tremendous respect for Clemson, a team that preseason forecasts projected as an ACC title contender. That's why Brooks wanted his team to play with an attacking mindset and with less than three minutes remaining before halftime, and

UK on top 7-6, he decided to reinforce that message. The coaching staff had noticed a flaw in Clemson's punt rush formation that should give Kentucky an opportunity to successfully execute a fake. And with the Cats facing a fourth-and-four at their own 20-yard line, Brooks called for "Raider," the fake punt play named in honor of special teams' coach Steve Ortmayer's long association with the Oakland and L.A. Raiders.

Punter Tim Mastay says he was all for it.

"I think that was the fourth punt of the game. The first two were really poor punts and the third (one), they blocked it, so by the time we got to the fourth punt, I was thinking the last thing we need to do is punt the ball. I was relieved that all I had to do was throw the ball—and Marcus made a great (catch)," Mastay said.

Up in the press box, then offensive coordinator Joker Phillips had some serious reservations. And when Clemson called a timeout, Phillips asked the head man if he was really sure about this gamble.

Photo by Tom Leach

Tim Mastay (right) conducts an interview with the boss for the Rich Brooks TV show on the Big Blue Sports Network.

> . . . Even if I never get to punt or kick competitively again, your belief in me and your persistence, patience, and integrity have made a mark on me and I hope to emulate those characteristics throughout my life. . . .
>
> *Excerpt from Tim Mastay's letter to*
> *Coach Brooks—See full text on page 307.*

"I said 'are you sure?' And he says, 'yes, I am sure,'" Phillips said, noting Brooks was emphatic in his response. "And when Rich says he is sure, I am staying out of the way. (But) I was hoping he would talk himself out of calling it."

Fat chance of that.

"They had partially blocked one punt, hurried (Tim) Mastay into some bad punts, and we felt the fake was there although they were showing something different than what we practiced against. I just felt the momentum had started to turn in their favor," Brooks explained. "Clemson called a timeout to conserve time, and I actually went over there and said, 'okay, we are going to run the fake but bear with me.' I started to coach them on the protection and to make sure to get the punt off so (the Clemson coaches) didn't suspect something on the other sideline."

(On the radio...

> *"Mastay to punt. The ball just across the Kentucky 19-yard line. Low snap, but Mastay's got it. It's a fake and it's a completion to Marcus McClinton. Breaks a tackle, across the 25 and out to the 30-yard line and a first down for Kentucky. How about Rich Brooks!")*

"Our snap wasn't great and Mastay had to handle the ball on the right and he is a left-handed passer," said Brooks. "He got the ball off about one step before he got hit and Marcus McClinton made a catch that was behind him a little bit and made a little run to get the first down. It wasn't easy, but if we had got the blocker out where he was supposed to be it might have been a really big play. But as it turned out, the really big play followed that."

(On the radio...

"Play fake and Woodson is setting up deep. He's going deep. DeMoreo Ford. He's got it. 30, 20, 10, 5, touchdown Kentucky!")

Photo by Victoria Graff

That 70-yard play-action touchdown pass from Woodson to Ford put the Cats up 14-6 and set the tone for the day.

"We talk about sudden changes and that is one of his goals, to win the sudden changes," Phillips said. "We went with the fake punt and that is the

A 70-yard touchdown pass to DeMoreo Ford broke open the game against Clemson.

sudden change that you need to win. We went up top and won that sudden change deal there. But when the guy makes a (move) like that, it makes your next call easier."

Ortmayer says he can only recall one fake punt or field goal that failed to work in Brooks' entire tenure at Kentucky. And Brooks, who gets a gleam in his eye when you tell him that stat, says the fake punt and the long TD pass that followed set the tone for Kentucky's triumph.

"Those two plays did so much to send a message to Clemson, to our players and to our fans that we didn't come here to just be in a bowl game. We came here to win it. We are going to go after it. We are not going to just sit on our hands, you know, try not to lose, we are going to go out and try to win," said Brooks. "I think that was very important in our approach to that game. By the end of that season, I don't think there was anybody that hadn't bought in (to Brooks' plan) and after that game, more importantly, other people bought in. Fans, recruits, players who were returning, they saw we could compete against one of the more respected programs in the country and beat them."

Kentucky built its lead to 22 points early in the fourth quarter and held off a Clemson rally for a 28-20 win, the first bowl victory since 1984 for the long beleaguered program.

(On the radio...

"Andre Woodson drops to a knee and raises two fists to the air. This one is over. The Kentucky Wildcats are going to win their third bowl game since 1951 and their first in 22 years and they get their eighth win of the season. 3,2,1, Cats win!")

And it set off a raucous celebration. Players carried the Music City Bowl trophy to a side of LP Field to give fans a closer look. In the locker room, the scene featured both exultation and reflection.

"Joker was sitting next to me," Archer recalled, "and he said 'we've come a long way since the locker room in Baton Rouge'. It was very emotional for a lot of kids and a lot of coaches."

This was the kind of moment native-Kentucky-son Jacob Tamme had dreamed of relishing. A star wide receiver at perennial power Boyle

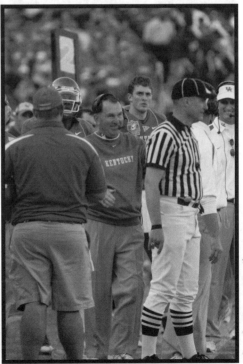

A smiling Brooks starts to savor UK's first bowl win in 22 years.

Photo by Victoria Graff

45

Photo by Victoria Graff

Athletics Director Mitch Barnhart congratulates senior Durrell White (9) on the bowl victory.

Photo by David Coyle/TeamCoyle

Rich Brooks celebrates in the arms of his players after UK beat Clemson 28-20.

County High School in Danville, KY, Tamme didn't respond quickly enough to a scholarship offer from previous UK coach Guy Morriss and saw it awarded to another prospect. When the coaching change occurred, Tamme contacted Barnhart to say he desperately wanted to wear the blue-and-white. A short time later, Brooks called with a scholarship offer. And late in his second year at UK, Tamme was moved to tight end by soon-to-be offensive coordinator Joker Phillips.

"We had chances for a lot of firsts, particularly in the last two years. Some that are so obscure that no one knows about them," said Tamme, who caught a touchdown pass in the bowl win.

Photo by Victoria Graff

Dicky Lyons, Jr. flashes the victory sign after the bowl triumph in Nashville.

"(Sports information director) Tony Neely would dig in the book until he found a first. He found first game-ever notes for everything and it meant a lot to the team. Some of those things were real important so we kept harping on them. When you hear something like first bowl win in 22 years, that's two decades and creating a culture around the program where bowl games aren't expected. And when you break through that and win bowl games, it changes the culture. Coach Brooks understood it and helped in changing it."

"I remember Lou Holtz coming on TV before the game and saying that Clemson will destroy Kentucky," Barnhart reflected. "This is a Clemson team that should be in a BCS bowl game and competing for the ACC crown and Kentucky has no chance. I remember those words, 'no chance'. I laughed at the end of that deal because we dominated that game. The score was not indicative of a game that was not that close."

"I believe a lot of it was Rich's will," said sportswriter Vaught on the reason for Kentucky's turnaround that season. "And it was that perfect

Photo by Victoria Graff

Wesley Woodyard shows off the Music City Bowl championship trophy.

combination of a coach that could lead the guys the right way and you had great leaders on that team to follow him. They wouldn't let this team fail. I think they felt they had put their reputation on the line, too."

The post-game celebration was a lovefest between the Wildcats and their terminally loyal supporters in the stands. After the trophy presentation, Brooks gave a thumbs-up to those fans as he jogged toward the locker room, where the tears of joy were flowing from players who had known almost nothing but adversity in their college careers.

"Elation" was Brooks' description of the scene. "Those are the type of things in situations you cannot get in normal life, that you cannot get if you are not coaching and probably one of the reasons why I am still coaching is because of the elation and doing something that other people didn't think we could do. By the midpoint of the season, they had written the team off, the staff off as dead, gone and history. To come out of that is one of the great lessons in life that athletics can teach you. The old saying 'it's always darkest before dawn, when the going gets tough the tough get going'—all of those things that are talked about happened to that team. To see all that come together, that is the real satisfaction I get."

Photo by TeamCoyle

The 50,000-plus Kentucky fans that came to Nashville got a postgame salute from Brooks.

Photo by Ken Weaver/TeamCoyle

DeMoreo Ford and Brooks celebrate the victory over heavily-favored Clemson.

Kentucky 28 | Clemson 20

2006 Gaylord Hotels Music City Bowl, December 29, 2006

SCORING SUMMARY

Clemson	0	6	0	14	-	20
Kentucky	7	7	7	7	-	28

UK – M. Johnson 1 run (Seiber kick) … 11:04 1st qtr.
CU – Barry 32 pass from Proctor (Early kick failed) … 8:14 2nd qtr.
UK – Ford 70 pass from Woodson (Seiber kick) … 2:14 2nd qtr.
UK – Lyons 24 pass from Woodson (Seiber kick) … 8:09 3rd qtr.
UK – Tamme 13 pass from Woodson (Seiber kick) … 11:29 4th qtr.
CU – Grisham 17 pass from Proctor (Proctor rush failed) … 7:25 4th qtr.
CU – Kelly 17 pass from Proctor (Palmer pass from Proctor) … 0:44 4th qtr.

TEAM STATISTICS

	Clemson	Kentucky
First Downs	19	21
Rush Attempts/Net Rushing Yds.	25/130	40/100
Passing C/A/I	23/39/1	21/29/0
Net Passing Yards	272	309
Offensive Plays	64	69
Total Offense	402	409
Fumbles/Lost	3/3	2/2
Penalties/Yards	5/50	8/84
Punts/Average	3/43.7	4/25.0
Third-Down Conversions	4-of-11	7-of-14
Time of Possession	26:16	33:44

INDIVIDUAL STATISTICS

RUSHING (ATT-YARDS-TD)
Kentucky - Little 17-57, Bankhead 3-37, Dixon 8-29, Conner 1-1, M. Johnson 2-1-1, team 1-0, Woodson 8-(-22)
Clemson - Davis 8-53, Proctor 9-32, Spiller 5-24, Ford 1-15, Stuckey 1-5, Merriweather 1-1

PASSING (COMP-ATT-INT-YARDS-TD)
Kentucky - Woodson 20-28-0-299-3, Masthay 1-1-0-10-0
Clemson - Proctor 23-39-1-272-3

RECEIVING (REC-YARDS-TD)
Kentucky - Burton 5-30, Tamme 4-59-1, S. Johnson 3-67, Lyons 2-50-1, Little 2-15, Dixon 2-2, Ford 1-70-1, McClinton 1-10, Pulley 1-6
Clemson - Kelly 6-66-1, Stuckey 5-93, Grisham 5-49-1, Davis 2-13, Barry 1-32-1, Ford 1-8, Harris 1-5, Merriweather 1-4, Palmer 1-2

TACKLES
Kentucky - Woodyard 12, McClinton 9, R. Williams 7

Chapter Five

Re-energizing the
Louisville
Rivalry

AS A PLAYER AT OREGON STATE and a coach at Oregon, Brooks got early exposure to the passion an intense college football rivalry can generate. And he got a booster shot when he lost his first game as Kentucky's coach to the school's arch in-state rival Louisville. With the Cardinals winning the next three games in the series, Brooks knew the goodwill he banked with the finish in year four might be wiped out if UofL scored another decisive victory in 2007.

The season began with Kentucky hosting Eastern Kentucky University, marking the first time since 1993 that the season did not start with the annual rivalry game against Louisville. Brooks caught tremendous heat in the media for pushing for that change, but he felt the chance to start a campaign without so much pressure on the first game would benefit a program still in the growing stages. He was a little surprised at how much of a controversy the move caused among some reporters and fans.

"It would have been one thing if, when I came in here, it had been going on 50 years or longer. But at the time I got in here, it had been eight years. It wasn't like it was a long-standing (tradition)," he said. "I know there was some added pressure that if we didn't win it, we would have been thoroughly abused and criticized by the media and our fan base for moving it from the opening game. What it did was it allowed us to break in some new players and give them some playing time, gain some confidence and be able to have an opportunity to figure out what turned out to be a new coaching staff at Louisville."

Veteran *Louisville Courier-Journal* columnist Rick Bozich was among the many in the media who spoke out against moving the UofL game out of the opening game slot on the Kentucky schedule. Still, he thinks it helped Brooks' standing with both his own players and the UK fans.

"I think in part it was because 'we've lost a bunch of games to UofL. We're going to stand up to them and do things our way'. He kinda rallied the troops and the fans behind him. I admire him for that on some level," Bozich said. "He was trying to take control at some level of his side of the deal. Did that help them win the game? I don't know, but it turned out well for them."

All of the bowl game emphasis on setting an aggressive tone carried over into the new season. On the bus ride to Commonwealth Stadium for the season opener, Joker Phillips decided he needed to back up his talk of an attacking mindset on offense with a deed—calling for a bomb on the game's very first play. Lining up at its own 49-yard line, Kentucky executed it to perfection as Andre Woodson connected with Lyons on a fly pattern down the left sideline and the Cats were on their way to a 50-10 victory.

Photo by Victoria Graff

Woodson looks for a little help from above as the Cats battled to end the losing streak against Louisville.

After a 56-20 win over Kent State, it was time for the main event. Louisville had won the previous four games over Kentucky in the Brooks era in decisive fashion, and the Cardinals brought a number nine national ranking into the 2007 matchup at Commonwealth. The Wildcats gained the upper hand early, converting turnovers on the Cards' first two series into a 10-0 lead, setting off a frenzied response by the Big Blue faithful. But the Cardinals rallied and the two teams traded punches for the rest of the night until a Brian Brohm touchdown pass gave UofL a 34-33 lead with only a minute and 45 seconds left in the game.

Woodson and company took the field confident they could get the winning score, but after driving into Louisville territory, Kentucky was pushed back to its own 43-yard line because of an unsportsmanlike conduct penalty. This was the kind of setback that had derailed many past upset bids, but not this time.

With less than 30 seconds remaining, Brooks and Phillips again decided on a bold plan of attack. Phillips called for a play named "Four Verticals," in which four wideouts each streak straight down the field parallel to each other. It had nearly worked on a long pass attempt just before halftime, and Brooks says they had noticed that a safety, charged with providing deep support, had shown a tendency to cheat toward the middle of the field because of tight end Jacob Tamme's earlier success. Just before Woodson left the sideline, quarterbacks coach Randy Sanders reminded him "don't forget about Stevie." Johnson lined up widest to the left, and Sanders thought number 13 might be the one who came open if that safety did indeed creep toward the middle of the field.

(On the radio...

"Woodson from the gun. Play fake. Steppin' up. He's throwing deep down the near sideline. He's got Johnson. 20, 10, 5, touchdown Kentucky! 13 is a lucky number.")

"We'd run that play a lot and we'd hit some big gains. You could see that look in everybody's eyes 'we're going to get something good on this play'. When you see that, there's not much you have to say as a quarterback," recalled Woodson. "We ran that play about three plays before and I missed Tamme, so I knew the safety was going to jump on Tamme and Stevie would be open. Right when I released the ball, the only thing in my head was 'Stevie, please don't drop this football'. When he scored, I never ever, ever heard a stadium get so loud. It was wonderful. You just can't describe feelings like that."

"Definitely, I can still see it. It seemed like it took forever to get there," said Johnson, "and then, like, for a second I thought I was going to get caught, because how long the ball seemed like it was taking to get there. And then, when I made the little turn in, which I knew that they were going to try to come and try to get my legs, I was like, 'OK, yeah, it's all good. Well, I'm in the clear, it's a touchdown.'"

Photo by Victoria Graff

Stevie Johnson's 57-yard TD sealed the upset of Louisville and set off an eruption of noise from the UK fans.

BROOKS STANDS BY HIS MAN

In Brooks' tenure at Kentucky, there are numerous examples of him taking a tough disciplinary stand against offenders even if it meant hurting his team's chances for success. But one of the things that endears Brooks to his players is that he will back them when he believes in their side of the story. And Johnson is a classic example of that.

During the week leading up to the 2007 opener, Johnson was arrested while on his way to visit teammate David Jones, who was in the hospital recovering from an appendectomy. The charges included driving without a license, driving without insurance and resisting arrest.

Johnson called Brooks soon after the incident occurred and explained his version of what happened. On the most serious charge—resisting arrest—Brooks believed what his player told him and Johnson was not suspended.

"I think anytime players do things that are against the law, which is obviously against team rules, I have always been a guy that is going to sit down and try to figure out what happened first," Brooks explained. "You sit down and look at the police report and then you get the player's side of the story and then you make a decision that is the best for the individual and the program. Stevie's explanation of what happened, I was not happy that he resisted arrest, if you will, but I did not feel it warranted a suspension or anything that severe. So I would let it play out in court to see whether my observation of what Stevie said was on the correct side. I believe Stevie is a good kid. He hadn't been drinking, and I think that it was overstated what happened and even though it was a lapse in judgment, it was not severe enough to penalize him any further and embarrass him any further."

Players know the only chance they have to avoid or lessen a penalty from their coach is to be straight with him.

"If I don't get the truth, players have been dismissed from the team, they have been suspended from games. I think that we have been fortunate to not have a lot of those issues, and I want to make sure the team has discipline. I think discipline takes a lot of different forms. One of the things that athletes get that a normal student doesn't get if they get in trouble is that they get thoroughly embarrassed publicly. That goes a long way in determining how they will act in the future, because," Brooks said, "I think that it is a pretty severe thing to be bantered about publicly as a person that has violated the law.

"Athletes are held to a different standard and they should be. There are a lot of different scenarios, and I have always been a guy that likes to give the player the benefit of the doubt until I learn what is going on. I try to ascertain the facts as best as I can, without trying to be a judge and jury, though I have to be in some sense. When players have had repeated problems, the axe falls a lot faster."

Johnson says he will never forget the faith Brooks showed in him.

"I basically can say sure I owe my season to him because, just like you said, any other coach, they didn't have to believe what would happen, with a kid getting into it with the law and everything, and it was a serious situation, and he didn't suspend me," Johnson said. "I mean, it has something to do with me because, I wasn't really one of those kids that was getting into that kind of trouble and everything, and I'm pretty sure he saw that in me. So that was huge for me, and a big decision for him to, you know what I'm saying, to trust me."

And before you point out Johnson's value to that season's team as the reason to stick by him, remember that Brooks dismissed a possible starting quarterback, Curtis Pulley, in a similar situation, prior to the 2008 season.

Kentucky 40 | Louisville 34

September 15, 2007

SCORING SUMMARY

Louisville	7	14	7	6	-	34
Kentucky	13	6	7	14	-	40

UK – Seiber 36 FG ... 13:58 1st qtr.
UK – Johnson 5 pass from Woodson (Seiber kick) ... 12:02 1st qtr.
UK – Seiber 31 FG ... 6:06 1st qtr.
UL – Allen 8 pass from Brohm (Carmody kick) ... 1:11 1st qtr.
UK – Little 10 run (Seiber kick failed) ... 12:43 2nd qtr.
UL – Douglas 3 pass from Brohm (Carmody kick) ... 7:16 2nd qtr.
UL – Allen 10 run (Carmody kick) ... 1:02 2nd qtr.
UK – Conner 7 pass from Woodson (Seiber kick) ... 9:46 3rd qtr.
UL – Guy 100 kickoff return (Carmody kick) ... 9:31 3rd qtr.
UK – Tamme 5 pass from Woodson (Seiber kick) ... 13:47 4th qtr.
UL – Allen 2 run (Brohm pass failed) ... 1:45 4th qtr.
UK – Johnson 57 pass from Woodson (Seiber kick) ... 0:28 4th qtr.

TEAM STATISTICS

TEAM STATISTICS	Louisville	Kentucky
First Downs	26	27
Rush Attempts/Net Rushing Yds.	27/101	35/185
Passing C/A/I	28/43/1	30/46/0
Net Passing Yards	366	275
Offensive Plays	70	81
Total Offense	467	460
Fumbles/Lost	1/1	1/0
Penalties/Yards	7/53	5/65
Punts/Average	2/38.5	3/47.3
Third-Down Conversions	8-of-13	9-of-17
Time of Possession	29:37	30:23

INDIVIDUAL STATISTICS

RUSHING (ATT-YARDS-TD)
Kentucky - Little 27-151-1, Dixon 3-27, Conner 2-7, Woodson 3-0
Louisville - Allen 18-96-2, Spillman 1-6, Stripling 2-6, Brohm 6-(-7)

PASSING (COMP-ATT-INT-YARDS-TD)
Kentucky - Woodson 30-44-0-275-4, team 0-2-0-0-0
Louisville - Brohm 28-43-1-366-2

RECEIVING (REC-YARDS-TD)
Kentucky - Burton 9-99, Dixon 5-29, Tamme 5-27-1, Lyons 4-33, S. Johnson 3-65-2, Little 2-11, Conner 1-7-1, Ford 1-4
Louisville - Douglas 13-223-1, Urrutia 5-72, Allen 4-21-1, Barnidge 2-10, Guy 1-23, Stripling 1-21, Spillman 1-3, Brohm 1-(-7).

TACKLES
Kentucky - Woodyard 13, McClinton 7, Jenkins 6, J. Williams 6

Commonwealth Stadium erupted after Johnson's touchdown catch and the Cats held off Louisville's last-gasp rally for a stirring 40-34 win. Another monkey had been removed from the back of the Kentucky football program—Brooks' boys had beaten Louisville.

"I don't think the players felt pressure. I think that it was squarely on me, because I was the one who talked about moving the game to later in the season," said Brooks of the circumstances leading up to the game. "We had lost four games in a row to Louisville. And particularly the way we lost to Louisville the previous year (59-28), it just had to at some point stop. And if it didn't , the criticism would have built up to a loud roar again. It was a huge game to win for the future of this program moving forward. It was a huge game to win to get to postseason play, to get some national recognition for beating your arch rival; but also we had not beaten a top 10 team in a long time (Penn State in 1977). All of those history things, which turn into positive history lessons, I think you can't overstate the significance of that win. I think that the naysayers would have had a field day had we not won that game."

Photo by David Coyle/TeamCoyle

Bringing the Governor's Cup trophy back to UK set up a wild postgame celebration in the locker room.

Jacob Tamme remembers that the players were still getting the impression that there were plenty of skeptics on the topic of whether Kentucky football had really turned a corner.

"That was a huge win. That was a special game for a lot of reasons. No one on the team had ever beaten Louisville. We wanted to start off the season with a bang because we knew it would be a great year," said Tamme, whose fourth-down catch kept the game-winning drive alive prior to Johnson's touchdown. "A newspaper reporter the Monday before the game walked in the hallway of the press conference area and he asked, 'so you think you guys have a chance?' (My thought was) 'did you watch the end of last year? Did you see us win 8 games? Did you know we have some pretty good players?' But I was like, 'yeah, I think we have a chance'. Of course we had a chance and that is part of the thing, not only did we think we had a chance but we thought we were going to win the game. That was how we felt about every single game we played that year, and I think that changed somewhere in those two or three years that not everyone else might not be there or think we have a chance but the team and coach Brooks felt that we should win.

"The Louisville game was priceless," he continued, "and we beat a good team and the way it finished made it special. I get chill bumps thinking about it."

Photo by Dick Gabriel

Brooks does his weekly radio call-in show in the IMG studios every Monday night.

The doubters had been silenced—for now. But it's the nature of sports that they will return, and Brooks is one coach who admits paying some attention to those critics.

"The concern I have is how the players react to what is reported, what is talked about in talk shows, what is on the blogs, and who is getting criticized and for what reason and all of that. My suggestion to them, and I don't do it, but I tell the players to not read things during the season," he said. "What you need to focus on after a game is to think about what I need to do to get ready for the next game and how do I get better as an individual and how can I get our team better and what part will I play in making that happen.

"I have some other very good friends in coaching who do not read the paper, will not listen to talk shows. They will still get feedback but they are also afraid to tell the coach what is being said because they don't want to get him upset. It is just my philosophy that I am not going to go out of my way to listen to something or read something, but when given an opportunity, if I am in the car and there is a talk show on, I am going to listen to it," he continued. "Sometimes it is not very pleasant, but you get a sense of what is going on, and I kind of get a feel for how I can approach my team better when I know what the overall temperature is, let's put it that way.

Ken Goe is a sportswriter for *The Oregonian* and covered Brooks for much of his tenure at the University of Oregon. He says it was the same way when Brooks was with the Ducks when it came to media coverage.

"Yeah, he read every word. I don't know if he's still that way, but he knew exactly what was in every paragraph of every story, and he challenged me a few times, on—it was usually facts, and he was almost invariably right, and I appreciated it," Goe said. "What I appreciated about him was that everything was out in the open. There were no hidden agendas."

Brooks believes staying tuned in helps him in counseling his players on dealing with things they see or hear. These days, with so many sources for opinions to be vented, Brooks knows players are going to find out what is being written or said, either directly or indirectly.

"A lot of coaches, they don't want anyone to know that they read the paper and follow it, but they really do," said Scott Stricklin, former assistant AD for media relations at UK. "It is my experience that no one is closed off to it. If they aren't reading it directly, they would have somebody close to them let them know what is being said and what is being written. They would ignore it and if brought up to them, they'd pretend that they didn't know about it, even if they did. Rich made no bones about it. He would almost wait until someone asked a question if he had something he wanted to bring up about something written or said. He would tie his answer with something that had been said leading up to it. He did it in a very clever way that told them he was paying attention. He was honest in his defense, if a defense was necessary, and he would disagree if he had a disagreement. There were some (media) guys who bothered him more than others but that is just the nature. He never seemed to take it personally when criticism came."

Despite Kentucky's success at the end of the previous season, there weren't

Photo by Victoria Graff

any football pundits proclaiming that the Wildcats were ready to contend for an SEC championship in 2007. Brooks, though, believed it was a realistic goal and so he didn't spend any extra time celebrating the win over Louisville. A week later, the Wildcats began SEC play as an underdog at Arkansas, which was led by running back Darren McFadden, a leading Heisman Trophy contender.

The game could not have started worse for the Big Blue. An early fumble by Woodson was returned for a touchdown and with

Brooks and his team prepare to come onto the field at Arkansas.

McFadden leading the charge, the Hogs piled up 230 yards on the ground by halftime. Late in the second quarter, Arkansas led 20-7 and had driven into UK territory but "Mr. Big Play" Lindley scooped up a fumble and took it to the house to enable the Cats to cut the deficit to just six by the intermission. Momentum swung back in favor of the Hogs in the second half, when a safety was followed by a kick return for a touchdown. Down 29-21, Kentucky once again rallied in the fourth quarter, scoring 21 unanswered points in the final eight minutes to pull out a 42-29 victory. It marked the second year in a row that Kentucky had won its SEC opener and the first time since 1984 that the Cats had accomplished that feat on the road.

Brooks' face reflects the disappointment over Kentucky's 38-23 loss at South Carolina.

Photo by Victoria Graff

"We scored the last 21 points, and I don't think that we would have had any chance at that happening if we hadn't finished '06 the way we did, coming back and beating Georgia, coming from behind and beating Louisville in 2007," Brooks noted. "To win against that kind of team with that kind of talent, on the road, was one of our best wins since I have been here, period."

When the new rankings came out the following Monday, Kentucky jumped 13 spots to number eight in the AP poll. Disco was still king of the music charts when that last happened—in 1977. And next up was a Thursday night ESPN matchup with the SEC's other big surprise team, unbeaten South Carolina.

Woodson fumbled on the Cats' second offensive play of the night and it was returned for a touchdown. Late in the first half, he threw his first interception of the season, at the USC two-yard line, and another fumble by the UK quarterback early in the third period was also returned for a score.

With four turnovers in all, Kentucky saw its winning streak come to an end with a 38-23 loss to the Gamecocks.

"That loss probably hurt as much as any other loss I had had to that point," Brooks said. "I felt we were a team that was as good as or better than South Carolina, and I felt that we should have won that game."

Brooks knew his team had missed a chance to make a statement about being a factor in the SEC East race. There was an opportunity to recapture that lost ground the next week, but to do it, the Wildcats would have to beat a number one ranked team in LSU. Given that UK's record in that kind of match up was 1-8 since the 1950 Sugar Bowl win over Oklahoma, virtually no one outside the Kentucky family gave Brooks and company much of a chance.

Chapter Six

Shocking the College Football World

WHEN IT CAME TO CREATING A BUZZ on the college football landscape, LSU was hotter than cayenne pepper as the Tigers prepared to visit Lexington, KY in October, 2007. Les Miles' team was coming off a dramatic 28-24 win over Florida, a game in which LSU converted three fourth-down plays in the final quarter. And the October 13 date for the Kentucky-LSU matchup was one day short of a full year since that rout in Baton Rouge.

"I think anytime you play the number one team in the nation, you have built-in motivation," said Brooks. "They all knew what had happened at LSU with the 49-0 embarrassment. They put that challenge into the rest of the 2006 season and took the challenge into 2007 and were ready to make a statement not only to our fans but to LSU—that the team you thumped down there, we are not those guys."

"Emotionally, I will tell you to this day, Wesley Woodyard, Keenan Burton, Jacob Tamme, and Rafael Little, those guys were the emotional heart beat of that team. "Barnhart noted. "They kept listening to what Rich did and (they were) the leaders of our team. They understood that he had been in big games before. He had seen the big scene and wasn't afraid of it. So many coaches walk in that locker room and they get afraid of that big game. I don't want to say that you don't go in there with nervous energy--everyone had nervous energy—but Rich never backs off looking forward to the big game. He takes it as a challenge, and I think that is the difference in a lot of coaches and Rich. He has put us in a position to be there in big games and be able to take people on."

Kentucky scored first, when backup tight end T.C. Drake caught a deflected pass in the back of the end zone. LSU responded with 17 unanswered points, part of a 27-7 run that saw the Tigers expand their lead to 27-14 on a field goal with 3:49 left in the third quarter. If UK was going to shock the college football world, it would mean the Cats' newfound confidence would be tested by the need for yet another fourth-quarter comeback, against a team that would eventually win the BCS national championship that season.

"I think that our players had a lot of confidence on offense to that point. I think at different points we were a fairly confident defensive team as well, but we seemed to still have those glitches on defense with a play here and a play there. I think our players felt that they had a shot going into that game. The fact that it was on national television was a big factor as well," Brooks observed. "There were so many different points in that game. There were so many sways—from the good to the bad to the good and back to the bad. Just knowing that physically we were able to hang with them as the game wore on was one of the biggest factors to me that our players knew that they could get this done. The year before, we had been thoroughly embarrassed by that same LSU team."

Lyons says the transformation of the mindset of the Kentucky players that started late in 2006 was now complete.

"I remember we were down like 10 at Auburn in '04, when they had Cadillac Williams in there, and everybody just gave up, and it was only halftime.

This game, we were down by 15 in the third quarter, and there was nobody that was worried. We knew that we were going to come back and win this game," said Lyons.

An eight-yard touchdown pass to Jacob Tamme with 1:13 remaining in the third started the rally for Kentucky. A Lones Seiber field goal brought them to within three midway through the fourth and then LSU decided to go for the knockout blow from deep in its own territory. Quarterback Matt Flynn threw deep but Lindley was blanketing his man and he came down with an interception in LSU territory. When the drive stalled for the Cats, Seiber drilled a 27-yard field goal at the 4:21 mark to tie the score at 27. With many of the UK fans no doubt thinking back to LSU's "Bluegrass Miracle" win at Kentucky in 2002, Tigers' kicker Colt David barely missed on a 57-yard field goal attempt at the buzzer and the game went into overtime.

The two teams first traded touchdowns and then field goals, sending it into a third OT. Kentucky got the ball first and drove to the LSU two, only to draw a delay-of-game penalty on third down. This was the kind of momentum-busting mistake that UK fans had seen derail so many upset bids over the years, but not this time and not with this team. Derrick Locke picked up a blitzing defender heading for Woodson's back just a split second before the QB released his pass.

(On the radio...

"Two receivers split left. Johnson back to the right with Tamme the tight end this way. Woodson from the gun and again, LSU looks like they're coming from both edges. Gotta get rid of it quick. Woodson, pump fake, he floats it. Man wide open. Got it. Touchdown, Kentucky! It's Stevie Johnson.")

A mandatory two-point conversion attempt failed, meaning LSU could win the game with a touchdown and a successful two-point play. Miles turned to the ground game, calling star tailback Jacob Hester's number on three straight plays, which netted eight yards. On the third-and-four run, Hester was shaken up on the hit from Kentucky middle linebacker Micah Johnson, so Charles Scott entered the huddle. With the game's outcome on the line, the Tigers prepared to do what they did with perfection against Florida—execute on fourth down.

Photo by Victoria Graff

Stevie Johnson's TD catch in the third overtime provided the margin of victory against LSU.

"They had called a time out on fourth-and-two. (Our players) came over to the sidelines and we are out there and linebackers coach (Chuck) Smith is talking to Micah, (defensive coordinator Steve) Brown is on the headset and I am looking at Micah thinking 'great tackle' and I see him grabbing his shoulder," Brooks remembered. "He had had a little (joint) problem and I said, 'are you alright?' He looked at me funny and I said, 'Braxton, get in the game.'"

Braxton Kelly had started from day one at Kentucky as part of Brooks' second recruiting class. As the highly touted Johnson began to make an impact in his second season, he and Kelly split time at the crucial MLB spot. The fact that the Cats had two players of that caliber to alternate was a testament to the depth the coaching staff was building.

As Brooks expected, LSU went back to the same well.

(On the radio...

"Scott is the tailback. Johnson the fullback. Offset I, two tight ends stacked right and now one of them goes in motion to the left. (Matt) Flynn turns. Leaves it with Scott. No! Hit at the 16. He did not make it. Victory, Kentucky! They have done it. Big Blue Madness on the football field at Commonwealth Stadium, as number one goes down.")

Game over. Kentucky 43, LSU 37. Teammate Wesley Woodyard then tackled Kelly in celebration as the fireworks went off above Commonwealth Stadium and a huge throng of Big Blue fans again came pouring onto the turf.

"I just remember I felt he was stopped and that he hadn't made it. But it was kind of like a long pregnant pause. It took like five seconds, 10 seconds,"

Photo by Dick Gabriel

When Braxton Kelly stopped LSU's Charles Scott on a fourth down play, Kentucky secured its first upset of a number one team since 1964.

Photo by David Coyle/TeamCoyle

Defensive coordinator Steve Brown and Wesley Woodyard were beaming with pride over UK's performance against number one LSU.

Brooks recalled, "and then you see Wesley (Woodyard) running around and guys jumping all over Braxton and the place just goes nuts. It is one of the greatest emotional moments. It is one of the reasons why you coach and play the game. It was just a very special moment.

"After the game, things are just crazy and I have (police) officers on each shoulder and I am trying to find Les Miles and you see Les Miles and officers running toward the tunnels so, I know I am not going to get him but I am running to catch him," he continued. "To my right is (UK associate AD) John Cropp and we collide and I hit him with my right shoulder he hits me with his left and he goes tumbling down on the field. That is one of the better hits I have given. It was chaotic to say the least."

"I think we were both walking on air," Cropp said.

For Brooks, the win, coming against a team that had victimized the Cats with that last-second miracle TD five years earlier, solidified the message he wanted his players to buy into.

Kentucky 43 | LSU 37

October 13, 2007

SCORING SUMMARY

LSU	0	17	10	0	7	3	0	-	37
Kentucky	7	7	7	6	7	3	6	-	43

UK – Drake 2 pass from Woodson (Seiber kick) ... 2:49 1st qtr.
LSU – Scott 1 run (David kick) ... 14:55 2nd qtr.
LSU – David 31 FG ... 5:42 2nd qtr.
LSU – Scott 13 run (David kick) ... 1:48 2nd qtr.
UK – Woodson 12 run (Seiber kick) ... 1:04 2nd qtr.
LSU – Dickson 4 pass from Flynn (David kick) ... 9:12 3rd qtr.
LSU – David 30 FG ... 3:49 3rd qtr.
UK – Tamme 8 pass from Woodson (Seiber kick) ... 1:13 3rd qtr.
UK – Seiber 33 FG ... 7:57 4th qtr.
UK – Seiber 27 FG ... 4:21 4th qtr.
UK – Locke 1 run (Seiber kick) ... 1st OT
LSU – Murphy 2 run (David kick) ... 1st OT
LSU – David 38 FG ... 2nd OT
UK – Seiber 43 FG ... 2nd OT
UK – S. Johnson 7 pass from Woodson (Woodson pass failed) ... 3rd OT

TEAM STATISTICS

	LSU	Kentucky
First Downs	22	24
Rush Attempts/Net Rushing Yds.	50/261	41/125
Passing C/A/I	18/37/1	21/38/2
Net Passing Yards	142	250
Offensive Plays	87	79
Total Offense	403	375
Fumbles/Lost	0/0	3/0
Penalties/Yards	12/103	7/62
Punts/Average	4/33.8	3/47.3
Third-Down Conversions	8-of-19	9-of-17
Time of Possession	33:21	26:39

INDIVIDUAL STATISTICS

RUSHING (ATT-YARDS-TD)
Kentucky - Locke 20-64-1, Dixon 17-45, Woodson 3-16-1, team 1-0
LSU - Scott 7-94-2, Hester 18-61, Flynn 10-53, Holliday 5-24, Perrilloux 5-15, Murphy 3-10-1, K. Williams 1-5, Tolliver 1-(-1)

PASSING (COMP-ATT-INT-YARDS-TD)
Kentucky - Woodson 21-38-2-250-3
LSU - Flynn 17-35-1-130-1, Perrilloux 1-2-0-12-0

RECEIVING (REC-YARDS-TD)
Kentucky - S. Johnson 7-134-1, Lyons 6-49, Tamme 3-33-1, Burton 2-13, Dixon 1-18, Drake 1-2-1, Grinter 1-1
LSU - LaFell 4-42, Dickson 4-33-1, Murphy 2-22, J. Mitchell 2-9, Scott 2-6, Byrd 1-13, C. Mitchell 1-8, K. Williams 1-5, Hester 1-4

TACKLES
Kentucky - Woodyard 11, Jarmon 10, Lindley 7, Warford 7, Cobb 7

Photo by Victoria Graff

Brooks gets a celebratory hug from UK president Dr. Lee Todd after the upset of LSU.

"It just signified that what I heard when I came here—the 'Commonwealth curse' and all that baloney—is truly baloney," he said. "Games are won by players and coaches on the field at the time and our players proved that."

"It was just a time of joy," said Tony Dixon, a junior tailback at that time. "You could even see it in the coaches' faces. That's something I'll never, ever forget."

"Tears of joy" is the term linebacker Wesley Woodyard used to describe the scene in the locker room. But Woodson says it wasn't shock.

"When we got in the locker room, it was kinda like 'we expected to win that game'. It was not like it was a surprise. We knew we had it in us. It's about time this happened," he said.

Brooks addressed the team and so did UK president Dr. Lee Todd.

Photo by David Coyle/TeamCoyle

Andre Woodson gives a thumbs up to the fans for their support in the upset of LSU.

"One of the things I will always remember at the LSU game, it was pure joy. People were euphoric," said Dr. Todd. "Just the joy of seeing the students, and not just the students but the older fans, the ones that have been sitting around me for a long time and have been through the LSU (miracle) and lived through the Florida interception, the games that we should have won and didn't, and all of a sudden to do it and see the joy of the stadium.

"After (that) game, when you looked at the stands, they were still full. People were still there and enjoying each other. You have to believe that

SEC DEVELOPS NEW SPORTSMANSHIP POLICY

BIRMINGHAM, Ala. — The institutions of the Southeastern Conference have approved new sportsmanship policies designed to limit access to competition areas for all sports, the league announced Tuesday.

The policy, which went into effect on Dec. 1, 2006 states that "access to competition areas shall be limited to participating student-athletes, coaches, officials, support personnel and properly-credentialed individuals at all time. For the safety of participants and spectators alike, at no time before, during or after a contest shall spectators be permitted to enter the competition area."

The policy imposes significant institutional financial penalties for violations in the sports of football, men's and women's basketball, at the discretion of the Commissioner. Institutional financial penalties range from $5,000 for a first offense to fines of up to $25,000 for a second offense and up to $50,000 for a third and subsequent offense.

"This policy is designed to create a safe environment for our student-athletes, coaches, staff and fans," said SEC Commissioner Mike Slive. "Our institutions felt that this was a step that needed to be taken to insure a safe atmosphere at all of our intercollegiate athletics events."

In addition to the financial penalties, the new policy also provides for institutions to penalize violators for entering the competition area with expulsion from the facility, arrest for trespassing and the loss of future ticket privileges. Violators who are students may be subject to institutional student disciplinary measures.

Institutions are responsible for publicizing and enforcing the policy, as well as the penalties associated with the violations.

there have been groups of people here for years that sit in their own little section and now they got a reason to stay longer. It was just a real high point, "added Dr. Todd, whose school had to pony up a $50,000 fine to the SEC office because the fans came onto the field for the third time in less than a year.

Photo by David Coyle/TeamCoyle

Mitch Barnhart congratulates Brooks on the upset of LSU, which propelled Kentucky back into the nation's top 10.

As day turned to night and the drama intensified, CBS' TV audience had grown substantially. Outside of the league championship game, only two other SEC matchups that season garnered more viewers.

"Amazing things happen when those kind of games are seen by the nation," Brooks said. "Kentucky begins being looked at in a different light and a different way. Like, 'hey, they play football too. And they are good and we can go there have fun and get national recognition as well.'"

There's always a gathering at the Brooks' home after a home game, but the scene was more festive than usual this time. Brooks did some celebrating with family and friends, watched some replay clips on ESPN but soon, it was time to get to bed because Sunday would start the preparation for another SEC heavyweight in Florida.

"It was just a normal night. I was just so worn out," he said. "You get so emotionally drained and physically tired of going through a game like that with so many swings and ups and downs. I don't think people realize how short of time you have to make those decisions and the strain it takes to make decisions and get it in on time and not slow the process down. It can wear you out."

In his postgame comments to reporters, Brooks lauded Woodson for an "All American performance." He had completed 21 of 38 passes for 250 yards and three touchdowns, but more impressive to the coach was the job Woodson did in preparing for LSU's defense and knowing when he needed to change plays. Brooks says those adjustments helped the Cats gain 125 yards on the ground against a defense that was allowing less than half of that amount. And although LSU led the SEC in sacks at that point, the Tigers never did get to Woodson.

Photo by Victoria Graff

ESPN's Chris Fowler, Lee Corso and Kirk Herbstreit brought their popular "College Gameday" show to Lexington for the first time ever in 2007.

Photo by Victoria Graff

A crowd estimated at more than 10,000 turned out to see the "Gameday" show.

Within hours of the upset of LSU, Scott Stricklin was taking a call from the producer of ESPN's wildly popular "College Gameday" show, saying they wanted to bring their crew to the University of Kentucky campus for the upcoming Florida game. "A million to one" was the response from one of the hosts, Lee Corso, when asked if he ever imagined doing that program at the University of Kentucky.

The "Gameday" set was erected near the bottom of a hill to the side of the William T. Young Library, providing an amphitheatre-like environment for thousands of Kentucky fans to crowd into the scene behind the on-camera hosts.

"You know, I don't think it was that a big a deal for me. I just think that it was recognition that hadn't happened in Kentucky football because ESPN's become an icon of college football. And I think it was nice recognition that we were now in the category of some of the more storied programs of having Gameday on their campus. That hasn't been a long-term phenomenon, where they've been moving it from site to site. So the fact that we were in that category was I think an exciting exposure for our university and our football program. The fact that you're on national TV game as well as being on Sportscenter, where they're broadcasting from your campus all day long, certainly doesn't hurt the visibility of recruiting to the people you're trying to get to who watch that stuff pretty regularly," Brooks said.

"We have never experienced such overwhelming hospitality from a school and a city in the 14 years of road shows," Gameday host Chris Fowler wrote on his espn.com blog the week after the trip to Lexington.

The game was a shootout between Heisman hopefuls Woodson and Tim Tebow, who would eventually win the award. They combined for 671yards through the air and nine passing touchdowns with the Gators holding on for a 45-37 victory. For Brooks, the loss meant his dream of getting this team to the SEC championship game was all but gone.

One of the things Brooks took from his coaching mentor, Tommy Prothro, was that no team can be at its emotional peak week in and week out. Prothro felt it could happen maybe four times per season, but Brooks thought you could perhaps do a little better than that—but not much. And after a five-week run that included two top 10 upsets, a road win at Arkansas and two disappointing conference losses—all on national TV—the Wildcats were prime candidates for what thoroughbred handicappers call a "bounce," the idea that a horse regresses off a taxing effort.

"I don't think there was any question that if we'd been able to defeat Florida right after defeating LSU that we would have been in a totally different stratosphere and in a different position going forward. Having said that, the loss was a real big letdown emotionally. I know a lot of players who put a lot on the line. We still had some people hurt. We got a few more hurt in that game. You know, the next week was a very difficult proposition," Brooks said.

A home game with Mississippi State was next up for the Cats and the perfect storm of bad circumstances was developing. You had a UK team that was emotionally spent playing against a Bulldog team it was expected to beat. And back-to-back slugfests against LSU and Florida had taken a physical toll. Three starters—including Burton and Little—were held out of the game with injuries, as were a couple of backups. And with Smith and Dixon shaken up during the contest, the Cats were down to their fifth-string tailback (Moncell Allen) by the end of the day. The weather was the final dose of bad Big Blue karma. It was a chilly, gloomy day and Brooks remembers that the turnout for the Cat Walk was considerably smaller than they'd seen the past few weeks.

In retrospect, the 31-14 loss to a State team that would eventually win a bowl game was not a shock. But that didn't lessen the disappointment. The defeat knocked Kentucky out of the top 25 polls and the effect seemed to linger through a hard-fought win at Vanderbilt, a loss at Georgia in which the Dogs erased a 10-0 UK lead and the first half clash with Tennessee, when the Vols built a 24-7 halftime lead.

On the brink of an embarrassing Senior Day blowout loss, the Wildcats took the advice Brooks gave them in his halftime talk and remembered what kind of team they were. Kentucky outscored Tennessee 24-7 in the second half to force the game into overtime. For a moment, it looked like the Cats would complete another fourth quarter rally, as they drove methodically

Photo by Victoria Graff

Brooks walks off the field after the Cats let a 10-point lead slip away in a loss at Georgia.

from their nine-yard line to the UT two in the final minutes. A potential game-winning pass from Woodson sailed over Burton's head on the back line of the end zone and Seiber then kicked a field goal to tie it a 31-31 on the final play of regulation.

"I did think it was finally going to happen," Brooks said of UK's bid to end the nation's streak of futility against one particular opponent. "I just felt we were going to win the game. I knew in my mind we were going to take the ball and put it in the end zone and win the game in regulation. I felt like it was going to happen, yes. The way we were playing, and we had them on their heels. We had started extremely bad in that game. In the first half, we played awful. And then all of a sudden, we started playing our kind of football again, and reignited, and I thought we totally dominated the second half of that football game."

In the second overtime, UK once again was poised to deliver the knockout punch. UT had the ball first but threw an interception, meaning the Cats needed only a field goal to win. Not wanting to risk having a pass picked off, too, Brooks and company kept the ball on the ground for three straight plays, setting up Knoxville, TN native Seiber for a 34-yard field goal attempt. It was blocked.

Does Brooks have any regrets about not employing a more aggressive play-calling approach after the interception? The answer is "no."

"I have regrets that we didn't make it. It was the right thing to do. It was the percentage thing to do," Brooks said. "And what had happened, earlier (335-pound) Christian Johnson, who was our right guard on the field goal team, had broken a finger, and he said he was having a hard time getting his hand down on that side and so we substituted (a smaller player). We had a combination of our line getting knocked back too far, and a low kick, and (instead of) a win that we should have had, we ended up going to another overtime."

In fact, it went two more overtimes, with the Vols finally pulling out a 52-50 win to extend the streak to 22 consecutive wins in the series.

"I tell people that the 2007 season was the craziest season ever," said Tony Barnhart, "and I can prove it—because I went to Kentucky three times to watch college football games. I've never done that. I saw three really good games (LSU, Florida, Tennessee) and each one of them had an impact on who won the SEC."

Unfortunately for the Cats, they lost two of them and the setback against UT killed any hopes Kentucky players had of getting to play in a New Year's Day bowl game. It would have marked just second such achievement in more than a half a century of Big Blue football and it was oh so close.

Kentucky had been a leading contender to represent the SEC in the Cotton Bowl, according to Rick Baker, president of the AT&T Cotton Bowl Classic. It would have been the Cats' first appearance in that tradition-rich game since 1951. Arkansas' upset of LSU a day earlier was the first blow to Kentucky's chances and once UK lost to the Vols, Baker says the McFadden-led Hogs became the "logical choice."

If both Kentucky and Arkansas had won—or both had lost—it would have been an interesting discussion as to which team to take, according to Baker. "We'd love to get Kentucky in our game. They have a lot of alumni in this (Dallas, TX) area and their fans travel great," he said, noting that Tennessee is the only SEC Eastern Division team to play in their contest. "I've known Mitch Barnhart for a long time and we have a lot of respect for Rich Brooks. There were a lot of reasons why we would have liked to have had Kentucky."

Instead of Dallas, the Wildcats found themselves making plans for a return trip to Nashville for another Music City Bowl and a match up with traditional power Florida State.

Chapter Seven

Making
More
History

WHEN NECESSARY, Brooks can verbally peel the paint off the locker room wall to challenge his players to perform at a higher level. But he likes to use history lessons to motivate his teams as well, and Brooks says he's been able to do that more frequently than ever at Kentucky.

In the wake of the heartbreaking four-overtime loss to Tennessee, Brooks leaned heavily on a couple of historical angles to get the Wildcats re-focused

Photo by Victoria Graff

Brooks and Florida State coach Bobby Bowden joke at a press conference for the 2007 Music City Bowl.

for a return trip to the Music City Bowl to face Florida State. He constantly talked up the chance to win bowl games in successive years for the first time since Bear Bryant-coached Kentucky teams won the Orange and Cotton Bowls in 1950 and '51. And with a win over Bobby Bowden's Seminoles, Kentucky would record an eighth win for the second straight year, something that had not been done at UK since 1977.

"With this group of young men, it has worked. And you never know whether the message you're giving is being received. You never know that. But certainly our players have responded to trying to do something that hasn't been done here for awhile, trying to do something that hasn't been done for 20 years, 30 years, 40 years, 50 years or trying to do something that has never been done here ," Brooks noted. "Honestly it's been a little easier to cite history things here on the football record than it has been in some places that I've been. And certainly I've never been to a school that holds some of their former athletes, whether it's football or basketball or whatever, in higher esteem and in such high regard.

"These players that have come through here and accomplished this have put themselves in the memory bank of an awful lot of the Big Blue Nation. And I've already started to witness it by seeing players that have been gone for a year or two come back and be introduced at a basketball game, or at a football game when they're coming off of a bye week in the NFL, and they come home and get introduced at Commonwealth Stadium," he continued. "It's an absolute thrill for me to see those players get the recognition after their career is done here, because of what they have accomplished here, and the fans remember them and hold them in such high regard."

With more than 30 FSU players sidelined with academic-related suspensions, the game lost some of its luster nationally. But *Louisville Courier-Journal* columnist Rick Bozich says it was still a significant win for UK.

"I remember I wrote a column before they played Florida State in the (2007) Music City Bowl," said Bozich, "and even though Florida State had all of those guys suspended, they had 20 or 30 more four- or five-star players than Rich Brooks had."

Photo by Victoria Graff

Brooks liked the way his team practiced for the bowl game even though the regular season finished on a down note.

When the Cats arrived in Nashville to finish preparing for the bowl game, Brooks was encouraged by what he was seeing. The practices were crisp and his players were winning the various competitions between the teams at pre-bowl events. It made the coach proud to see how his players were taking care of business even though the season had not turned out as well as they thought it would after the LSU upset. And Brooks says his players were buoyed by how their fans stuck with them, turning out more than 50,000 strong once again.

"Yeah, I think there's no question it did," Brooks said of the crowd. "I mean, it equaled or surpassed the year before. We were also playing a nationally-respected team, even though they had some problems with some of the players and eligibility. It still was Florida State and if we had hung on to the ball a little better, that would have been, I think, a very impressive win rather than being just a good win in a bowl game."

On the eve of the game, Brooks had to dismiss senior guard Jason Leger for a violation of team rules.

"It is heartbreaking because Jason Leger had been one of the cornerstones in our turnaround as far as toughness, his unselfishness going from defensive tackle, which he didn't want to do, to the offensive line, and he was a very good player in that game (at Florida) and for the rest of his career. We have some hard and fast rules and one of them on the bowl trip is that if there is a problem, they will be sent home, period. And it doesn't make any difference who you are. He had an unfortunate incident and you either follow through with your policy and discipline or you risk having chaos, but it doesn't make it easy to suspend a player in his last game who had worked so hard and done so much for this program," Brooks said.

Joker Phillips remembers it was an emotional time. And Brooks took it perhaps hardest of all. "You know who was crying like a baby," Joker asked rhetorically, pointing across the hall at Brooks' office.

Karen Brooks says while the losses hit her husband hard, it is handling some of the disciplinary issues with his players that often takes the biggest toll on his psyche.

"I think dealing with kids that let you down, when you expect something from the kids and they let you down (is tough). And kids screw up all the time, but if they continue to do it, I think that it is disappointing. You think you have kids that, you know, you are making progress with and all of a sudden he lets you down. That, I think, is a hard thing to deal with," she observed. "You can't save every kid you have got. You really think you have a kid with all that huge talent (like Curtis Pulley) and you think you are going to do some things with and you can't save him from himself. Those are hardest I think. That hurts him."

Steve Hellyer (Director of Football Operations) says one of the best parts of retirement for Brooks, when it comes, will be avoiding those kinds of issues. Having seen it firsthand through two coaching stops, Hellyer says he can tell Brooks agonizes over those kinds of decisions.

"It kills him. There are (assistant coaches) that just, it is obvious that they are at the end of their rope with a young man and he will talk to him and say he is the boss and it is his decision," Hellyer noted. "He is the guy who says we are going to keep working with this guy and try to improve him. Everybody is different but there are guys that have had it up to here being late, inattentive, not studying or whatever it is they do. It is always him that says he is worth saving. If he is screwing up it might be the coach's fault. He is one of the few guys I have worked with who doesn't always blame the student athlete.

"I know he had a tough upbringing in Northern California and he made some mistakes when he was a young man, too, and I think he understands

Photo by Victoria Graff

Brooks leads the Wildcats onto the field for the 2007 Music City Bowl.

that kids make mistakes and do stupid things. He is a compassionate guy," he continued. "There is no doubt, even though players were afraid to go talk to him in his early days because he can be gruff. Those that did were glad they did. He is one of those guys that if you come clean with him and not feed him a barrage of excuses, he is fair."

The New Year's Eve game against Florida State provided a showcase for many of the veterans around whom the team had rallied in the dark times in the middle of 2006. Woodson won his second consecutive MVP trophy by completing 32 of 50 passes for 358 yards and four touchdowns. Little rushed for 152, Burton overcame an ailing knee to catch seven passes, Tamme scored a touchdown, Johnson had two scores and seven receptions and Woodyard recorded a game-high 15 tackles as Kentucky held on for the victory.

(On the radio...

"*Weatherford gets the snap. Three-man rush. Flushed out of the pocket to his left. He sets at the 50. He heaves it down the far sideline. Into the end zone. Batted down. David Jones, I think, batted it down in front of Carr about seven yards deep in the end zone. The Kentucky Wildcats win it 35-28. Kentucky has its second straight bowl win for the first time since Harry Truman was in the White House in 1952.*")

Burton says those 2007 seniors came from successful high school programs and they combined to lead with a mentality that put winning above any individual needs or goals. And he says he's proud of the foundation that he helped lay under Brooks' leadership.

"Oh, it makes me feel good. It makes me feel like all our work wasn't in vain. It makes me feel like we headed in the right direction. You know, it's bowl game here, bowl game there. But now I think it's kind of like, well maybe we can get to a national championship one day. Maybe guys will start, you know, seeing us and saying, 'you know what, if we come to Kentucky, this can happen. You know, if we believe, then anything's possible,'" Burton said.

"One thing I can say is that we came from different places and different ties, but we were all willing to pull together like a brotherhood and that is what

Rafael Little rushed for 152 yards in the 35-28 win over Florida State.

Photo by Victoria Graff

Kentucky 35 | Florida State 28
2007 Music City Bowl, December 31, 2007

SCORING SUMMARY

Kentucky	7	7	14	7	-	35
Florida State	7	7	0	14	-	28

UK – Tamme 14 pass from Woodson (Seiber kick) ... 10:39 1st qtr.
FSU – Weatherford 6 run (Cismesia kick) ... 1:49 1st qtr.
UK – S. Johnson 13 pass from Woodson (Seiber kick) ... 8:28 2nd qtr.
FSU – Carter 24 interception return (Cismesia kick) ... 3:28 2nd qtr.
UK – Little 2 pass from Woodson (Seiber kick) ... 6:49 3rd qtr.
UK – Dixon 4 run (Seiber kick) ... 0:04 3rd qtr.
FSU – Weatherford 1 run (Cismesia kick) ... 8:02 4th qtr.
UK – S. Johnson 38 pass from Woodson (Seiber kick) ... 5:19 4th qtr.
FSU – Carr 7 pass from Weatherford (Cismesia kick) ... 2:14 4th qtr.

TEAM STATISTICS

	Kentucky	Florida State
First Downs	29	22
Rush Attempts/Net Rushing Yds.	36-143	33-204
Passing C/A/I	32/50/1	22/50/2
Net Passing Yards	358	276
Offensive Plays	86	83
Total Offense	501	480
Fumbles/Lost	5-3	1-0
Penalties/Yards	7/45	10/102
Punts/Average	5/39.8	6/41.7
Third-Down Conversions	6-of-14	6-of-16
Time of Possession	30:25	29:35

INDIVIDUAL STATISTICS

RUSHING (ATT-YARDS-TD)
Kentucky - Little 28-152, Dixon 4-17-1, Woodson 4-(-26)
Florida State - Smith 17-156, Weatherford 12-48-2, Parker 2-1, Holloway 1-0, team 1-(-1)

PASSING (COMP-ATT-INT-YARDS-TD)
Kentucky - Woodson 32-50-1-358-4
Florida State - Weatherford 22-48-2-276-1, Parker 0-1-0-0-0, team 0-1-0-0-0

RECEIVING (REC-YARDS-TD)
Kentucky - Little 8-50-1, S. Johnson 7-124-2, Burton 7-56, Lyons 5-78, Tamme 3-35-1, Dixon 1-8, Grinter 1-7
Florida State - Parker 8-105, Carr 6-99-1, Fagg 5-51, Owens 2-10, Smith 1-11

TACKLES
Kentucky - Woodyard 15, Kelley 6, Moore 6, Warford 5, McClinton 5

football is about," said Woodyard, "building that bond and allowing people to have friends and connections for the rest of your life and that is something we definitely did."

Photo by David Coyle/TeamCoyle

Wesley Woodyard and Keenan Burton kiss the 2007 Music City Bowl championship trophy.

"I am proud that we gave people something to be proud of," added Tamme. "I have been so busy I haven't had time to really reflect, but I get misty thinking about these moments. It is really special and to keep going and keep progressing. Something I have always thought to be proud of is if you and your class leave with things better than when you came in as freshman, and I can stand here and know that when we left it was better than we inherited, it was done with a lot of work. Even when the wins weren't coming necessarily, there were guys putting in the work to get better, like the Tommy Cook's, the Draak Davis's."

And Woodson says the players could tell how proud Brooks was for what they had accomplished.

"He knew what we all went through, with fans booing us, people not having respect for us, to all of the things we had to fight through, that's something I'll always remember about Coach Brooks," he said, "is how much he loved us as players."

For Lyons, the love Brooks has for his players was illustrated clearly on the day after the 2008 NFL draft. Despite the impressive numbers posted by the Wildcats and the big wins, no UK player was taken higher than the fourth round.

Kentucky players taken in NFL draft in Brooks era

2004	Derek Abney, WR/returner	7th round	Baltimore Ravens
2005	Vincent "Sweet Pea" Burns, DE	4th round	Indianapolis Colts
2008	Jacob Tamme, TE	4th round	Indianapolis Colts
	Keenan Burton, WR	4th round	St. Louis Rams
	Andre Woodson, QB	6th round	New York Giants
	Stevie Johnson, WR	7th round	Buffalo Bills
2009	Myron Pryor, DT	6th round	New England Patriots
	Jeremy Jarmon, DE (taken in supplemental draft)	3rd round	Washington Redskins

"He was just like distraught about why none of our guys went higher. I mean he was just so upset that nobody believed in them as much as he did," said Lyons. "I'd never seen him that upset about it, and that's when I really looked at it and realized how much he cared about us."

In preparing for the 2008 season, Brooks again pounded away at a history lesson to set the tone for his team. Kentucky's success in football had almost always come in two-year spurts, he repeated time and time again, and the challenge for the upcoming season was to sustain the momentum that had been established by reaching postseason play for a third year in a row. With so many big-play guys leaving on the offensive side, Brooks and his staff knew the key to achieving that goal would be an improved defense and the ability of the offense to eliminate sacks, fumble returns and other negative plays that Woodson and company often overcome with ease.

Over the summer, the battle between Curtis Pulley and Mike Hartline to succeed Woodson was the main focus of the media and fans. Shortly before training camp started, Pulley got into legal trouble and on media day, which marks the start of training camp, Brooks stepped to the podium and announced that Pulley was no longer on the team.

"It was just a violation of team rules, and I don't like to go into specifics. He had had previous transgressions, and part of the scenario is once you have been on probation or missed a game and something else comes up, the penalty gets more severe if you repeat your problems. And that's what happened, and the timing of it was bad, and the scenario was bad. The fact that he had been in trouble and hadn't told me made it worse. So we just moved on. And I had the information that I needed to have. I made the decision that I felt was right for the program," said Brooks.

As was the case with Jason Leger on the eve of the 2007 Music City Bowl, the decision was easy from a discipline standpoint but extremely difficult to make personally.

Photo by Victoria Graff

Wesley Woodyard and Brooks answer media questions after UK wins a second straight bowl game.

Photo by David Coyle/TeamCoyle

The bond between players like Jacob Tamme (18) and Brooks helped carry the program through a rough start to his tenure at UK.

"The toughest thing personally I deal with is what we call in the coaching profession 'breaking somebody's plate', taking their opportunity to play the game away from them," Brooks said. "Most of those are controlled by me. The decision isn't difficult, but the emotion of it is difficult. Once they've gone past the breaking point, to have a team, you have to draw the line. I don't have any problem drawing the line but it's very disappointing. In large respect, I feel like I've failed those individuals, that I haven't gotten through to them. I suppose that is one of the most difficult things that I do. That won't be missed (when I retire).

"You don't really remember the ones you help. You remember the ones you lose and you don't get through to," he continued. "They just eat at you. That's a terrible thing to say but that is the truth."

With that course set, the coaches focused on getting little-used sophomore Mike Hartline ready to assume the role as Woodson's successor at quarterback. And with Louisville getting its turn to host the annual rivalry game, the contest was once again set as the opening tilt.

While the days of Brooks working himself into a vomit-inducing frenzy in the pregame speech have passed with age, Karen Brooks says her husband's body language still gives off signals as a new season approaches.

"Building up to a game, his eyes get smaller. Especially the first game, like the Louisville game here. His eyes get smaller and smaller until they're little pinholes by game day. I guess it's tension," she observed. "The big games, he's probably more nervous. But he gets quieter as he gets nervous. But I can know what's going on inside him by just looking at his eyes."

The idea that the Cats could now win with defense was demonstrated in the 27-2 season-opening rout at Louisville. The defense produced two touchdowns via fumble returns. Ashton Cobb provided the first, while the second came from a most unlikely source.

(On the radio...

"*(Hunter) Cantwell drops back. Hit and the ball's loose. Johnny Williams hit him. Picked up by Myron Pryor. Can he outrun (Louisville center Eric) Wood. Yes, he can. Pryor opening up. At the 30, at the 20, 10, 5, touchdown Kentucky!"*)

Photo by David Coyle/TeamCoyle

Myron Pryor (98) returned a fumble for a TD at Louisville to get the 2008 season off to a good start.

Brooks felt the performance "put a stamp on" what the coaches were selling to the players, about winning in a different way.

"I don't think there's any question they took some pride in that," Brooks said of the defense, "and then went out and earned that respect, and earned some accolades for how they played defense. Most of the bouquets (the previous two years) had been for the quarterback, and the receivers, and the running backs, and the tight ends, and you know, defense was kind of an afterthought. Even in some of the key wins in the previous two years, the defense had made spectacular plays to help us win those games. You go back to Trevard Lindley's interception in the end zone in the first Music City Bowl. You go back to him recovering a fumble in that same game. Jamil Paris, who stripped the ball out when Clemson was driving and we recovered it. And then you go into the LSU game, and remember those defensive plays. There's been a lot of things, but that (Louisville win) was a, from start to finish, great defensive game."

One of the season's high points came in week seven, when the Wildcats came from 13 points down in the final five minutes to beat Arkansas 21-20.

Photo by Karen Czar

Brooks stalks the sidelines during a hard-fought win over Middle Tennessee in 2008.

Photo by Tom Leach

Randall Cobb was the star of the game in the win over Arkansas with two late touchdown catches.

Commonwealth Stadium was half-empty by the time the Hogs fumbled at their own 41-yard line. A 32-yard touchdown pass from Hartline to freshman Randall Cobb was followed by a three-and-out stop by the defense that gave UK the ball in Arkansas territory after the punt. And when Hartline and Cobb hooked up for another score, the fans that were left seemed to make as much noise as if the house had been full.

"That is the head coach's personality and never giving in. We just kept going, going, going to the final whistle, whether we win, lose or anything," said defensive coordinator Steve Brown. "Because of Coach Brooks and the character of the players, the fans are realizing that it isn't over. And if half the stadium is left, they still believe we are going to pull this out. And that is the Rich Brooks era. That is what they are going to do and those players are going to fight to the bitter end. Win or lose, they will compete to the end and that is his personality coming down to the players."

Big Blue radio network analyst Jeff Piecoro played at Kentucky (1981-84) before he joined the school's radio team in 2001. That means he's been a part of many games in which Kentucky lost in the fashion that it rallied to beat Arkansas.

"I don't think that is the mindset of this team anymore. I think he's been able to turn it," Piecoro said of Brooks. "And I think games like that Arkansas game are a byproduct of that mentality."

A lopsided loss at eventual national champion Florida led to a quarterback change, with Brooks starting a true freshman at that position (Cobb) for the first time in his coaching career. The versatile rookie led the Cats back from another 13-point deficit to win at Mississippi State and then a late turnover spoiled what might have been another upset of Georgia. From there, the regular season finished with disappointing losses to Vanderbilt and an underachieving Tennessee team.

"I think the season was very frustrating because I felt like we would improve as we went along. (But) two things happened. We didn't improve; our young players didn't improve as much as I'd hoped they would, so we continued to struggle. And we really struggled on third down," Brooks said. "Defensively, we got three guys hurt in the Middle Tennessee game and really set us back on defense. I know Micah (Johnson) was affected for the entire year, so that really hurt us as we moved forward because I think we went from being on top of our game on defense, to being better but not as good as I felt we were going to be in the league season. And offensively, our (scoring) woes kind of just kept getting worse, and I think the pressure also on some of those young players became fairly intense and the scrutiny, it was very, very difficult."

Still, with six wins, Kentucky accepted a bid to the Liberty Bowl in Memphis, thereby achieving the goal of reaching a third consecutive bowl game for the second time in school history. Brooks knew UK might forfeit some level of its fan support by choosing the Liberty Bowl and a longer trip to Memphis over a third-straight appearance in the Music City, but he also knew his players wanted a fresh experience. It was not a slight against the game in Nashville—it's just that his players wanted to see a different city, participate in different pregame events and perhaps most importantly, get a different goody bag of items each bowl presents to participating teams. The coach was just happy to be back in a bowl game, especially one in which he had played during his days at Oregon State. But he also wanted his team to be in the best

Photo by Victoria Graff

A lopsided loss at Florida in 2008 kept Brooks and his team frustrated all day long.

frame of mind, in hopes of keeping the postseason winning streak going.

"It was really crucial, and Coach Brooks definitely came to a few of us, to understand what's at stake here, that we have been making so much progress over the last couple years, that it was just crucial that we don't have a relapse, that we don't fall back to where we were," said defensive end Jeremy Jarmon. "It meant so much to our football team to come back the next year, get enough wins (to qualify) and win our bowl game. It just says a lot about the character of the guys, their ability, and also just a great job by the coaching staff to get us ready."

"I think it was critically important that we got to postseason play, because the history of Kentucky football, since the early 50s has been, if they were good, they were good for one year, or the maximum two years," Brooks explained. "I was disappointed that we weren't better than we were. I felt we would be, because I felt we'd improve during the season and we finally got better during bowl practice. But the other side of it is, is that it kept some continuity of finding ways to win football games, of continuing to win some games that people didn't think you could win, to being in a position to win some of those other ones that we fell short again. But it's all to me like climbing a ladder, you know. It's hard to climb a ladder when a rung is missing, and postseason play is the rungs on any ladder if you want to climb to the top of the ladder. So I really think that it's critically important that we maintain postseason play as we try to build toward our goal of winning an SEC championship."

Photo by Victoria Graff

Brooks says regular trips to bowl games is crucial to elevating the UK program in the rugged SEC.

Photo by G. Privet

Woodson and Brooks at the 2007 Music City Bowl

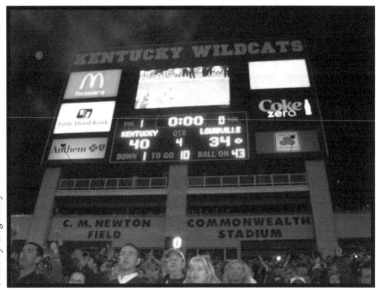

Photo by Greg Petrey

The scoreboard tells the story of the 2007 win over Louisville at Commonwealth Stadium.

Chapter Eight

Memphis
Meltdown

RICH BROOKS' COMPETITIVE FIRE is legendary to those close to him. Steve Brown says when he played for Brooks at Oregon, there was always a trash can in the locker room because the coach would get so worked up that he would vomit at some point during his pregame speech. With age, Brooks has toned it down a bit but when he's provoked, that competitive spirit will reignite. In the Liberty Bowl game against East Carolina, a lackluster first-half performance that saw his team trailing 16-3 set Brooks off.

"I was very surprised we played as poorly as we did in the first half. I was really very upset because the attitude and everything had been real good, and and we started (the game) okay and then all of a sudden, we just had a slump and I thought we lost focus. I thought it was obviously less than our best, and I just felt we really needed to turn the dial up, because part of going to bowl games is also representing the SEC in my opinion," he said.

"At the (Liberty Bowl) luncheon, (ECU's) quarterback (Patrick Pinkney) got up and talked about 'we're real happy to be playing a team from the SEC' (pronounced like first syllable of 'section'), kind of like the WAC," he remembered. "I'm sure he didn't mean anything by it, but our players didn't like that reference and took it as a little bit of a lack of respect, and I kind of reminded them of some of those things at halftime."

It wasn't so much what Brooks said in that locker room but the way that he said it.

"I kind of just go with what my gut tells me and certainly, I was extremely upset at halftime because we were not playing with the same intensity that we started the game with. We were 30 minutes away from making UK history and we were playing like we didn't care for the last 20 minutes of that half," Brooks said of what sparked his rage. "I was out of control for about three-to-four minutes when we got in there. I went off. I can't totally tell you exactly what I said but I said it with a lot of passion. I didn't kick anything or throw anything. I have done things like that in the past and hurt myself, so I have gotten a little smarter than that."

His oldest son, Denny Boom, has seen plenty of these halftime tirades but this one was unlike most of the others.

Brooks has no trouble showing the passion he has for his team when the situation calls for it.

"He got into their face pretty hard. Probably the hardest I have ever seen. I have seen him very vocal and much fired up at half time and challenges them, but usually it is for a short few minutes. Then the coaches will come in and do their changes and checks of what they saw in the first half. But this was probably the longest time that he lit a fire under them that I have seen," Boom noted. "He was very emotional and very loud and vocal."

"He said a couple of foul words and looked us in the eye and said 'this is not Kentucky football'," recalled tailback Tony

Dixon, a senior co-captain on that team. "He really told us what we needed to hear. After it was over, you could see it in the players' eyes that we were not going to lose that game."

"Most of the time he doesn't get angry but he was really, really angry at halftime for the way they played," said Brook's friend, Dr. Stephens. "I have never heard so many cuss words in my life come out of his mouth. He made everybody that wasn't on the team leave the locker room but, we could hear him in the hallway."

Stephens says the impact of the tirade was visible when the players came out of the locker room.

"You could see it in their eyes. There was more focus, more intensity. You could just tell that they were going to get it done. The players were very quiet when they went out and that is not usually the case. So you can just see it in their eyes," he said.

Dicky Lyons wasn't even playing (having been sidelined by an injury) but he was fired up.

"He usually gets emotional, and it's not angry. But he was so upset at how we were playing. We were kind of just laying an egg, and he let them know that he was disappointed so it got me pumped. You could just feel the anger in him," Lyons said, "that this team was beating us like that, knowing the talent we had, and you could tell he was pissed off, and I mean it rubbed off on everybody."

Once he said his piece, Brooks backed off and returned to a typical halftime mode of discussing adjustments and having his assistants point those out.

"I have been in this business so many times where you think you get a response and you don't and when you don't think you get through and you do," Brooks said, explaining that he didn't know for sure how his team would respond to the tirade. "It was almost therapeutic for me to get it off my chest, and I think the players were a little shocked. They hadn't ever seen me go quite as nuts as I did."

The response was immediate.

(On the radio...

"The kick is going to back Jones up to the one-yard line. He's going to head up the right hashmark at the 10, 15, 20, 25, 30, look out! Down the far sideline at the 50. He is going to the house. Across the 30, 20, 10, 5, touchdown Kentucky!")

Kentucky's David Jones, who had promised special teams coach Steve Ortmayer he would return one for a touchdown if given the chance, did just that. The 99-yard score put a charge back into the UK sideline and the pro-Cat crowd and the rally was underway.

Kentucky pulled even at 16 only to see East Carolina go back in front with a field goal late in the third. That meant it would take the ninth fourth-quarter comeback in the past two-and-a-half years to get the history-making bowl victory and UK started the rally with a field goal, to tie the score at 19.

Midway through the final period, an interception by the Wildcats and later a fumble return for a touchdown were both negated by penalties. Then, after a long gainer by the Pirates into UK territory, Pryor forced a fumble and fellow defensive lineman Ventrell Jenkins grabbed the loose ball and took off.

(On the radio...

"At the 41, it's second-and-seven East Carolina. Pinkney turns, gives it to Whitley, runs into his own man, tries to reverse his field, drops the football. This one's picked up by the Cats. Heading off to the near sideline is Ventrell Jenkins. Across the 30, stiff arm across the 20. Breaks a tackle, touchdown Kentucky!")

Jenkins' rumbling return to pay dirt including the highlight-reel stiff arm of a defender at the 20-yard line, gave the Cats their first lead of the game. The point-after was blocked, but Kentucky stuffed ECU on its next series and the Cats then ran out the clock to complete a 25-19 win.

Kentucky 25 | East Carolina 19

Liberty Bowl, January 2, 2009

Scoring Summary

Kentucky «	0	3	13	9	25
East Carolina	3	13	3	0	19

Team Statistics

Team Statistics	Kentucky	East Carolina
First Downs	16	17
Rushes - Yards	37-106	31-101
Passing Yards	204	296
Return Yards	75	16
Passing (Att-Comp-Int)	31-19-1	38-18-0
Punts - Average	6-41.8	8-47.8
Fumbles - Lost	1-0	2-1
Penalties - Yards	4-35	4-17
Time of Possession	30:43	29:17

Individual Statistics

Passing

Kentucky	Att	Comp	Yards	Int	TD
Mike Hartline	31	19	204	1	1

East Carolina	Att	Comp	Yards	Int	TD
Patrick Pinkney	36	18	296	0	1

Rushing

Kentucky	Att	Yards	Average	TD
Tony Dixon	28	89	3.2	0
Alfonso Smith	5	28	5.6	0
John Conner	1	1	1.0	0
Mike Hartline	3	-12	-4.0	0

East Carolina	Att	Yards	Average	TD
Brandon Simmons	10	44	4.4	1
Norman Whitley	7	31	4.4	0
J.R. Rogers	3	23	7.7	0
Michael Bowman	1	3	3.0	0
Patrick Pinkney	10	0	0.0	0

Photo by David Coyle/TeamCoyle

Brooks, E.J. Adams and Mike Hartline hold up the Liberty Bowl trophy after Kentucky's third straight bowl win.

"What changed is defensively, we played like we played at different stages during the season. We basically took over the game on defense. Our offense was more efficient, and we executed in some third down situations to keep possession. We obviously started with a big jolt with the kickoff return by David Jones. I have been around a lot of football games in my life, and I have never seen a sequence, which happened in that fourth quarter. It was almost like our defense had made up their mind that we were going to do whatever we had to, to win this game," Brooks said. "And for those plays to follow back-to-back for those three plays, I have never seen such a thing."

Brooks especially enjoyed seeing Jenkins (named the Liberty Bowl's MVP) make the game-winning play, as the senior had overcome a troubled background in his Columbia, SC hometown to make it to the University of Kentucky. Also impressive to Brooks was the toughness shown by his quarterback, as Hartline fought through a severe bout with a virus to lead the Cats to the come-from-behind win.

"I think that is just a lesson in perseverance. A lot of guys would not have responded well after being benched after eight games," Brooks said of

Hartline. "When he was benched after being 5-3, he could have had a sour attitude, not continue to work and improve. But he didn't go that route. He continued to bide his time and wait for another opportunity and ended up being the offensive MVP and also did a great job dealing with adversity physically during the game, as well as rising above the criticism and doubters, if you will, and showing he is a capable player."

By now, fourth-quarter rallies had become old hat for the Wildcats. But Brooks says not everyone has become a true believer yet. He related a day-after-the-game story at the team's headquarters in Memphis, the famed Peabody Hotel.

Special teams coach Steve Ortmayer and his wife, Merylee, were riding the elevator with a couple of Cat fans decked out in their UK apparel. After congratulating the coach on the team's win, one of them admitted they had left the Liberty Bowl stadium after halftime, thinking Kentucky's fate was sealed.

"Merylee said something like 'haven't you learned by now that with a Rich Brooks-coached team, you don't leave until the end of the game,'" said Brooks, adding that he thinks the majority of fans are now confident in the Cats ability to overcome obstacles.

The players, said free safety Marcus McClinton, had jumped on the bandwagon long ago.

"First, I think it's personnel. The guys that coach has recruited. Guys that have a lot of heart. And I think it's just him teaching us never to quit. In practice, we go hard. (And) it's just him in general. He's not a quitter. He's a standup guy and that's the kind of attitude that rubbed off on the team," he said.

With the success Kentucky has enjoyed, as well as the continued improvement in recruiting, a decision on when to pass the torch to head coach-in-waiting Joker Phillips will not come easily for Brooks.

Daughter Kasey Brooks Holwerda says the family is not in any hurry to see Brooks hang it up.

"I think we were all down at BB King's after the bowl win in Memphis and saying 'oh gosh, don't stop coaching now. We love it'. For us as a family,"

Photo by Victoria Graff

Brooks made sure to thank the UK fans who made the trek to Memphis to see the Cats beat East Carolina in the 2009 Liberty Bowl.

she said, "it is something just hard to describe because we have lived it our whole lives. For us, even as adults to come together and be pulling for the same direction, it is so much fun. It is fun for me to see how the fans react to my dad and see him with Kentucky people. It is a really exciting, satisfying, thrilling experience.

"One of the things I thought as a parent, the first time he retired, was that my kids never had the opportunity to share those experiences because they were too young when he was with the Falcons," Kasey added. "They had been around it but never understood it. For them to have the opportunity now, my son will stand down on the sideline with my dad and kind of shadow him around. It is fun for me to know they will have these experiences with their grandfather and it is special to me that they were able to share it, too."

Chapter Nine

Closing the
Talent
Gap

RICH BROOKS' FAVORITE MOVIE is "The Dirty Dozen." The
players he and his staff recruited in those first few fateful years at Kentucky
didn't have the questionable behavioral records of that fictional collection of
prisoners-turned-soldiers. However, the challenge they embraced, reversing
the football fortunes of long-suffering UK program, was as unlikely to succeed
as the mission of The Dirty Dozen.

In Brooks' first season at Kentucky, the team featured one player—
Derek Abney—who could run the 40-yard dash in 4.5 seconds or less. In
the 2009 intra-squad game that ended spring practice, a linebacker—Danny
Trevathan—had enough speed to be used as a kick returner. Those two facts
say a lot about the degree to which Brooks and his staff has upgraded the
speed in the UK program.

Between 2003-07, Brooks and his staff signed a total of five players ranked
at the four-star level by Rivals.com. Of those, only three—Andre Woodson,
Micah Johnson and Corey Peters—ever started a game for the Cats. By way
of comparison, LSU signed 21 players ranked with at least four stars in the
2007 class alone.

The 2009 class of signees put Kentucky in the top 30 nationally in some
recruiting analyst rankings. That was the best showing yet for this staff and

Photo by Tom Leach

Defensive coordinator Steve Brown also played for Brooks at Oregon.

it still was rated behind 10 other SEC schools on most lists. Brooks doesn't lose any sleep over the ratings because he's confident they are continually closing the talent gap on the teams they're chasing in this league and the results give credence to that feeling.

"I think that this recruiting class and the ability to get a few more players with a few more stars (in the rankings) is all a process. I think that the brand of Kentucky football is changing. What they had seen was three years of good football at Kentucky—not national championship football, but three years of really good football, defeating quality teams, winning bowl games, and it is a process of raising your level of exposure, the level of awareness," Brooks said. "Because young people have short memories. They don't know about history and really don't care that much about the history, in my opinion. What they do care about is: 'Am I going to a place that I care about? Am I going to a place where I can win? Am I going to a place where I can play and play early? And am I going to a place where I can utilize my talents?' Once you establish an identity, which I think we have at Kentucky football with the style we are going to play, players can see themselves fitting into that style. They can see themselves fitting into that style as well in a successful manner rather than going in and getting their brains blown out."

Before Steve Brown coached under Brooks, he played for him at Oregon. Brown was one of those players without many stars by his name. His best sport in high school was tennis, but when he flashed big-time football talent in a late summer all-star game in California, Brooks quickly offered him a scholarship to play for the Ducks.

"That is the one thing that is one of the biggest things coach has the ability to do. I guess he has an eternal crystal ball because he has the ability to see the possibility. He has a great ability to evaluate players and see the possibility of what they can be in two or three years," Brown said. "That is how he built the Oregon program and that is how he built it here. He takes guys that were one or two stars, and we teach them and see their abilities of what they can do and they blossom into really good players, a la Trevard Lindley."

That ability to find players good enough to win in the SEC that are overlooked by other programs is always the challenge facing a coach trying to move up his team up the ladder in what is regarded as the nation's toughest football conference. Jeff Drummond covers recruiting for *The Cats Pause*, and he says Brooks and his staff have had a higher batting average than most in those situations.

"The success rate has been a lot higher. They've been able to hit on more of those guys than previous staffs. I think that's always been part of what Kentucky has had to do from a strategic standpoint because the state's population base doesn't provide it with enough players. And you're going head-to-head with (some) big-time programs in other states," he explained.

At Oregon, then athletics director Bill Byrne says finding those hidden gems was as crucial to Brooks' success as it has been at Kentucky.

"I think he can evaluate talent as well or better than any other coach I've ever worked with. I think he has an eye, and that's a gift, for evaluating young people and projecting young people as to whether or not they can play," he said. "Our middle linebacker at Oregon was a kid named Larry Wilson from Irrigon, OR. You wouldn't stop in Irrigon because they don't have a stoplight and yet, he took him out of six-man football to starting middle linebacker in the Pacific 10 conference as a freshman. He would have been a National Football League player if he hadn't been injured. Rich can pick guys out and Rich can line them up in the right spot. He just needed more of them. That was the issue we had at Oregon."

The "style of play" component gave Brooks some pause in 2008 when considering a commitment to Cobb at quarterback, because it would mean utilizing less of the pro-style approach and more of an option-oriented attack. He wanted Morgan Newton and Ryan Mossakowski, two highly-touted signal-callers planning to attend UK, to know the offensive system to which they committed was still the first option for the long term.

"There was definitely some thought about that in my mind. What kind of message are we going to send if we go all of a sudden, we go from a pro-type offense to an option-type offense? That decision was one that was made at the time on a short-term basis to win," he said. "We are still going to be the type of offense which got us here and the type of offense that I feel helps us continue advancing up the ladder."

Brooks makes the final call on whether or not to offer a prospect a scholarship, but the evaluation process is a collective one with all of the coaches watching game tapes and able to offer their thoughts on the potential that player has.

"We sold playing time, but what helped us is that we were all on the same page," said Phillips, who was Brooks' first recruiting coordinator at UK. "We sat in the staff room and watched tapes of every kid. Rich would also be there. We would all watch the kids, so when the player went on campus everyone knew him. I have been places where the position coach watched him, the coordinator watched him, or the recruiting coach had watched him. So very few people knew him or had seen the kid play. We had the whole staff in there. If Steve Brown liked a DB (defensive back), I was sitting there looking at him and say 'okay, I see what he is looking for'. And if I liked a receiver, he could say 'I see what Joker is looking for.'"

"It is a source of pride for us when we present a player and get him accepted (by Brooks)," added Brown.

When it comes to the in-home visit to seal a recruiting commitment, Brown says Brooks' salesmanship skill stems from timeless qualities of honesty and sincerity.

"He puts the parents at ease and lets them know we are going to look after your son and care for him. He also lets them know that you won't be there to discipline him, so we will make sure that they are doing the right things.

He is kind of the glue that seals the deal," said Brown. "He is comfortable in any type of household, whether it is the CEO of a company or single mom or dad, he can relate to people and is comfortable in all those settings."

"He is legendary on recruiting visits," noted Hellyer. "He will get a recruit that wants to play him in ping pong or pool and he doesn't let up on him. He does not let him win. I think he finds out that the kid appreciates that—if the kid is competitive, he wants to compete. He (Brooks) is competitive in everything. (But) he does it in such a way that he is good at rubbing it in."

Karen Brooks says the fact that her husband has a job that requires him to deal with young people has kept him from getting set in his ways.

"I think it keeps us young, keeps him young. Dealing with kids and kids are different now than they used to be. I think both of us have become much more accepting of things than a lot of our friends our age. When you deal with young people, you can't get into the way things should be. You meet people of all these different ways of life and life really isn't always that straight

Photo provided by Denny Boom

Karen and Rich Brooks at the 2008 Derby Ball in Lexington.

and narrow. So, I think that you become much more liberal in your attitudes about people and ways of life. I think you become more knowledgeable, and I think it is great for everybody to get out of their comfort zone, especially as you get older," she said. "I think this has been good for him. I think he learns something new every day, and I think it is good. He has really enjoyed it."

Mitch Barnhart says he marvels at the energy level of his 67-year-old head coach.

"They go out there and get after it and Rich, at age 67, has as much energy (as anyone). I am not sure anyone loves the chase (of recruiting), but he is active in it. He has a clear eye for evaluating talent," observed Barnhart. "And sees people that might be a bit undersized, underexposed, and he thinks he can put 15 or 20 pounds on him, move him to a different spot and make him do something else. When he walks into a home with a mom and a dad and a young person, he is genuine and it is believable. It is not a fake. It is not insincere. It is genuine. In recruiting, people want someone they can believe and you can believe Rich."

And once players are in the program, Neely says Brooks does a "great job of communicating expectations" and making sure they know none of the criticism they get is personal.

"His doghouse has a two-way door. I've dealt with some coaches that once a player got on a coach's bad side, he couldn't get out again. Coach Brooks is not like that. He doesn't give up on them. He gives them every reasonable chance," noted Neely.

As you might imagine, a lot more doors are opened now to pitches from Kentucky than was the case when Brooks arrived. In 2003, the new staff had to deal with significant reductions in the numbers of scholarships UK could offer because of the NCAA sanctions placed on the program for violations in the Hal Mumme era. The 2008 season marked the first season that the school was able to field a team with a full complement of 85 players on scholarship.

"The biggest thing was negativity, job security, and whether we were going to be here to see the process through," Brooks said of the issues UK faced on the recruiting trail in those first few years. "I don't think it suddenly

Photo by Victoria Graff

Micah Johnson (4) is one of the highest rated recruits signed by Brooks and his staff.

changed at any point and there is still some of that out there. But a lot of the reasons for that to have had any credence at all are disappearing by positive results on the football field, which makes it more difficult to negatively affect the people we are going after. In some situations, now we are finding that when we identify or offer a prospect, there is a rush right behind us saying, 'maybe we missed this guy, maybe we should check this guy out'. Similar things happened like that, I think, when I was at Oregon. We would go into LA and recruit players and eventually beat out UCLA and (U)SC. And after that, we went down there and identified players and they would go and recruit them."

Despite the obstacles, Kentucky landed the likes of Woodson, Tamme and Burton in the first class of recruits. Year two brought players like Woodyard and Little. Brooks says those kinds of players laid the foundation for the resurgence the UK program has enjoyed.

"Those kind of guys, when they come into your program, they are what I call true difference-makers. Not only do they turnaround your program, they are really good players. Those three guys didn't have stars by their names but they had stars in their eyes and they convinced other people that this could get done as well. If you don't have that in some of your players, it is more difficult to turn the tide in the environment," Brooks said. "Our best recruiters were our own players. Once we got some new players in here, they became our best salesmen, and they are probably the biggest reason why we are sitting here and talking about winning three straight bowl games."

UK radio analyst Jeff Piecoro says Brooks hasn't done it alone. Piecoro credits the quality of the staff Brooks put together with being a driving force in the talent upgrade that had to happen for the Cats to achieve their goals.

Photo by Victoria Graff

Finding overlooked players like Jacob Tamme (18) who developed into stars has been a key to Brooks' success.

"When you look at the past four or five years, they're some of the best classes Kentucky has ever had. I think that's what has been able to elevate Kentucky football. They've always had good players—they just didn't have enough good players. I think it's the players and the dedication of the coaching staff that makes luck. There was a great saying that Coach (Jerry) Claiborne used to have on the wall from Vince Lombardi that said 'luck is when preparation meets opportunity'. I think that's a perfect saying for Rich Brooks. The preparation is meeting the opportunity now. They're getting better players."

Drummond says the one-on-one relationships built in the recruiting process now seem to trump other factors, i.e. TV exposure, tradition, when it comes to signing recruits.

"Without a doubt, these days, the biggest factor these days is that relationship with the recruiting coach or the position coach. It used to be that guys looked at a school's tradition, the prestige but we've seen a big shift in recent years to a much more personal type of recruitment," he said. "I think one of the reasons, maybe, is so many teams get the exposure nowadays."

Rob Gidel is a freelance-recruiting analyst with a particular fondness for the University of Kentucky program. He says an early move Brooks made with that staff, bringing former Wildcat star Joker Phillips back to his alma mater to coordinate the recruiting effort, paid big dividends in overcoming the effects of an NCAA probation stemming from the Coach Hal Mumme era.

"They had 68 scholarship players at one time, and I think it's safe to say that 20 or so of the players that Guy Morriss (Mumme's successor) brought in were not really SEC-caliber players. The biggest thing for Coach Brooks was bringing in Joker and putting themselves in houses they had never been in before in South Carolina and Georgia," Gidel noted. "The NFL ties were very helpful. His genuineness (is a plus). Coach Brooks has this attitude of he's just going be himself and if that's not good enough for you, he'll go his separate way. Kids appreciate that. Coach Brooks just sells his program and hopefully that's good enough.

"The most important thing in college football recruiting is the official visit and 95 percent of that visit is spent with the players (already on the team). Guys like Keenan Burton and Micah Johnson who not only came to this program but took it upon themselves to help bring in more talent," Gidel added, "and to be so inspired by what Coach Brooks is putting into this program that they want to sell it to other kids."

Brooks says the types of players the staff recruited proved instrumental in getting the program turned.

"I'll never forget Wesley (Woodyard) when he came here. When I offered him a scholarship, I could just see it in his eyes. They showed he had the enthusiasm and the belief that he was really looking forward to coming to Kentucky and playing college football. That energy and enthusiasm was critically important for a program that didn't have enough of it," Brooks said.

Woodyard vividly remembers the visit to Lexington, too. Brooks talked about football being "fun" and then followed through on that promise.

"That is what the game of football is about—have fun. Coach Brooks, a lot of people wouldn't think he was a guy that could have fun, but he is a guy who can bring the best out of you and make sure you are going to have a lot of fun on the football field. It is his intensity," Woodyard said.

"He lets them be themselves," Joker Phillips said of Brooks' approach. "A lot of them jaw back and forth at each other and the offense and defense go back at each other (in practice)."

"He comes out with a smile on his face and hoopin' and hollering," said tailback Tony Dixon, a senior on the 2008 team. "When you see an old man doing that, it puts a smile on your face."

David Jones, another member of the 2008 senior class, says he bought what Brooks was selling because the coach came across as genuine—and very passionate.

"I saw that in him when he talked with me at my house. I just saw a passion in him. I know about the passion in a coach because my high school coach (Belfry's Philip Haywood) is a legend. Just being around him for a long time, I can read coaches and I believed (Brooks)," Jones said.

And Jones says keeping the faith is what got the players through the early years of the Brooks era, when wins were few and far between.

"The first time I ever lost in the state of Kentucky was here at the University of Kentucky. We had a 4-8 season and everybody doubted us. We'd go to the mall and people would laugh. Now, we go out with our Kentucky stuff on and everybody is coming up and saying 'I love UK football' and 'Coach Brooks is doing a wonderful job,'" he said.

Ortmayer says the coaches see that new attitude when they go into the schools and homes of prospective recruits.

Photo by Victoria Graff

Brooks' fiery demeanor on the sidelines is evident when things don't go well for the Cats.

"It has grown each of the last 3 years, to the extent that there was a time here when a year or so ago, if we are talking to a kid in Atlanta who is also talking to Auburn, Georgia, and Tennessee, we are not even getting in the door. And we now can. That kid is listening to us now," he said.

Linebackers coach Chuck Smith is the Cats'

recruiting coordinator, as well. He joined the staff in 2005 and he says the run of three consecutive bowl wins had a dramatic impact on the program's efforts at landing better players.

"I know the game that probably has stuck out more than any is the LSU game. You'll talk to coaches, secretaries at the desk of these school and they'll say 'we saw that LSU game'," he said. "These players want to play on TV. That's one of the top things as far as they're concerned. That's how we get the attention of some of these kids. They've seen Kentucky. They know what the uniforms look like.

"I think we're establishing our own identity as far as Kentucky football.

One of the things I think is underappreciated is how good the facilities are," Smith added. "The thing we have to do is get them on campus and let them see the facilities and meet the coaching staff. Then, we've got our best chance to get them. Once they get here, they're pretty impressed with what they see."

When Brooks came to Kentucky, he had not been involved in the recruiting game for nine years. He quickly noticed the biggest difference was the attention paid to the process by the media and fans.

"Night and day," he said of the change. "Not only different because of the Internet and talk radio but different because of the intense scrutiny of the entire recruiting process in the SEC. It is a lifestyle. SEC football is a lifestyle and a religion. Everyone wants to know 24/7 what is going on with their program," he said. "I will never forget my first year, I went into Georgia to a player's home on a visit and came out of that home, flew back to Lexington, got in the car and was listening to a talk radio show about my home visit. This was just three hours later. They had everything the kid liked and didn't like about the visit, and I am thinking okay, this is a little different environment than I was recruiting in, in Oregon in the early and mid 1990s."

Brooks says his assistants are more internet savvy than he is, and while all of that coverage makes the job more difficult, with players knowing who else you might be after at their position, there are also ways to use the situation to one's advantage.

"Sometimes you get information that you are not given by the recruit when you interview (him). The Internet service and radio talk show guys that are calling all these recruits and you can pick up information in the process. One, how you are standing with a guy or whether the guy is just working you because he really isn't going to come to your place. You think you have a great shot at him but you find out you need to cut the bait and go fish someplace else because you are going to be wasting your time. The worst thing you can do in recruiting is put all your eggs in one basket and somebody who is giving you an indication they are interested but really aren't," he noted.

As an example, Brooks admits they made a mistake in thinking they had a realistic chance of getting highly-touted quarterback Brian Brohm away from Louisville in 2004.

Photo by Victoria Graff

Brooks signs autographs at the annual UK football Fan Day event.

ANOTHER EXAMPLE OF HOW THE INTERNET
HAS CHANGED THE GAME FOR COACHES

Keeping secrets in the Internet age can sometimes be an impossible task. Take the 2005 game at Indiana. Kentucky decided to move backup quarterback Curtis Pulley to receiver, to take advantage of his athleticism, but Brooks wanted to keep it under wraps. On Tuesday, that new offensive set was implemented into the game plan for practice. Later that day, a post on the Cats' Pause message board detailed what was happening. It turns out, a student manager had told a friend who then made the post without the manager's knowledge. To say Brooks was mad would be an understatement.

"That really bothers me because you don't know where it is coming from, whether it is a player talking to somebody, a manager talking to somebody, or someone taking a peak through the fence. You are not sure. Those are the things that really do disturb me. I think there are some things that still have the sanctity of the practice field and the sanctity of the locker room that are not for public consumption," he explained, "unless you decide a practice is open for public consumption. In today's age, public consumption covers a wide range, where in the old days it did not cover that big of a range. I am not stupid enough to think that it won't happen again. I think it will be an ongoing problem and something you have to be aware of. The worst thing that can happen to the coaches if you are trying to do something different and make it a surprise for the opponent and it is not a surprise because they found out one way or another. There is not a lot that you can do anymore to come as a surprise because we give them all of our videos. They know all the statistics. You've got news reports, newspaper, TV, radio. There is so much out there that when you do have something that you might want to do, you don't want the opponent to find out. It is like putting in a fake punt. You don't want that opponent to know that you are working on a fake punt that week or when the punt might be."

At Indiana, Pulley lined up at receiver for the first play. He went in motion and took a handoff on an end around play. He was tackled for a loss, in a game the Hoosiers ended up winning in dominating fashion. "That was not a good game period," Brooks said of Kentucky's 38-14 loss in Bloomington, IN.

Chapter Ten

The Job
Nobody
Wanted

"WHO?"

That was the collective reaction in the state of Kentucky to the news that Rich Brooks had been hired as the new head football coach of the Wildcats. A west coast-based coach through most of his career, Brooks had not coached in college since leading Oregon to the Rose Bowl after the 1994 season. And he'd been out of coaching altogether since deciding he was tired of being an assistant coach after four years with the NFL's Atlanta Falcons. The fact that Brooks had losing records at both Oregon and in his two-year stint as head coach of the NFL's St. Louis Rams—even though the situations he inherited in both cases required major rebuilding work—only added to the skepticism in the bluegrass.

"I never had a job that anyone else wanted. In the head coaching jobs that I got, they were turned down by a lot of people before they got to me. It never bothered me—maybe it should. I think that some people are fortunate enough in life to do something and have their talent match a certain situation that is almost like the perfect storm. The perfect storm in college football is to have talent and one of the top five or 10 jobs in the nation. Well, then it is pretty hard to screw those things up, but most people don't get their jobs that way," Brooks said. "Some people take lesser jobs and then get to the big job.

Some people never get to the opportunity of the big job. I am not just talking football but in life. Whether you are selling insurance, working for smaller companies and butting heads with the bigger companies. There are just all those situations in life and all you can do is control what you can do. And you better work your fanny off because no matter what happens, in the end at least, people will respect that you were a hard worker, that you were honest and straightforward. Those are the three things that my father taught me."

Brooks was initially involved as a consultant for UK. Associate athletics director Greg Byrne had known Brooks from childhood because his dad, Bill, was then the AD at Oregon. And from working briefly in the Oregon athletics department in the early 80's, UK AD Mitch Barnhart was casually acquainted with Brooks. Barnhart respected Brooks' reputation and had Byrne get Brooks' thoughts on different coaching candidates under consideration at Kentucky.

One of the first things Byrne did was call Brooks, to get his input on candidates Kentucky should consider.

"As I was about ready to hang up the phone, he says, 'if you all can't get comfortable with somebody, you tell Mitch I still have 10 years left in my belly'. That was in the first conversation," said Greg Byrne. "I thought so highly of him but I wasn't sure if that was the right fit at the time. We thought we had an opportunity to talk to Bill Parcells at that point and I didn't tell him that."

For a program in Kentucky's situation, the Parcells name was one the administration felt it had to explore if there was a chance of landing him.

"We had heard that Bill was interested, so we took a swing. When it didn't work out, we looked at 'who is the guy that can make this work'," said Barnhart.

"There was a real effort to bring him (Parcells) in and a few times, I think there was a good chance of that happening," Byrne added. "But at the end of the day, in hindsight, the absolute right coach got hired." As the process continued, Barnhart says Brooks kept reminding him that he was confident he could do the job. And that desire started to appeal to Barnhart.

"As people began to find out about the sanctions, they didn't want any part of it. When you'd tell them, you could hear the phone go dead at the other end," he said. "There wasn't anyone jumping up and down saying get me the job when you lose 20 scholarships and are unable to make it to post season play. It wasn't a real lucrative deal. There wasn't a lot of depth on the squad and wasn't a lot lined up for people to say this is a way to extend my career. Knowing that he wasn't afraid of the fight was real important to me. Knowing how tough he was important to me. Knowing how organized he was was important. A young coach would not have been able to survive those first few years here. You would not have been able to make it based upon the lack of scholarships and depth in our program. To fight through all that would have been very difficult."

The more time Barnhart spent time on this path, the more he started to see that the qualities he observed in Brooks at Oregon back in 1982 had not changed.

"The jaw was set the same. His demeanor was exactly the same. The same toughness, thought processes were very

Brooks trades in his trademark straw hat for a toboggan when the November wind turns cold.

evident. He had a plan and didn't need to write it down. It wasn't some blueprint or organizational chart. He could say it in a very articulate manner and knew what he wanted to do and knew what needed to be done," Barnhart said.

"He had done at Oregon what we needed done at Kentucky," added John Cropp, who was part of UK's interview team. "He had taken a losing program in a tough league and made them into winners. He had walked the walk."

When it came time for Brooks to meet the president, Dr. Todd came away impressed with the fact that the coach did not try to sugarcoat the situation he was walking into.

"When I first met him, he said you have no size and no speed and you are playing in the SEC. He said I will get you size and speed but it will take awhile," Dr. Todd recalled.

Sons Brady (far left) and Denny at a family Thanksgiving dinner with their dad.

Photo provided by Denny Boom

On Christmas Eve, 2002, Brooks got a call to see if he was indeed serious about exploring this opportunity.

"I am at my daughter's (Kasey Holwerda) house in Lake Oswego, OR and he said, 'it looks like the guy we thought we had a shot at we are not going to get and would you be interested in talking to us about it'?" Brooks recalled. Two days later, he flew to Cincinnati for a meeting at a hotel near the airport, expecting to fly back home the next day. They met for "two or three hours," and then Barnhart, Byrne and associate AD John Cropp said they had to return to Lexington for a basketball game. A short time later, Byrne called Brooks and said they wanted him to come back to Lexington to see the UK campus and facilities.

"I was almost shocked at the facilities I saw. They were pretty big time in my opinion, and I looked at that and thought 'how can they not be better here?' Later that day," Brooks said, "I was offered the job."

Brooks says his wife, Karen, was the only member of the family not excited about his return to coaching, but she remembers it differently.

"That isn't entirely true. I probably would not have been excited if it had been somewhere else," said Karen. "I am not kidding you—I had always wanted to go to Lexington, Kentucky. When we left Atlanta, on our trip back to Oregon, I planned the whole thing so the movers could get there and we could go through Lexington on our way home. Our movers were really late and it was too late, so we went through Nashville and I was so disappointed because I had always wanted to go through Lexington. I have always been horse crazy as a kid—I love horses. Kerri (our daughter) had done some basketball games here (as a CBS Sports videographer) and said 'it was one of the most beautiful places you have ever seen'. So when we heard it was Kentucky, it is not entirely true that I was not happy. I was happy because he was not a good retired person—at all. He was too young. Some guys at his age would be ready to retire but he wasn't ready. You could fish and you could play golf, but he really has always loved coaching and he was not ready to give it up yet."

His kids could see that, too.

"We were shocked but also excited because we missed having him coach and it was a big thing for our family," Kasey Holwerda said for herself and her siblings. "We spent a lot of time together during football season and it brought a lot of people in our lives together. We missed it. We were all just so excited for him because we knew how much he missed it and how good he was at it. I think he was shocked at how excited we were trying to convince him to go coach again. When he retired from the Atlanta Falcons, we had a feeling that he wasn't ready to be retired and he still had a lot of coaching left in him. I think he missed the college game and being with kids. I feel he still had a lot to prove to himself and he had a lot left to give. We didn't feel like he was happily retired. I think he wanted to bring another program back. I think that was a part of the appeal of Kentucky. He enjoys the process. We knew he could get it done there and are just gracious that Kentucky had enough patience to see it through."

Brooks' brother, Wayne, was a bit surprised by the move, though.

"I thought he was retired and I was surprised. He called me up and told me he was going to make that move and I was kind of floored. I was happy for

Photo provided by Kerri Brooks Robinson

Brooks family photo from July 4, 2008. (Front row, from left) Siri Brooks, Sini Holwerda, Kisky Holwerda, Denny Boom. (Middle row) Brady Brooks, Rich Brooks, Karen Brooks, Kasey Holwerda, Gunnar Holwerda. (Back row) Brooks Emerson with mom Kerri Brooks Robinson, Brent Robinson, Steve Holwerda.

him but I know what was going on in his mind, that he didn't fulfill destiny yet. I did the same thing when I finished coaching the local team here (in California) and got it out of the system. I think Rich had some unfilled needs to finish off. I am glad he made the move and I am sure he is, too," Wayne said. "There had always been some thought that he should have stayed at Oregon, shouldn't have gone to the pros. He could have finished his career at Oregon and had all those good teams that (Mike) Belloti did. But he wanted to get to the next level and when it didn't work out long term, going back to Kentucky (was important). He needed to prove that he could do what he did at Oregon and make it successful."

Perhaps no sport requires a greater commitment to "team" than football and Dr. Todd was quickly taken by Brooks' ability to put together a coaching staff with impressive resumes.

"Why would anyone come to a school on probation to work for an old coach unless they had a ton of respect for him, guys like Steve Brown.

Actually, he brought in Joker Phillips because he had met him at a conference in Atlanta. I don't think he knew how great of a recruiter Joker was at that time. But I watched the people he brought on board at that time and was impressed with how he built the team and how much respect there was within that group," Dr. Todd said.

Phillips is a Franklin, KY native and played for Jerry Claiborne on teams that went to consecutive Hall of Fame Bowl games in 1983 and '84, winning the second one over Wisconsin. That connection to UK was strong, but Phillips had some trepidation about coming home, given that he was part of a staff under Bill Curry that got fired.

"I am not sure that I was ready to come back and there was so much talk about coming back. I wasn't sure if I was ready at the time and had to make sure everything was right when I did come back," Phillips explained. "Talking to Rich, he kept saying 'come on back here and let's have some fun'. He kept saying that. And then I asked him what areas would be recruited and he said he would put me in charge of recruiting. And I said 'where did he think we needed to recruit' and he said 'it is up to you'. He basically kept saying 'come on back here and let's have some fun.'"

One of the reasons Brooks was able to assemble such a high quality staff is the respect those coaches had for him. One of them was a former Oregon Duck, Steve Brown, who played for Brooks and later coached under him in the NFL with St. Louis.

"I was living in St. Louis trying to figure out what I was going to do. I was in contact with him because he turned down Wake Forest and turned down San Diego State. I was already on his ready list. So I called him and he was at the airport and I talked to his wife Karen and she said he was on his way to Portland to catch a flight to Kentucky. I said 'Kentucky?' and she said 'yes, he is being interviewed'," Brown said. "He (Brooks) called me before he took off for the flight and said 'there is a chance that I might get this job, what do you think? Would you come?' And I said I would be there tomorrow. He called once he got the job and said 'I am taking the job, you want to come?' And I said 'I will be there'. I knew that I wanted to be apart of what he is doing because he doesn't take jobs just to be a part of them. He takes jobs with the possibility of being a winner. And obviously it took a couple years, but we did it."

Special teams coach Steve Ortmayer initially resisted Brooks' overture but after a visit to the UK campus, he was sold.

"He called me right after he got the job and said, 'Ort, why don't you come over here and have some fun for a change'," he said. "Up through the 1980's to like 1989 or so, the NFL was a great place to be because it was all football people. But as the (Art) Rooneys, (George) Halas and ownership started to get old and fall off, the corporate ownerships picked up and changed the NFL power structure. It changed the bottom line and became a business situation instead of a football situation. So, when he came here that is what he said, 'let's come here and have some fun'.

"I said 'Rich, I don't think I can do this now, I have been in this league for 22 years and I think I need to stay' and he says at least come and look at it. I promised I would," Ortmayer continued. "I-64 runs right from St. Louis to

Photo provided by Kerri Brooks Robinson

Siri Brooks and Sina Holwerda perform as former presidents with their grandfather at a 2008 holiday outing.

126

here and I drove down to look at it and for me, the facilities and the situation was such, that at this point in my life, what was important to me was to have the opportunity to win it all, which, if it's in the NFL, it is the Super Bowl and if it's college football, it is the National Championship. Quite frankly, in my mind, when you play the SEC East, if you can win the East you have a good chance to win the national championship. So when I saw the facilities, I said 'gee, this looks nice'. The opportunity to get back with Rich was huge for me. I just felt that he was very, very good at what he does and I think we have a good relationship so it was great for me."

At the news conference announcing his hiring at UK, Brooks' reference to the "Southeast" Conference only served to embolden his many skeptics. And soon thereafter, a story broke about a recruiting violation that occurred very early in Brooks' tenure at Oregon. For a program just coming off NCAA probation, you can imagine the media firestorm ignited by this development. Dr. Todd says the media reaction was overblown and there was never any doubt they were going to stick with Brooks.

"It was a nightmare because of the NCAA probation that we had back in 1979 at Oregon that I thought was totally gone and past. And then I actually offered Mitch, 'if this is a problem, I will step out of this' and he said 'no, that would probably just make it worse'," Brooks recalled. "So I put my head down and went forward."

Dr. Todd has been continually impressed by the way Brooks has gone about the job, even during the darkest hours.

"Whether it is a CEO of a business, a school president, or the coach of a team that needs to have talent, you must respect within that talent. You need to have skills and he put it all together. And I like the way he did it," Dr. Todd said. "He (Brooks) never broke a promise on anything, never whined about anything. I often talk about Jim Collins (author of "Good to Great") and he talks about level five leaders. The major thing I remember in that book is that they put the institution ahead of themselves. If you look at when Rich was in trouble, when people thought he was in trouble, he could have pulled redshirts off some kids six games into the season because he needed to get another couple wins or two. But he didn't do that. He knew that they weren't ready and it was for the good of the program. I saw many times that he would put the program ahead of his own personal gain and that meant a lot."

While skeptics of Brooks' hiring abounded among the Kentucky media, as well as national college football observers, Tony Barnhart was not one of them. The longtime *Atlanta Journal-Constitution* writer knows the ins and outs of the SEC as well as anyone on the beat. From his familiarity with Brooks' rebuilding job at Oregon, Barnhart—no relation to Mitch—was confident that UK had found the right man for the job.

Photo by David Coyle/TeamCoyle

Brooks gets a grateful handshake from UK president Dr. Lee Todd after the 2007 upset of LSU.

"When he got the job at Kentucky, I remember telling some people here in Atlanta 'that's gonna work, if they will be patient.'" What coach Brooks has done there has not really been a surprise to me," he said. "He's the perfect combination of fire and ice. He knows what he's doing and how he wants to do it. But at the same time, even though he's sorta cool in his approach, he really gets fired up when things are not going well. He treats his players like men and if they don't do what they're supposed to do, he gets after them. I always thought he had the best combination of technical competence but compassion about the game. If you watch him on the sideline, he's still pretty passionate."

That passion—and that of the UK fan base—would be tested severely over the next three-and-a-half seasons.

Photo by Don Fowler

Don Fowler and friends. (l-r) Stephen Sawyer, Karl Sawyer, Don Fowler, Terry Settles, J Sosh.

Photo by Richard Mullins

Butterfly on Coach Brooks' finger. K-Day golf tourney Paintsville June 2007.

Chapter Eleven

Staying the Course

MOST NEW COACHES GET A HONEYMOON PERIOD with the fan base, but Brooks wasn't exactly feeling the warm embrace of the Big Blue faithful. He didn't have the big-name appeal and there were plenty of questions about his age and negative perceptions about a so-called west coast guy's chance of succeeding in the south. When Kentucky lost 40-24 to arch rival Louisville in the new coach's first game, the bandwagon grew considerably lighter.

The team he inherited had only 68 scholarship players, 17 fewer than the number allowed by the NCAA. And Kentucky was missing several key members from the squad that won seven games the year before—SEC player-of-the-year Artose Pinner, wideout Aaron Boone, All-SEC punter Glen Pakulak and defensive tackle Dewayne Robertson, a first-round NFL draft pick—but hopes were high for 2003 because of two key returnees. One was folk hero quarterback Jared Lorenzen and the other was superstar wideout/return specialist Derek Abney, who needed just one more kick return for a touchdown to set an NCAA record.

Fan frustration grew as Kentucky let a 21-3 lead evaporate into defeat against Florida. A seven-overtime setback against Arkansas and a dismal showing in a loss at Vanderbilt killed any chance of achieving Brooks' stated goal of playing in a bowl game and the Cats finished the season at 4-8.

"I actually felt pretty good about the team starting the year. They were trying to do it, and I think that loss (to Louisville) made it more difficult, and I think it fractured a little more as the season wore on," Brooks said, noting that some players were working under their third different head coach. He noted that the situation was made worse because a group of players had gone to bat to help Morriss get the job two years earlier, and they were hurt that a change had occurred such a short time later. "My stated goal was to get to post season play that year and we didn't. I think that unrest and unhappiness was to be expected. The one thing I didn't want to happen was to have it fall at the players' feet. It does, eventually it gets there whether the boos are directed at coaches, the players or me. It all ends at their feet anyway because of the negativity and that is just the nature of the beast."

Lorenzen says Brooks and his staff inherited a somewhat toxic environment, because a popular coach had left on the heels of a seven-win season.

"It was unbearable on the seniors when Coach Morriss left. We were devastated. We were promised that he wasn't going anywhere. We felt that we went to bat for him and begged Mitch Barnhart to hire him because we thought that he was the best coach, and then to have him just kind of turn his back on us is the way we felt," Lorenzen said. "Coach Brooks just came right in and understood that completely. He didn't get on us right away. He understood that we were going to have some harsh feelings, not towards him, but just about the experience in general. But he was great, bringing us all in and making us feel like we were a part of something special.

"You knew who was in control," he added. "He had that presence of when he walked into a room, he commanded the respect. Like he just would sit there, and you just, you knew that he was in the room. Call it intimidation or call it respect or whatever it may be."

Joker Phillips says the coaches recognized the issues they were dealing with, but Brooks was not going to compromise on what he believed it was going to take to advance the Kentucky program.

"I can remember the first time we were in a hotel before a game, there were guys in the lobby playing the piano and visiting with family, and I grabbed one of them and said 'get off the piano and get in your room! Think about the game!' And his response was, 'hey coach, we won seven games doing this last year'. But that was not Rich's way. That was not what we had to do," he said. "So we had to convince those kids that we knew how to win also. That also came with conditioning. Rich had convinced those guys that he knew how to win and conditioning was his way. Some bought in and some didn't. That's reason we didn't win right off the bat, because we had (some talented) players. For the first year, we were 4-8 and had a chance to beat Florida. And went seven overtimes against Arkansas and lost to Vanderbilt late. We had some chances to win and get to a bowl game, but we didn't have people to buy into Rich's plan to win."

Fans didn't want to hear that. They just knew that a team that won seven games the previous season was only able to get four wins in Brooks' first year. That just intensified the skepticism that accompanied a coach who spent most of his career on the west coast and who had a career losing record, no matter how poor the circumstances he inherited when he had taken over at Oregon.

But that experience in transforming the Ducks' football program had solidified Brooks' belief in the approach that was needed at UK. And he wasn't going to compromise.

"I think he was the perfect guy for this job. I say this because, a young guy, young coach would have come in here and when things got bad he would start veering off and changing his plan," Phillips said. "We, as coaches, thought we needed to change some things, too, but the old man said 'this was the way we were going to do it' and kept on the straight and narrow. We got the players here to believe in what we are doing. He knew how he was going to do it. He was stubborn. Nothing changed and we did the right things, which was blocking, tackling and being mentally tough and finding the things we needed to do to win."

Despite the disappointing results for the team that first year, Brooks found himself marveling at what Lorenzen and Abney did.

"That first spring, Jared was down to 266 (pounds) and he really looked good. His movement was great. Then (in the summer) he was 306. But he was a special guy on the field. He would throw a play at you on the field and you would just say, 'wow, this guy is really special'. Then he would do some things that would say, 'you can't do those things'. He was and is one of the most gifted guys. I have never seen a guy that big who had the skill that he had. Obviously the arm strength was there, but his footwork. His feet were good. Very competitive guy," Brooks remembered.

As for Abney, Brooks knew it was important for the fans to see the popular senior get that return record. A punt return TD that might have sealed the upset of Florida was called back for holding ("a horrible call," Brooks said) but Abney later got another chance to break the record, against Mississippi State at Commonwealth.

(On the radio...

"Abney backing up. He'll get to return this one—from his own 20. Circles off to the right, gets a block and cuts it up at the 25, 30, 35, 40—look out! To the near sideline at the 50, breaks a tackle, just one man to beat. He's across the 30, to the 20, Derek Abney to the 10, to the five and into the end zone. Touchdown Kentucky!")

"He and Lorenzen were like rock stars. I had never been anywhere where players were thought of quite as highly when there wasn't the great success that has gone with wins or bowl games and things like that. They were outstanding, they were playmakers and what Abney had done the year before is almost unheard of with scoring the touchdowns. It was really important because Abney was one of those guys, he was a warrior and he left it all on the field," Brooks said.

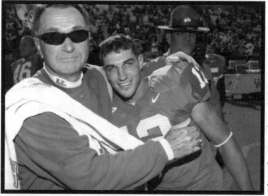

Brooks hugs Derek Abney after the senior broke an NCAA record for kick returns for touchdowns in 2003.

Photo by David Coyle/TeamCoyle

"He really was very, very happy for me, and I really do remember when I came back from that (record-setting TD)," said Abney. "That's actually one of the things I really remember about Coach Brooks in terms of game time situations, that after I had done that touchdown against Mississippi State, him grabbing my head, I remember that, and (how he was) really genuinely happy for me. I think Coach Brooks, and for me I think it's that, to be able to connect like that, knowing that in his inside circle and how he connects with people inside versus people he doesn't know as well, it shows kind of the special relationship he has with his players and his coaches."

Abney says Brooks seemed to understand the bitterness some players felt about the circumstances that had transpired. But Lorenzen says anyone who thinks he harbors any hard feelings toward Brooks is mistaken.

"To the casual fan, yeah I can understand where they would think that. But I was very happy. I'm sure he had to put in some good words to get me with the (NFL's New York) Giants, and apparently he did," said Lorenzen. "I mean they're going to talk to your head coach to see what kind of person you are, and he was obviously the head man, so he got me there (the NFL) for three years, and I wouldn't trade that for anything. But I couldn't be happier for him, especially the way he's turned around what we're doing now."

Photo by Victoria Graff

Brooks comforts an injured Tony Dixon at a 2004 spring practice.

Things got worse in Brooks' second year, starting with a 28-0 loss in the opener at Louisville. A month later, Mid-American Conference foe Ohio University upset the Wildcats in Lexington and the howls of the fans' grew louder and louder.

Offensive coordinator Ron Hudson became a target of fan criticism during the 2004 season.

A big dose of the criticism was directed at offensive coordinator Ron Hudson, whom Brooks staunchly defended. Brooks is as loyal as he is competitive and when Barnhart indicated it was time for a change, Brooks dug in his heels.

"I have fired several coaches over the years but not very many because I feel it is my responsibility to get them to do something better if they are not doing it well. It basically came down to a situation where, I was told that the administration was not going to renew his contract," Brooks recalled.

Did he consider walking away himself, rather than fire a coach he believed in? "Yep. It got close to that," Brooks said. "It wasn't a good time at the Nutter Training Center. I discussed it with Ron and he said 'that is crazy (for the staff to risk their jobs). That is not right' and he resigned because he didn't want to have anyone else out of the job," Brooks continued. "So, he sacrificed, in my mind, a great deal. I still feel very bad about that but it also, I suppose, bought a little time to help turn this thing around."

Hudson left with one game left in the season, and Brooks put Phillips in charge of the offense for the finale at Tennessee, with the head man and also offensive line coach Paul Dunn sharing the play calling role. With an open date preceding that game, Phillips used the extra time to insert Jacob Tamme at tight end and the little-used redshirt freshman responded with two early touchdown catches as Kentucky built a big lead, only to see the Tennessee Vols rally in the final minute to win 37-31.

"It ended up being our best offensive game of the year," Brooks noted.

"One is because Shane Boyd played a great football game and he played,

Shane Boyd (7) nearly led the Cats to an unlikely upset of Tennessee at the end of the 2004 season.

in that game, like I hoped he would have played all year long. He was accurate. He got the ball out. He made great decisions and except for a couple of late calls that went against us, we could have hung on to get that upset."

Lost in the disappointment of a two-win season in 2004 and the controversy surrounding Hudson was a noteworthy achievement in the season's next-to-last game.

Down 13-0 to start the fourth quarter at Commonwealth against Vanderbilt, the Wildcats rallied for two scores to win 14-13. The game-winning pass came on a floater from Boyd to Glenn Holt.

(On the radio...

"Holt to the near side, into the shadows. Splitting wide into the sunlight on the far side is Scott Mitchell. Backs are in an I. Boyd with a play fake. Setting up deep. Has time. Pats the football, pumps, throws it for the end zone. Man out there—Holt. Touchdown Kentucky!. On the back line of the end zone, it was like Glenn Holt was fielding a punt.")

While not pretty, the victory marked a significant achievement.

"I went to Tony Neely and asked when is the last time Kentucky came back from a 13-point deficit to win a game in the fourth quarter. He said 'I don't know, let me look'. He looked and looked and looked and could not find one," Brooks said. "That was the biggest comeback in Kentucky football history, which shocked me—absolutely shocked me. To me that was something to build on, something very positive to build on. Even though it was an ugly game, the winning touchdown pass was not the prettiest, but it was a win where you normally have lost games like that and not even had a chance to come back and win them. I think once you grasp something positive, you have to drive that nail home. You have to hammer that nail and pound it all the way into the wood and make sure it sticks. No question that was significant, absolutely."

Year three started with a thrilling game against Louisville, but a big second half comeback led by Woodson fell short in a 31-24 loss. A week later, UK was facing a potentially devastating home loss to Idaho State when the coaches inserted Rafael Little as a kickoff returner.

(On the radio...

"The kickoff is very high and it's going to come to Little at the two. He heads up the left hash mark, veers to the outside at the 20, breaks a tackle at the 25, 30, look out. 40, back into the middle of the field at the 50. At the 40, to the 30, to the 20, 10, five, Touchdown Kentucky!")

Photo by Victoria Graff

Brooks oversees the pre-practice stretching by his players at a 2004 spring workout.

Kentucky dodged the upset that night, but then lost five of the next six games, getting blown out by the likes of Indiana, Florida, South Carolina and Auburn.

"For the first few years, I had my doubts," Jim Host said of Brooks' hiring. Host is a UK alum whose former company, Host Communications, developed the University of Kentucky's radio network into the largest in the nation. Host said he wondered if Brooks had been away from the college game too long, but UK administrator John Cropp reassured him. Cropp had been a successful assistant coach before moving into administration, so Host respected his opinion and felt better about Brooks when Cropp said "he's doing all the right things."

Host also grew to appreciate Brooks' style.

"He was always dead honest," he said. "He never changed. He was unflappable."

Combs, whose publication (*Cats Pause*) began covering UK sports in the mid 1970's, agrees.

"I've been around a lot of coaches, and I've never been around a coach that is more of a straight shooter than he is. That's what I've always respected going to those Monday press conferences during the season—you knew he was going to shoot it straight to you," he noted. "There's a lot of media guys around here (Kentucky) that don't want to be reminded about what they wrote about him those first three years."

Brooks' family had supported his decision to return to the sidelines, but there was a growing uneasiness for them as the prospect of his firing was looming larger on the horizon. With the Internet, the Brooks' children could see and hear the criticism increasing, but it was Karen who had to live the experience at the epicenter.

"The first year was fine, I think because not much is expected the first year. I am kind of oblivious, or try to be oblivious, to things I don't want to hear. I would try, not the first year but the second year, to not read the newspaper if I didn't want to read it. I would never listen to talk radio, which Rich listens to all the time. But I just wouldn't listen to things like that, so I would just bury my head in the sand, I suppose. That third year, it got really bad," she said.

"I remember getting a letter that was weird. It was just a plain white envelope and it was just an ugly letter. Oh my God, it was horrible. It came to my home and that was what pissed me off," Karen continued. "I was not going to tell Rich about it because I know he gets all kinds of stuff like that but it came to my home and the fact that someone knew where we lived really bugged me. In it, (the letter) had said something about copies to Barbra Archer (wife of UK defensive coordinator Mike Archer) and Mitch Barnhart. So I called Barbra Archer and she had got one also. The two of us were just furious about it, and we just kept thinking about what it was that we should do. There was not that much to do about it, so it ended up that she had told Mike so I eventually told Rich about it. I just thought that people are so ugly at times. There was no return address. It was almost like they had cut out things from a magazine so you couldn't trace the typewriter or anything. It was bizarre."

Photo provided by Kerri Brooks Robinson

Karen and Rich do their impersonations of Lovee and Thurston Howell from "Gilligan's Island" at a July 4, 2008 outing.

Karen Brooks is no shrinking violet in the role of a coach's wife. At Oregon, she earned the nickname "Purse Lady" at Oregon for hitting an unruly critic with her purse. A then 14-year old Kerri once punched a fan who was critical of her dad, and when fans at Kentucky were calling for Brooks' head on a platter, she took to a message board to try and set them straight.

"He was not thrilled with me but I think he understands that he raised me and that I am a fighter who is going to stick up for my dad. I am sure that we were all shocked that it got blown up to what it did. It got into Sports Illustrated and all those crazy things. But I am going to stick up for my dad. I think he was proud of me," Kerri Brooks Robinson said.

"I was so upset about that because I knew he hadn't gotten a fair shake in Kentucky yet. I know we live in a society with instant gratification, but to go into a situation and a program that was so screwed up as Kentucky was, you can't fix it with a band aid," she continued. "I got sick over it and couldn't sleep. It was just that bricks were stacked against him. If people only gave him a chance, I knew that people would love him. I knew that people would come to like my dad. I knew he wasn't getting a fair shot yet. I knew once he had been around and people realized he was a good guy, and funny, that people would like him."

Lexington talk show host Dick Gabriel wasn't hearing from many callers who liked her dad in those days, though.

"There were a lot of people that were absolutely livid. It was hard to figure out who they were (more) mad at—Brooks or Barnhart. Of course, that prompted people to call and defend Brooks, but there wasn't that much to defend in terms of wins and losses. There were people who would call in and say they were going in the right direction," he said, "but there are a lot of people who flatly stated that it was about wins and losses and that it was time to make a change, oblivious to the fact that (UK) didn't have enough good players."

Despite the negative reviews from the fan base, Smith left a role as a multiple state championship-winning coach at Boyle County High School to join Brooks' staff in 2005. Why leave a position so secure for which one that could have put him in the coaching unemployment line if Brooks didn't succeed?

"I really liked the way he was doing things. I am a graduate. I played here. I love Coach Brooks' old-school mentality, because I've always thought that was what was needed at Kentucky, to get this program going in the direction that it needs to be going. It didn't matter to me at that point because I wanted to help get this program on the rise and be a part of that," said Smith.

"When Coach Brooks tells you something, that's the way it is. He wants his players to play hard and tough and practice (that way), but he cares about his players. He's going to drive them to be the best they can be but he's also going to put his arm around them and love them," he continued, adding that his defensive coordinator when he played at Kentucky—Charlie Bailey—had that kind of approach. "That's the way I was brought up in the business."

Sanders joined the Kentucky staff for the 2006 season. He had been released from his job at offensive coordinator at Tennessee the previous year, in a move many media types wrote was an effort to find a scapegoat for a bad year in Knoxville.

Sanders says he accepted Brooks' offer to coach the quarterbacks at UK because he, too, believed in the direction the head man was taking.

"It was pretty easy to see how Kentucky was getting better. You could see how hard the kids played. You could see a lot of things that, in my opinion, are the result of coaching," he said, referring to that intensity the players showed. "He has really good administrative skills. As an assistant coach, you know what's going on. You have a common purpose that you're working for. You know what your plan is and how to go about getting there."

UK Media relations guru Scott Stricklin says Brooks bought himself some goodwill with the reporters who covered him with his candor and truthfulness.

"I think the media probably came to appreciate that before the fan base did. You have got to appreciate his honesty, and they went out of their way to let people know that because it was refreshing to them and because we are in an age where coaches give canned quotes and say stuff that is generic. Rich isn't that guy," Stricklin pointed out. "He says things that are meaningful and

Photo by Victoria Graff

Brooks' straight forward answers at news conference won him respect from the media even when wins were hard to find.

I think it helped the media do their job, so he earned their appreciation. He didn't always agree with some of the shots they took, but I think any time you are in a market or area where people care passionately as they do in Kentucky and the team isn't performing as well as they want them to, there is going to be a perception that people are attacking. I think Rich's maturity allowed him to have a better perspective of that than another coach might in that situation."

Nationally, however, Brooks wasn't getting much love. Before the 2005 season, SportsLine.com writer Dennis Dodd suggested fired UK coach Hal Mumme had a better chance to win in his new job at New Mexico State than Brooks had at Kentucky. And *Sports Illustrated* college football writer Stewart Mandel put the UK headman on his worst coaches list. "A disaster from Day 1" is how he described Brooks' performance, on his si.com blog.

When Kentucky was blown out 38-14 at Indiana early in that 2005 season, longtime *Louisville Courier-Journal* columnist Rick Bozich wrote that it was no longer a matter of "if" Brooks would be fired but "when."

"He was at a point, I don't know what percent but there was a decent percentage of media people that were rolling their eyes and their fans saying 'we need to get a younger coach, a more vibrant coach,'" Bozich said. "He just kept saying 'I know what I'm doing'. And he was right. He never panicked. He didn't take any shortcuts. He, at least publicly, ignored all that (criticism), always took the high road and just kept working. He finally got it going and never really said 'I told you so'. He got it going in the right direction better than anybody I can remember at UK in the 30 years I've been here.

"I've even apologized to him, saying I was wrong and he was the right guy," Bozich added.

Kasey Holwerda says she goes online to follow what is happening with her father's program, and when she and her family visit Lexington, she gets a firsthand account from those naysayers who surface when things aren't going well.

"It is really crushing when you are the child of a coach or the spouse of a coach. My dad handles it much better than the rest of us do. We take it personally and it really hurts us," she admitted. "Each sibling handles this in a different way. Some of us are very interested in all the message boards and everything. I am at a point in my life where I don't want to dig up and read negative things about my dad. It doesn't make me happy, so why do it. I try and stay out of the message boards, but I read the Kentucky papers online. I go to Kentucky.com and read the Lexington sports page. When I am there, I listen to the sports talk shows driving home from the games because my dad listens to it, but I don't dig into it to the extent that other siblings may or may not admit to you. It upsets me, and I don't want to get upset about it because it is just too hard."

Her brother Brady has some of those same issues. He watches as many games as he can with his dad's longtime friend in Sacramento, CA, Russell Porter. Brady Brooks says it wasn't very enjoyable in those early years.

"I'm the pessimist of the family. (Russell) and I watch games together and those first couple of years, we were wanting him to hang it up. It was just too painful for us," Brady said. "My sisters are always positive. I'm a little on the negative side. It really physically bothers me, it's seriously stressful. When people are putting him down, it gets really hard."

It was a stressful situation to be sure, but Karen Brooks says it had been worse other places for her and Rich. She remembers the time in 1975 when Dick Nolan and the entire staff (including Brooks) of the San Francisco 49ers got fired.

"He was only paid for about six months. He couldn't find a job and we had a mortgage and three little kids," she said. Brooks ultimately found an assistant coaching role with UCLA and a year later, got his first head coaching job at Oregon.

"I would not have wanted him to go out like that," Karen said of where Kentucky stood after Brooks' first three-and-a-half years. "That would have

Photo by Victoria Graff

Brooks leads the Wildcats onto the field for a 2004 matchup with Indiana at Commonwealth Stadium.

been a real bummer. It is so nice now that he can go out when he wants to go out, on his own terms."

Brooks could see the potential in the players in the freshman and sophomore classes, but with the coach having won only eight of 31 games to that point, the rumors were growing that another change was coming at UK. The assistants were hearing the negative vibes when they made their recruiting contacts, so Brooks asked Barnhart to let him know whether he was going to be back or not, thinking a show of faith might stop the bleeding in recruiting. It came during the week that followed the 49-27 loss to Auburn.

"I basically was asking Mitch to either say I'm gone or say I'm going to be back for next year. It took several weeks, but I think it came out before

Photo by David Coyle/TeamCoyle

Brooks cuts up with the 2007 seniors at Picture Day.

the Vanderbilt game that I would be back. Your coaches are on the road on a Friday before a home game and going out and still trying to identify recruits and sell a positive message, and if all the talk is negative, that you're not going to be there, then you're wasting good energy, you're wasting money, you're wasting a lot of things," Brooks said.

For Barnhart, a key element was what he was hearing from the players. After the Auburn game, Scott Stricklin remembers Woodyard putting his arm around Barnhart and urging the school to stay behind Brooks and the team. Other leaders on the team—Woodson, Tamme, Little, Burton—came to Barnhart to echo that plea.

And then Dicky Lyons, Jr. remembers Barnhart putting the question to the entire team in a meeting—"do you want a new head coach?"

"Not one guy on the team raised their hand," Lyons said. "There was never a doubt in our mind that we wanted anybody else, because we knew that what he had set up for us to do was just going to take some time. We believed in him. I remember the meeting like it was yesterday, because just nobody, you know he asked and not one person raised their hand."

"We were honest with him, that he needed to stick with Coach Brooks," Woodson added. "Once we found our way, we definitely got things going in the right direction. We felt like he was the right man for the job but we just needed time. I think Mitch listened to us. He always wants to know what the players have to say—about anything. The players felt very strongly about keeping Coach Brooks around."

Stricklin says he received a call from Barnhart the night after the Auburn game and the AD wanted to come out with a public statement of support for the coaching staff.

"We helped him craft a statement, and I said 'there is no wiggle room in here'. A lot of times an AD giving confidence is just to relieve some pressure, but Mitch didn't want it to be short term. So he came out and said we are going to give Rich another year, and I believe in the job he is doing and the young kids he is playing. He said he is seeing evidence with the players that they are able to play in this league, that it just takes time but it is also time for us to start winning games, and next year I expect us to win some games," said Stricklin.

Dr. Todd gives Barnhart credit for taking a strong stand that was far from universally popular. And he says it was the players expressing their feelings to the AD that got that ball rolling.

"He said 'Wesley Woodyard came into see me and said we want to play for this coach and win for this coach'. Andre Woodson came in about an hour later (followed by others). It says a lot that they stood up for the coach. Mitch was committed and I was committed. Everything he was doing was right, and we were in a tough league to build and we were getting better. The players who (bought in) got something from the coaches, they liked the coaches, so it was building a new environment with respect internal to the coaching staff we had. Those players were rising. Mitch and I were listening to all the heat from the outside, but if you looked inside, you couldn't ask for anything better I didn't think."

Tony Barnhart heard and read his colleagues in the media questioning the hiring of Brooks from day one and that only intensified as the losses piled up in those first three years.

Close losses to rival Tennessee have been a source of great frustration for Brooks and UK fans.

Photo by Victoria Graff

"What they were saying is 'this guy is past his prime. The game has passed him by'. Obviously, that was not the case. It was just a matter of giving him and his staff enough time," he said. "You don't get three losing seasons in a row in this league anymore. That's why it was so unusual, what Mitch Barnhart and Dr. Todd did."

For Brooks, the strong support of his team was gratifying.

"I probably wouldn't be here talking to you and doing this if there weren't some players on the team at that point that were positive about what they wanted in the program, and they wanted the coaching staff basically to be here, and I think they expressed those views to Mitch, and I don't know, but I assume it had some influence on me being here," said Brooks.

Buoyed by the statement of support for their coach, the Wildcats went on the road as an underdog to face Jay Cutler-led Vanderbilt, which was playing for a chance at a rare bowl trip. UK jumped on top early and held off a Cutler-engineered rally down the stretch for a 48-43 win.

Oscar Combs figured Brooks would be, in effect, an interim coach at Kentucky. He remembers thinking that Brooks was a solid choice to stop the bleeding of probation, since the bigger names Kentucky pursued turned the school down. But Combs figured if the Wildcats made a turnaround, there would be a different coach driving the bus. He happily admits he misread that part of the deal.

"I never thought I would see another Jerry Claiborne (but he is)," Combs said of Brooks. "He's done, as far as I can tell, the second-best job in Kentucky history, only behind Bear Bryant. Really the only difference between Jerry and Coach Brooks is that Coach Brooks maybe has more of a sailor's tongue at times. They're not caught up in their ego. They're just solid people."

The players still believed in Brooks, but there weren't a lot of fans with them on that bandwagon, especially after the Cats ended 2005 with lopsided losses to Georgia and Tennessee. UK opened 2006 campaign with a 59-28 defeat at Louisville on national TV, but still, Brooks kept grinding forward every day, preaching to his players to believe in their potential

"He never got that frustrated and I never heard him say that he had bitten off more than he could chew," said Brett Setzer. "I mean he never lost focus. He always goes to the office early, win or lose. Always recruiting

Photo by Victoria Graff

The mood was festive at the 2006 Picture Day even though few outside the family were predicting success for the Wildcats.

148

and looking ahead. He was always positive and the kids love him. Which is something that probably wasn't going on in the early years as it is now because kids don't like to change. But these kids know where they stand with him because he doesn't sugarcoat anything."

"Rich didn't have highs and lows. He didn't BS them," said Brooks' former UK defensive coordinator Mike Archer. "And I think the players would tell you that's what they appreciated most. He told them just like it was and they responded to that."

"Coach Brooks is a good guy," said former UK free safety Marcus McClinton. "In this world, sometimes it's hard to find passionate people who are also good people. Coach Brooks is a genuinely good person. He was somebody I could really look up to. And everything adds up with him. He'll tell you straight out. He won't sugarcoat nothing but he's somebody you can talk to. He cares a lot about his players. I had a great experience at Kentucky. It felt like family. I always felt like I could talk with Coach Brooks if I had to."

Tommy Cook was one of the seniors in 2005 that had played for three different coaches and not known much success. But as he left the program, he could see things starting to change.

"The people that were always second-guessing things were slowly heading out the door and everybody that was there had bought into Coach Brooks' system. There was a feeling of family a lot more," he said. "It's rewarding to see the success that they're having now. It's one of the best feelings in the world."

Head coach of the offense Joker Phillips says there was one very bright spot in that blowout loss to Louisville at the start of the 2006 campaign. Both Phillips and Brooks say that's when the coaching staff was finally sold on Woodson as their quarterback. Even though the Cardinals jumped on Kentucky to the tune of 28-zip, Woodson took hit after hit from a very good UofL defense and kept competing as hard as he could, even completing long touchdown passes to Burton and Lyons. That kind of toughness was given a voice later that season when Woodson challenged his teammates in that post game speech after the LSU loss.

"There had been instances the two previous years that he would not have responded to taking that kind of beating," Brooks said "and I think that showed that this was a different Andre Woodson."

There weren't many high points in those early years, but one event that always brought a smile to Brooks' face was the Military Appreciation Night games at Commonwealth. Hundreds of soldiers from Kentucky bases would get tickets and they delivered loud and consistent support—come rain or come shine.

"I think people lose sight in your normal daily life, you lose sight of the freedom, the lifestyle we have and what other people are doing to ensure that stays the same. We can all look back at 9/11 and understand a lot of things that could be going on here or you could be in Afghanistan, living in Iraq, living in Iran. What we are able to enjoy, a lot of people don't think about. If it wasn't for what the military had done and is doing, a lot of the lifestyle and freedoms we have in life would not be possible," he pointed out.

Photo by Victoria Graff

The annual Military Appreciation Night games are ones Brooks especially enjoys.

"They are as enthusiastic as anyone who comes in. One game it was raining and thundering and even when they decided to evacuate and get under the stadium for a while, they were boisterous and supportive. We have quite a few players who have family in the military as well."

In 2007, Brooks received a letter from some Kentucky soldiers who were stationed in Iraq. The writer wanted the coaches and players to know how much watching the upset win over Louisville meant to them:

-----Original Message-----
Sent: Sun, 31 Aug 2008 8:34 pm
Subject: Mr. Barnhart, GREAT WIN!!! -- Pls fwd to Coach Brooks

Mr. Barnhart,

 I was unable to find an email address for Coach Brooks on the UKAthletics.com site and was hoping for your assistance in congratulating him and the players for a great game tonight.

Coach Brooks and the Wildcats,

As I sit at my workstation at 3:07 am on the Syrian border with Iraq, I and dozens of my Marines are likely too excited to sleep any time soon. A short time ago your game vs Louisville ended with a much deserved win. I am the First Sergeant for Military Police Company Alpha headquartered in Lexington, KY. As we are a Reserve unit many of our Marines are Kentuckians with close ties to the University of KY and are faithful fans of UK Athletics. More than a few are UK students that have put their educations on hold to serve their nation.

I want to congratulate you on your sincere and focused effort in Louisville tonight. You displayed great preparation and determination in achieving your goals. You did not allow the distractions of the heat, crowd or noise sway you in successfully completing your mission.
This was most evident in the small number of penalties assessed your team. This was a tremendous victory that I'm sure you will remember for your entire lives.

Coach, on a personal note, I would like to thank-you and your team for providing my Marines the welcome distraction from our duties here in Iraq. Watching your players perform at such a high level and with joy and motivation against their greatest rivals certainly raised the morale of my Marines. It also provided them with a welcome bit of home and family during their deployment overseas. I know many of them keenly look forward to attending games later in the season as we will likely be home in early November.

*Semper Fidelis,
--1stSgt Tony Reynolds

-----Original Message-----
Sent: Mon, 8 Sep 2008 9:05 am
Subject: On Behalf of Coach Rich Brooks

Sgt. Reynolds,

Thank you so much for your kind email. I am glad we can provide some diversion for you and the troops in a very positive way. The Louisville game was a very physical, hard-fought football game and one that I am extremely proud we were able to win. We have a great group of young men who are trying very hard to improve the image of Kentucky Football, and that game goes a long way in that direction.

We can't thank you enough for everything that you do to make our lives and pursuits possible. Your sacrifice and hard work make it possible for people like myself to enjoy a stress free life of safety and confidence that we will be safe from the people who want to do us harm.

I am hopeful that you get back here in November and that we will continue to give you some diversion as we move forward this season as quite a few of our games should be on TV.

Thanks again for everything you guys do and best of luck for a safe return home.

Sincerely,

Rich Brooks

Chapter Twelve

Goldminer's Son

IN JULY 2008, on a fishing trip to Oregon's McKenzie River, a 15-foot drift boat carrying Brooks, his son Brady and a friend capsized. They escaped serious injury and swam to safety but it served as a metaphor for Brooks' life and coaching career—no matter the obstacles, he is a survivor.

Kentucky's football program has taken more than its share of body blows since Bear Bryant left town in 1953. And in Rich Brooks, the Wildcats found just what they needed—a coach who could take a punch and find a way to counter.

Boxing played a key role in Rich Brooks' early development. It was one of many sports at which he excelled in the small northern California community where he spent part of his youth.

"In my high school we had a two-week break from football to basketball and in that time, we had boxing. Everyone would box in PE and then they would pick certain boxers to box in what they called 'the Smokers' (tournament). And it was a big fundraiser for the school," Brooks said.

In four years, in which matches in "the Smokers" were made based on ability and not age, Brooks never lost. He did, however, come very close to defeat in one particular match, and Brooks said he learned a good lesson about the need to stay focused on the task at hand and not get caught up in thinking about the bigger picture.

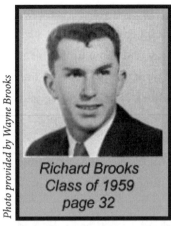

Richard Brooks
Class of 1959
page 32

Rich Brooks' 1959 yearbook photo at Nevada Union High School.

"My senior year, I am boxing a guy that weighs 25 more pounds than I do. And in the second round, I got him on the ropes and I think I am going to knock him out. I lose my focus a little bit because all I want to do is knock him down. He hits me with a haymaker, a defensive mechanism, and I am not paying any attention to defense because I am trying to land one. So his haymaker hits me and I am (stunned)," Brooks recalled. "I get woozy and the tweety bird is calling me and I back off. He doesn't even know he is hitting me hard because he is almost knocked out. That taught me, you have got to always be in control. You can't forget and lose sight of what got you to that point. You cannot throw caution to the wind and you have to understand that situation. I won the fight but I almost got knocked out."

Boxing was but a part of Brooks' athletic resume at Nevada Union High School in the small northern California town of Grass Valley. He played football, basketball, baseball and ran track, eventually earning a gridiron scholarship to play for coach Tommy Prothro at Oregon State University. Brooks came to Grass Valley from Alleghany, CA. Alleghany's population numbered fewer than 150 people but was home to one of the most famous gold mines, the Sixteen to One, in California history. Brooks lived in the tiny mining town with his father after his parents divorced. It was the athletic skills that prompted Dick Brooks to send his son to live with his mom in Grass Valley, where the opportunities to participate in sports would be greater. But it was in Alleghany where Brooks learned the value of hard work that shaped his coaching philosophies.

"My dad worked in the gold mines. I think hard work and trying to get better is just a part of my upbringing. My dad was a very hard working guy," Brooks said. "I will never forget the summer between seventh and eighth grade year, I got a job as a painter in Alleghany. The job was to paint the three-room schoolhouse (I attended). I get this job with this painter as his assistant and the first day, I come from the job, my dad came up from the mines and said 'how did the job go?' And I said, 'it went pretty good'. He said 'how much you making' and I said 'I am making a buck 35 an hour'. He said, 'congratulations, you are making more than I am'. He was making a buck 25. My teeth just dropped. He had been working all his life, and I get my first real job and I am making more money, and it was just for five weeks and painting while he is down (underground) mining and blasting and taking ore out. I will never forget that as long as I live."

Perhaps that tells us something about why Brooks, as a coach, has welcomed challenges others turned down—building a program where no tradition existed at Oregon, taking over the NFL's worst team in St. Louis and taking a job at probation-ravaged Kentucky when others were saying "no thanks."

Photo provided by Karen Brooks

Dick Brooks (Rich's father) was a longtime deputy sheriff in Alleghany, CA.

Brooks' father may not have earned a great deal of money but what he did earn was respect. And when it came to honesty, the apple did not fall far from the tree.

"The minute I met his father I thought, 'oh, my gosh, this man has so much integrity', " Karen Brooks recalled. "He was just an amazing person. He was such an honest man, lived his life the right way. I was just so impressed. His dad came from a family that was well educated and his sister had been an entomologist at (the University of California). But his dad wanted to be a gold miner. Why? I don't know, but he worked hard his whole life and then became a deputy sheriff up there (in Alleghany). He was a deputy sheriff for the last probably, 20 years of his life I suppose, and then finally retired. But, I was just really impressed and Rich is very much the same way, I think."

In every interview conducted for this book, the subjects universally mentioned "honesty" as one of the qualities they most admire about Rich Brooks.

"He will tell you the truth and he doesn't back off," said Bill Byrne, who became Brooks' boss as Oregon athletics director in 1984. "Now he's not out there to hurt your feelings or anything like that, but if you ask Rich a question you will get an answer, and you better be prepared for that when you deal with him, because he is totally honest. And I always loved that about him, I just absolutely admired him. He was my confidante. I didn't make a decision at the University of Oregon without consulting Rich Brooks."

"What stood out," close friend Brett Setzer said, "was that if he said he would meet you at 5 o'clock, your ass better be ready at a quarter to 5. If he says he will pick you up at 5, he will be there at a quarter till and whatever he told you was absolutely the way it was. I mean, there is no pretense. He is just absolutely a man of his word—good, bad, or indifferent. He always tells it like it is."

Childhood friend Russ Porter says Brooks is "intensely loyal" to everyone around him. At times, Porter thinks that trait can work against a head coach who needs to make a change in personnel or on his staff.

"Looking back at how many coaches Rich has fired or thrown under the bus, you won't find hardly any. He is so loyal, that when they aren't doing a good job, he will work with them so they do a better job. He accepts responsibility for things and stays with it. He and I talk often and I say 'so and so is terrible' and he will get mad at me because he is so loyal," said Porter. "Five years later, we will talk about it when that coach has moved on and he will admit 'yeah, that coach was (not getting the job done)'. But that is just the way he is. I think it is a wonderful trait as a person and has its pluses and minuses when you are running a program and are a head coach."

Whether it was boxing as a young man or games like golf or ping-pong these days, Brooks' competitive drive is legendary among those who know him.

"We were coaching buddies but at the same time we just competed against each other like it was a death struggle in damn near everything that we could think of," recalled San Jose State coach Dick Tomey, who coached with Brooks at UCLA and against as head man at Arizona. "We just both were highly competitive individuals, and then we found that about each other. And then when we played golf, we took it to a whole different level, when we played basketball, it was serious, and we went for a jog at noon, it became serious. And it was fun."

Steve Brown fishes with Brooks and they occasionally go golfing, but he says one thing Brooks won't do is play him in racquetball.

"I was playing pro football at the time, and I went back to Oregon and played him in racquetball and knew I could beat him, no problem. So I get up on him and I relax. He starts coming back because I relax, he beats me, puts the racquet down says I will never play you again. I will always be better than you. He has never played me in the last 30 years—he won't do it because he owned me. That is his deal. He wants you to compete against him and wants you to try to crush him, because if he wins, he's got you," Brooks explained. "If you beat him, you have got to beat him into the ground because if not he is going to fight you tooth and nail. He talks to our players about that and they feed off that because he is a competitor and is tough."

Wayne Brooks says his brother exhibited that burning passion to win at an early age.

"He wrote in his diary that he kept when he was young that 'I want to be better than my brother in all sports' and he certainly did achieve that. We were both athletic and he took it to a different level than I did. Ever played a game of darts with him? It is like you are in the Super Bowl," Wayne said. "I think it is the same way when he plays golf with his buddies. When I went to Oregon one time, we were at a place up in northern Oregon, and we had a place we were staying at and his kids were young and mine were young. We got out to the diving board and started doing flips and everything I would do he would do, and do it better. He was competitive. I think our dad was athletic. Our dad held the mile record at Redlands High School here in California for many years after he graduated and my dad was an excellent skier. I think that my background with athletics gave him something to go after—to be better than his brother and he was."

Brooks' thirst for competition even carries over to his hobby of fishing. There's a part of it that is relaxing, but as fly fisherman, he also gets to feed that need to excel.

"You have to be able to place the fly in the right spot. This is dry fly fishing, so you have to place the fly in the right spot and it has to float like a natural bug. Then, you have to watch it and you have to see the fish come up and strike it. If you do any of those things wrong, you are not going to catch any fish, so it takes a lot of concentration and really blocks everything else out of your mind," he said. "It takes a relative amount of skill to be good at it. You have to be able to cast it, which I grew up doing. I did all my fly fishing back casting under trees and roll casting and things where you couldn't get your line

Photo by Karen Brooks

Brooks shows off a bass he caught in the pond beyond his Kentucky home.

caught in the bushes or trees. The spoiled fly fishing I have now, I go out on my boat and can cast without restrictions. It has become easier in my old age."

Besides the competitive fire, Brooks' humor is a well-known characteristic to those closest to him.

"He knows when to tease you and when to back off," said Bill Byrne. "He's very, very quick-witted. He loves to tease you and he likes to get teased himself. He is just—I mean he's so much fun to be around. And he notices things about you. And if you don't like to be teased a little bit, you're going to have trouble around Rich because he'll pick something out and let you know about it. It's fun. I just, I love being around him. I really do. I miss not being with him."

He's not the only one. When Kentucky plays a home game, the Brooks' house is often filled with guests. It might be coaching acquaintances, former players or buddies from Rich's youth. Postgame parties also include the new friends they've made in Kentucky

"He has the best friends. He has always cultivated his friendships and some men don't do that," said Karen. "I think women have more of a tendency to do that. He has friends, like Russell (Porter), from grade school. These are friends he has known for 60 years. Then, he has his college friends. His Phi Delt (Phi Delta Theta fraternity) friends are really close. We still vacation with those people. So he still has close friends from so long ago that I think it is such a huge help when you have people to talk to."

And there isn't anything Brooks would fail to do to help a friend.

"I had a back problem," Brett Setzer said, "and couldn't move around very well, and my wife had to go somewhere and had called Karen to help me with the babies. I couldn't pick them up and was having a terrible time moving around. I am sitting in the babies room and I look up and here comes Rich. He comes walking in and I said 'what are you doing here?' And he said, 'the furnace is broken at our house and the guy is coming to fix that and Karen knows more about it, so where is the food and stuff. I came here to change the diapers'. He was just was glad to be there helping and I got a good picture (of him)."

Dr. Stephens remembers Brooks' challenging him to lose weight. Brooks asked Stephens how much weight he thought he could drop before an upcoming football season and Stephens replied, '100 pounds.' Brooks bet him $1,000 and two sideline passes. Come September, Brooks paid up, after having Stephens step on the scales at the UK training center to document the weight loss. Stephens says there was a lot of good-natured ribbing along the way, but he knew Brooks' real motivation was sincere. "He said 'I don't want to out-live you'," Stephens said.

As a player at Oregon State, Brooks was a defensive back on one of the Beavers' best teams ever. The 1962 squad won nine games, including a 6-0 victory over Villanova in the Liberty Bowl and teammate Terry Baker won the Heisman Trophy.

It was during that time at OSU that Brooks met his future wife, while coaching her in a powder-puff football game among sororities. They started dating soon after and when school ended, Karen remembers Rich making a trip to the upscale neighborhood near Portland, OR when she grew up, to meet her parents.

Photo provided by Denny Boom

Brooks with friends Brett Setzer and Royce Pulliam at the 2008 Kentucky Derby.

Photo provided by Karen Brooks

Karen and Rich Brooks' wedding photo.

"He was in his flip flops and shorts. That is what he wore all year round. He drove up to meet me and drove to our house and said 'oh, my God', because my situation was so much different than his," she said. "He had a son that he had in high school, Denny. I am not sure if he told my parents then or when he asked my parents for my hand in marriage—he might have fessed up right then and there. He is such an honest person that might have just said that this is the deal. I was just shocked because my parents had no objections, which I was surprised at. It all worked out. I think how sad it was that my father didn't get to see him be the head coach of Oregon. My father just loved watching when he was at Oregon State. My mother got to enjoy him being the head coach of Oregon but, my dad didn't. And (Rich's) dad died the first year we were there."

Wayne Brooks says the fact that Rich fathered a son at age 16 made his brother mature faster than most.

"Rich grew up real fast in that regard. His dad wasn't around and he didn't have his older brother to lean on. I helped Rich make a decision at that point. It wasn't a popular one with his girlfriend but it had to be done because Rich had a future, and I didn't want him to be working in the saw mills, trying to raise a young kid," Wayne said, noting that their parents covered the child support while Rich was away at college.

"It does help Rich understand his players when things happen," Wayne continued. "Arlene and Danny (Boom) did a tremendous job raising Denny. It was all very good and Denny is just a tremendous (person). As a young man, he went back into Rich's life and Rich has done his part. Denny and Rich grew very close."

Brooks is up front with his players about this part of his background.

"I have brought that up to numerous players who come in with difficulties or problems, just so they understand that I have been through some things like that. That I wasn't born with a silver spoon in my mouth. That I also had some (issues) as a teenager that I had to accept responsibility for," he said.

Are these players surprised to hear that?

"Very. Very surprised," Brooks answered.

While pursuing a master's degree at Oregon State, Brooks signed on as Prothro's freshman coach. After a one-year stint as a high school coach, he returned to the OSU staff for five years as an assistant coach on defense, working under headman Dee Andros.

"It was a great time because I was going back to my alma mater. And I was working with a guy that was fun to be around. My defensive coordinator was Bud Riley (father of current OSU head coach Mike Riley). It was a good group of people and it was kinda like going home. And we were really good," Brooks said, noting that the Beavers beat an O.J. Simpson-led Southern Cal team that year (1967). "We had two years (in which) we finished in the top

Photo by Karen Brooks

Terry Donahue (left) liked Brooks' honesty and hired him as an assistant coach at UCLA in 1976.

10 in the nation. The thing was, in those days, if you didn't win the Pac 10, you couldn't go to a bowl game."

In 1970, Brooks was reunited with his old college coach when he followed Prothro to UCLA. And it was Prothro who had perhaps the greatest influence on shaping the kind of coach Brooks would become.

"I think that I learned a lot from everybody I worked under but I think Tommy Prothro was a major influence on my background as far as fundamentals of blocking and tackling, and he also was very good at coming up with a trick play now and then, and I think that I kind of caught that bug from him," Brooks explained. "The ability to work for Dee Andros at Oregon State. He was probably one of the most inspirational coaches, you know, the old Knute Rockne pregame speech, halftime talks. He was as an emotional a guy who could get his teams emotionally high as anybody. You have to take that and try to work it into your own personality, and sometimes the oratory is a little more difficult to translate, and you have to still be yourself. Terry Donahue was a very young (coach), his first year as a head coach (at UCLA in '76). He hired a staff that almost all of them were older than he was, which included me. He was an extremely organized guy. I mean, he helped me with the organizational aspect, the planning, the off-the-football-field preparation in a lot of areas, which is remarkable for as young a coach as he was. And Dick Nolan, who was the head coach at the 49ers, was an outstanding x-and-o guy too, and I learned a lot of defensive principles from Dick Nolan."

Shirley Prothro says her late husband and Brooks both had football in their blood and that's what brought them together.

"They just hit it off. Rich was kind of enough to say that Tommy had a great influence on his life in many ways, which is so nice of him to say. Tommy was always so interested in Rich's successes where he coaches. Rich says that he used so much of Tommy's techniques and ideas in his own coaching," she said.

And any UK players whose mistakes evoke Brooks' wrath can thank Prothro for the way the message is delivered.

'The depth of learning is directly related to the volume of the lesson,'" Brooks remembers Prothro saying. "The amount you remember a mistake

Brooks with 1962 Heisman Trophy winner Terry Baker at an Oregon State alumni function.

Photo provided by Karen Brooks

is in direct proportion to the amount you suffer when you make the mistake. And that's why I sometimes seem to go overboard on the sideline on silly, stupid penalties or things like that, mistakes that really shouldn't happen, but almost always happen. But they shouldn't happen with the same guy twice, and that's the lesson I learned from him, that when you do something wrong you're going to hear about it, and that should help prevent you from doing it again."

But when Brooks erupts, he makes sure not to cross a line that causes him to lose the player's respect.

"I think it's a judgment call, because some guys are harder to get to do it right than others. Some guys are more stubborn than others. But the one thing that, and I've probably crossed that line particularly as an assistant coach and maybe once or twice as a head coach, but anytime you're going to go nuts on a guy, or discipline him, or single him out for something that he has done poorly that you know he can do better, you can't back him into a corner and leave him no place to go to escape," Brooks noted. "You have to have an opportunity to come back, and put your arm around him and say, 'hey, you know, we know we can get this better, so let's get it done'. And if you give him no way out, you're going to break the connection, you're not going to have a connection where he's going to continue to try to do it right for you. He'll go the other way. He'll say, 'screw you'. Sometimes a fine line and sometimes there's a big gap on how much a guy can take. Some guys really can't take criticism at all."

For Brooks, the way to understand where that line is comes from getting to know each individual as best he can, on and off the field, so that he doesn't take a one size-fits-all approach to every disciplinary issue.

"If you go by the seat of your pants and have a totally standard rule, sometimes you're going to wash out a lot of really good people and a lot of really good players," he said. "I do a lot of roaming during practice, trying to get a feel for how players are reacting to different assistant coaches and

Photo courtesy of Karen Brooks

how they're being coached, trying to determine whether they need to be coached harder or somebody needs to put an arm around them, try to get closer to them as far as their personal lives and what's going on, their family, or girlfriends, or school, and not make it all about football, because I think if that happens, I think they don't think you care about their development as an individual."

Joker Phillips will one day inherit the UK coaching job

Brooks with his longtime coaching mentor, Tommy Prothro.

from Brooks, so he constantly observes the way "the old man" goes about his work.

"Rich is hard on kids, but is one of those guys that as soon as you get off the field, he puts his arm around him and says I am trying to make you a better person and a better football player, make you a better father (when you become a father). A lot of kids don't have that in their lives and he is that father figure for them that they trust," said Phillips. "I think that has helped us be able to push our team and have them lay it on the line for us. When you see (him) walking down the hall, you don't duck into the nearest door. And I have been in places where players do that, but they don't mind going by him and cutting up with him. Places I have been to, the coach is coming and the player is coming and they will duck into another room so they don't have to talk to him. That is what other coaches do with the players and with the assistants. We don't have that here. It is not a real tense working environment."

Brooks admits he's still learning how to be a better head coach, but he relies on honesty and consistency as core values. He says his approach may be "old fashioned" but to a man, the players interviewed for this book say those are the very qualities which eliminate problems a 60-something coach might have dealing with 20-something young men.

Tony Neely says Brooks cares about his players just as much off the field as he does when they're on it. As an example, he noted a time when Dominic Lewis was considering a change to a more difficult academic major and faced the possibility of losing eligibility because he wouldn't have logged enough hours in his new field of study.

"Coach Brooks was absolutely furious and it was not about the fact that (Lewis) might not be able to play. I remember him pounding the table and talking about that," said Neely. "He sticks up for his guys."

Brooks followed Prothro from UCLA to the Los Angeles Rams in 1971. After two years, he returned to OSU as defensive coordinator under Andros and returned to the pro game as an assistant in San Francisco. Brooks interviewed for assistant coaching jobs in Green Bay and Cleveland after

Nolan and the staff was fired in San Francisco in 1975. When he failed to land either of those jobs, Brooks seriously considered getting out of the coaching profession.

Brooks was making plans to buy a gift shop in Grass Valley with the prospect of selling insurance on the side when Donahue convinced him to join the coaching staff at UCLA in 1976. One year later, Brooks got his first head coaching job, with the challenge of trying to rebuild an Oregon program that had produced just one winning season in 12 years.

Chapter Thirteen

The Oregon Years

THE FOOTBALL FACILITIES at the University of Oregon are now among the best in the nation. That's because of the largesse of alumnus and Nike founder Phil Knight, who has donated hundreds of millions of dollars to the school's athletic department. To say it wasn't that way when Brooks arrived would be a massive understatement. Combine that situation with the school's lack of consistent winning tradition and you know why so many other coaches before Brooks said "no" to Oregon's overtures.

"They tried to get Bill Walsh, and he pulled out of it and turned it down. Jim Mora, who was an assistant at the University of Washington at the time. They offered him the job, and he turned it down. And I think Monte Kiffin and I were the two guys left. He was at Nebraska at the time, and I was at UCLA, and the interesting thing to me is that I had been a player at Oregon State, coached at Oregon State for six years and had never lost to Oregon, so I don't know whether that helped me or hurt me in the process. I guess, I was one of the only viable guys left and they didn't want to start the process all over again, I guess," opined Brooks, adding that "some things are meant to be" so he wasn't bothered by others getting offered before him.

"Awful" is how Brooks describes the football facilities at Oregon. He says the fans the Ducks had were loyal, but there weren't enough of them to halfway fill Autzen Stadium. There were no meeting rooms for the team, so Brooks and his coaches gathered the players in the tunnels under the stadium that lead onto the field. In the late fall and early winter, with the wind blowing, the atmosphere for concentrating on the chalk talks was not conducive to sharpening one's focus. So along with trying to upgrade the talent for Oregon football, Brooks also took on the task of raising funds or creatively bartering to improve the working conditions.

"It was a long, hard process, and really I don't think we made any significant progress until Bill Byrne took over (as AD). He tried to get a cigarette tax. He got a sports lottery going, trying to raise money any way he could for the athletic program, not only at Oregon but they went in conjunction with Oregon State on the sports lottery, and then he finally got us over the hump a little bit. I had raised money to get a team meeting room up on the east end of the stadium from a lumberman named Don Barker, named it 'The Barker Room', and we finally had a place where we could meet with our team and look at film and stuff," Brooks said.

Photo provided by University of Oregon

Brooks led his Oregon players onto the field at Autzen Stadium.

UPGRADING THE KENTUCKY FACILITIES

When Brooks made his first visit to the UK campus, he was impressed with the football facilities he saw. The situation was a stark contrast to the substandard situation he had walked into at Oregon in 1977.

Nevertheless, he has pushed hard to improve that part of the Kentucky program because of the need to keep pace with the rest of the SEC—and have a chance to compete for the kind of recruits it takes to move the Wildcat program forward.

"The fact that we have made some upgrades to our facilities is critically important. We had great facilities before but we are playing in a league that has some of the best facilities in the nation, and we need to constantly be in the process of upgrading. The locker room in the stadium for example," Brooks said. "When I came here, the fact that we were 50 yards apart with offense and defense not in the same room just blew my mind."

When he was told no previous coach had complained about the setup, Brooks was surprised. He says it's hard to have a unified team with that much distance between the offensive and defensive squads in their game day locker room.

"So we got a new locker room there, thanks to Greg Wells who stepped up and donated a significant amount of money. We got our practice field (improved) so we don't slip and slide in the mud when it rains and we don't play on the freeway when it is hot and dry. Tim Couch donated some money with that," he continued, "and Dick Barbella gave some money to re-do our locker room (at the Nutter practice facility). We have a new team meeting room and we are going to continue to add to our facilities to update them and upgrade them and I think that is critical."

UK defensive coordinator Brown says Brooks is always looking out for the long-term good of the program more than his own personal gain.

"He is not out there for the Rich Brooks resume—he is out there for Kentucky. That is the beautiful thing about it, when it came to signing a contract, there were things written in it, so instead of him taking money, he gave money to coaches, did things in his power to upgrade facilities and that is something people don't realize," Brown said. "They just don't realize what he has done. Whether it is the (practice) fields, the indoor turf, the locker rooms, he has done everything he can to upgrade this program."

Byrne remembers walking into an office that housed four of Oregon's assistant coaches. One was watching game film on aluminum foil stretched over a window. Another was under a desk, making a recruiting call. A third was in a corner with a flashlight, preparing a game plan. And he and Brooks had to strike a barter deal with a local carpet retailer to get new carpeting for the offices.

Byrne wanted to remove the distraction of subpar facilities, so Brooks could focus all of his energy on the arduous task of upgrading the Ducks' talent. Oregon wasn't going to out-recruit the best teams in the Pac 10 but if they could at least close the gap, Byrne knew Brooks' coaching ability could then get them over the hump.

"He was very smart, very observant. He knew the lay of the land. He was just very astute. Great football coaches are terrific leaders, and he understood leadership," Byrne observed. "He got the very best out of his assistants, he got the very best out of our support staff, and he always got the best out of our athletes. It was a pleasure to attend practice and watch what he would do. I always loved the trick plays he would put in, and watch him set them

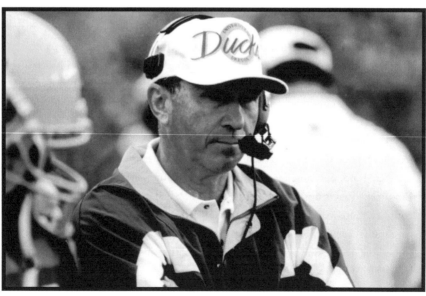

Photo provided by Karen Brooks

Brooks says the rebuilding job he undertook at Oregon was even tougher than the one at Kentucky.

up. I think what he did at Oregon, from where we were to where he got the Ducks, was one of the greatest coaching jobs I've ever seen. It was a pleasure to work with him."

Neither Oregon nor Oregon State was having much success in those days, so when the Ducks began to control the rivalry, Brooks' recruiting improved and Oregon was eventually landing most of the state's best high school players year in and year out.

After winning just two games in each of his first two years, Brooks' fourth team won six games and finished in the top half of the conference, earning him the Pac-10 coach-of-the-year honor. The Ducks lost more games than they won in five of the next six seasons before going 6-5 in 1987. There would be only two more losing records in Brooks' final eight seasons at OU.

"I think where we turned the corner at Oregon and where we turned the corner here was when we got a quarterback that could make plays," said Hellyer, then the sports information director at OU. "We had a guy named Bill Musgrave at Oregon who was maybe coach's most cerebral player. He was not very talented but very cerebral. That guy came in and in my opinion is the most valuable player in Oregon history because what he did was incredible."

Oregon was 6-1 in Musgrave's junior year, fueling dreams of a Rose Bowl run, before he was lost for the season with a broken collarbone. The Ducks didn't win another game that season but they also never had a losing record in Musgrave's four years there.

The 1989 season was a pivotal one, as the Ducks went 7-4 and had a chance to play in the Independence Bowl, which would mark the school's first postseason appearance in 26 years. Brooks credits Byrne with leading the charge to convince school officials that they should agree to the ticket sales guarantee it took to land the bowl bid. And Oregon won the game, beating Tulsa 27-24.

"It ended up being the biggest investment in Oregon football history in my opinion. We ended up taking almost 15,000 to 18,000 fans to Shreveport, Louisiana, and ended up beating a very good Tulsa team. Bill Musgrave

Photo by Karen Brooks

Kisky Holwerda with her grandfather at the 1989 Independence Bowl.

was the catalyst for that, and we'd had two really good years before that."

A 1990 trip to the Freedom Bowl marked the first-time ever the Ducks had reached the postseason in consecutive years. In the next four years, Oregon played in two more bowls, culminating in 1994 with the first appearance in the Rose Bowl in 36 years. Joe Paterno and Penn State defeated Oregon in that Rose Bowl game 38-20, but Brooks won numerous national coach-of-the-year awards for the team's amazing run. And like the 2006 season at Kentucky, the turnaround came at one of the lowest points in Brooks' tenure.

After a season-opening win, the Ducks lost 36-16 at Hawaii. A 34-16 defeat at the hands of Utah in the next game left Oregon at 1-2. But Brooks kept battling and so did his team. Two weeks after the Utah loss, UO scored its first win over traditional Pac 10 heavyweight Southern Cal in 23 years. After a loss to Washington State, Oregon ripped off six straight wins, clinching the Rose Bowl slot in the next-to-the-last game of the season, a 55-21 rout of Bill Walsh's Stanford team.

Late in that win, Brooks inserted backup quarterback Tony Graziani with instructions to run out the clock.

"I told him to run the clock and damned if he didn't audible out of a running play and drop back and throw a 60-yard touchdown pass. I ripped him when he came to the sideline," Brooks said. "I'll never forget shaking Bill Walsh's hand and saying 'I did not call that pass play.'"

Karen and Rich arriving in Pasenda for the 1995 Rose Bowl.

Several years later, Brooks and Walsh were at the same event and Brooks' grandson, Gunnar Holwerda, wanted an autograph.

"I go ask Bill and he says 'what should I put, your granddad beat the hell out of me in our last game together and ran the score up on me?' So he didn't forget," Brooks added.

With the Rose Bowl trip secured, Brooks then led his team to a 17-13 win at arch rival Oregon State, clinching the first-ever outright Pac 10 title for the University of Oregon.

"He was always at his best when the situation looked most dire," said Goe, the Oregon Ducks beat writer for *The Oregonian* newspaper. "Somehow, he had a way of bringing the best out of his players when the situation looked hopeless, and that's sort of what happened. The team rallied around a pretty good defense, actually had some NFL players on the defense, and the offense just got the maximum out of what it had, had a quarterback (Danny O'Neil) who didn't have much of an arm strength, but was really smart and understood the game really well, and was really adept at reading defenses."

"There were circumstances which he didn't have the best things to work with but he was always able to pull together teams," recalled Oregon president Dr. Dave Frohnmayer. "And I mean that as what a leader does to bring together a team rather than individual performers. That was probably no more evident than in the effort that he did to get us to the Rose Bowl in 1994. Everyone recalls that we lost (two games early), and Rich was walking off the field after a defeat and some fan was in Rich's face and he was stoic about it and didn't react at all. What a tough job that is and he and the team

Photo provided by Karen Brooks

Brooks shares a moment with Penn State coach Joe Paterno before the 1995 Rose Bowl.

turned it around in what is really a story book ending to a season to take the Pac 10 championship and go to the Rose Bowl."

Hellyer says Brooks had better teams at Oregon than the one that made it to Pasadena, but none were more resilient.

"That Rose Bowl team we had wasn't the most talented team you have ever seen, it just had a bunch of guys who gave you every ounce they had. That team was so indicative of in my mind taking on the personality of their coach," Hellyer said.

Throughout the early struggles and various setbacks, Brooks says he was always "stupid enough" to think a Rose Bowl bid was possible for Oregon. But seeing the dream come true provided a special memory.

"I do remember on that field, the awe of looking up and seeing almost 50,000 fans in Oregon colors and almost disbelief for a lot of the fans that they were there, their utter joy and feeling this is something they'll treasure and remember all of their lives," he said.

Brooks credits the administration at Oregon for helping him and his coaches complete the transformation of the Ducks' football program. When

Brooks left for the NFL, one of his assistants took over. Mike Bellotti was able to build on the foundation that had been laid in leading Oregon to nine straight winning seasons and occasionally putting the team in the national title picture.

"It transformed from one of the jobs that no one wanted to one of the jobs that was much more highly thought of," Brooks said. "We made Autzen Stadium a very difficult place to play for opponents because of the size of the stadium. The fans are right on top of you and it is one of the noisiest places in the country. We were able to transform what was a hopeless situation into a viable program that continued with Mike Bellotti and six of the coaches that were on my staff. The continuity of what we built there and the enthusiasm coming off that Rose Bowl team continued to develop the money support, booster support, facility support and now Oregon has some of the finest facilities in the country, period."

Was the challenge of building a winner greater at Oregon than at Kentucky? "Yes," said Brooks.

"I think it was more difficult at Oregon. The difficulty was in fan base, facilities, the financing. And (no) recruiting base within a close proximity to

Photo provided by Karen Brooks

ABC-TV's Lynn Swann shares a laugh with Brooks and Oregon alum Ahmad Rashad at the Rose Bowl.

Photo provided by Karen Brooks

Brooks got a victory ride when the 1994 Oregon team was honored with enshrinement into the University of Oregon Hall of Fame.

Oregon's 1994 Rose Bowl season (9-4)

Portland State	58-16	W
Hawaii	16-36	L
Utah	16-34	L
Iowa	40-18	W
USC	22-7	W
Washington State	7-21	L
California	23-7	W
Washington	31-20	W
Arizona	10-9	W
Arizona State	34-10	W
Stanford	55-21	W
Oregon State	17-13	W
Rose Bowl: Penn State	20-38	L

Photo by Oregon Media Services

1994 Rose Bowl team for the Oregon Ducks.

Brooks' achievements with Oregon football

- left as winningest coach in Oregon football history
- first coach to lead Ducks to four bowl games
- 6-5 record in 1979 was first winning record in nine years at UO
- back-to-back winning seasons in 1980; first time at UO in 16 years
- ranked in top 25 in 1987; first time in 17 years
- 1989: Independence Bowl win over Tulsa was first bowl win for UO in 26 years
- 1990: Freedom Bowl marked first back-to-back bowl bids in UO history
- 1994: first-ever outright Pac10 title, first Rose Bowl in 37 years
- 14-3-1 record v. archrival Oregon State

your campus. Here, you have a much more accessible talent base that can get in a car and drive to your campus," he noted. "Now, to win the SEC championship, that gap level between three straight bowl wins (and that level), may be a more difficult climb (than he had in getting to the Rose Bowl at Oregon)."

The "Ditch Rich" bumper stickers had been torn up by the time the Ducks made it to the Rose Bowl and the next season, after the coach had left for the NFL, Oregon honored Brooks by naming the field at Autzen Stadium after him.

"He could have been elected governor probably," Goe said of Brooks' popularity. "I would bet there probably isn't another coach in America that has a losing record at the school where they've named the field after him."

Brooks was able to return for the naming ceremony.

"We had taken a program from nothing to something and since it has gone to something outstanding. I really think it is something that happens in life that doesn't seem like it happened or could happen. How it happened, I don't know," Brooks said, "but it certainly is an honor."

Chapter Fourteen

NFL
Opportunity

WHY WOULD BROOKS LEAVE OREGON after his best season ever to coach the St. Louis Rams?

"I had been there 18 years (in 1995), and I like to say that when you are in one place long enough, usually there is a percentage of the fans that like you, there is a percentage that don't like you, and (a percentage that is) somewhere in the middle and hasn't made up their mind yet," he said. "After 18 years, there wasn't anyone left in the middle."

That is, no doubt, an oversimplification. In reality, Brooks says he was ready for a new challenge. And there were substantial financial reasons to make the move, as he ended up tripling the money he was making at Oregon, even though he had also served as athletics director for the last two years. His four-year deal to coach the Rams paid him $625,000 annually. Brooks says his former boss at UCLA, Terry Donahue, would have probably taken the job if the Rams had not been making a move from Los Angeles to St. Louis. Brooks, however, was excited about the opportunity to test his mettle at football's highest level—even it was another reclamation project. As the LA Rams, the team had suffered through five consecutive losing seasons, averaging fewer than five wins per year and now the franchise was moving to St. Louis.

Brooks had experience in the NFL as an assistant under Prothro with the Rams in the early 70's and then with the 49ers under Dick Nolan. But now he was a head coach in that league for the first time while also managing the relocation of the organization halfway across the country. To say that added to the challenge would be an understatement.

"When we took over the Rams in St Louis, there wasn't anything on the ground. There wasn't a training site, no offices. All of this had to be done between approval date in March and moving date of mid-April. That was a very, very stressful 30 days which involved Rich and myself," said Ortmayer, then the Rams' general manager. "We played in Busch Stadium because the dome was not complete. Essentially, we were the worst team in the NFL, the worst of 32. Actually it was 30. It was an unbelievably tall mountain."

Brooks' first game was scheduled for Green Bay's Lambeau Field and Ortmayer says the Rams were a 17-point underdog.

Despite the obstacles, Brooks' first team started fast, upsetting the Brett Favre-led Packers. A key play came from a staple of his coaching philosophy—special teams—as a blocked punt by wideout Isaac Bruce turned the tide in a 17-14 upset. St. Louis followed with three more wins in a row before reality started to set in and the Rams finished 7-9. Still, that was a three-victory improvement over the previous year.

Before the 1996 season, St. Louis traded running back Jerome Bettis to Pittsburgh and drafted troubled Lawrence Phillips out of Nebraska. The experiment with Phillips failed miserably and starting quarterback Chris Miller, who had played for Brooks at Oregon, was lost for the year to a concussion in the preseason. The team struggled to a 6-10 record, although it did win three of its last four games. Not good enough. Brooks was fired.

Photo by Karen Brooks

Kisky (left) and Gunnar Holwerda enjoy a pregame visit with grandpa before a St. Louis Rams game in 1995.

"The transition in getting the team back there, starting training camp, the whole process was a lot of logistical problems and a management that was still based in LA but was part time in St. Louis. For whatever reason, they decided to cut us loose after two years and then brought Dick Vermeil in," Brooks said.

Ortmayer thinks the lack of opportunity to see that job through is something that still eats at Brooks.

"And justifiably so. I think Rich Brooks is a tremendous realist. I think that he saw that as an unrealistic conclusion to the progress, which was on the right track. And so I think that he would have a hard time reconciling that," Ortmayer observed.

Ortmayer's instincts are correct. Brooks is bothered by the fact that he didn't get the chance to see the job through in St. Louis.

"On the grand scale of things, I think we were headed in a better direction than before I had taken the job. I was upset that I wasn't given more time. But that's life. I don't look back at it now and get angry," he said. "Did it bother me? Yes, it bothered me. But I knew I had to move on."

Brooks could feel the negative vibes against him as that second season was unfolding, but says he was "stubborn enough to think that I could change the outcome." That led him to pass up an offer to succeed Donahue as head coach at UCLA.

"Until I got the Kentucky job, that always stuck in my mind that maybe I had made an error there," he said.

"I think (Rams' president) John Shaw hired Rich because they were moving the Rams from LA to St. Louis and it was a mess," Karen Brooks suggested. "He probably knew he couldn't get some big names, so he'd get some guy who would work hard and get it going. He didn't even really give him a chance.

"I think he (Rich) is still a little bit frustrated because (Dick) Vermeil ended up going in there and going to the Super Bowl, and I think if they had stuck with Rich a couple of more years," she continued. "He would have gotten things turned around, too."

Karen was at least confident her husband did not miss the sometimes eccentric ways of the Rams' late owner, Georgia Frontiere.

"She invited us up to her box after the first game (in 1996). She has an opera singer up there—with a poodle—and they're playing 'Let Me Entertain You', and she says to Rich, 'let's dance'. And she starts singing 'Let Me Entertain You' and I'm about to die laughing," she said. "I'm trying to keep a straight face but it is so bizarre."

Karen Brooks thinks a storyline on the TV show "Coach" must have come from scenes like that one. In the show, Craig T. Nelson's character gets a pro coaching job working for an eccentric female owner.

Confident he could succeed if given the time, Brooks opted to stay in the NFL in hopes of landing another head coaching gig. He joined Dan Reeves' staff in Atlanta as defensive coordinator. And in his second year there, Brooks found himself in a Super Bowl.

Reeves actually underwent heart bypass surgery with two games left in the campaign and Brooks took over, leading the Falcons to a pair of wins to culminate an improbable 14-2 record.

"He stepped up and we didn't miss a heart beat," remembers Bill Kollar, one of Brooks' colleagues on the Atlanta staff. "Things went really well and the players respected him and things went on as they always did."

With Brooks coordinating the defense that season, Atlanta ranked second in the league against the run, fourth in points allowed and eighth in total yards allowed. Three years earlier, the Falcons had given up more passing yards than any team in NFL history.

Reeves returned for the playoffs but the road to the Super Bowl went through a 15-1 Minnesota team and Brooks' defense had to slow down an offense led by Randall Cunningham and wideouts Randy Moss and Cris Carter. That unit had established a new NFL record for points in a season.

Brooks knew Moss was the key to that high-powered attack,

Defensive coordinator Brooks applauds after a Falcons victory in 1998.

so he devised a plan to roll the Falcons' pass coverage to Moss, no matter where he lined up. The rookie sensation caught the game's first touchdown pass, but he had only five more receptions, for a total of 75 yards. And in the second half and overtime, Moss managed just one catch for four yards.

A rare late-game miss by field goal kicker Gary Anderson opened the door for the Falcons to send it into overtime, where they prevailed 30-27, earning them a spot opposite Denver in Super Bowl XXXIII.

Brooks remembers the Media Day zoo ("answering the same question over and over and over") and the numerous requests for tickets from old friends that he had not talked with in years. But most of all, he remembers an incident on the eve of the game that dealt a blow to Atlanta's hopes of upsetting the John Elway-led Broncos. Free safety Eugene Robinson was arrested for soliciting an undercover police officer for sex.

"I was up, Dan Reeves was up, half the team was up pretty late that night. That kinda took the edge and the shine off our chance. And it was going to be difficult anyway because Elway was just red hot. It became a lot more difficult after that happened," Brooks said. "I would have liked to have gone into the game without something like that disturbing the preparation."

Robinson got beat on an 80-yard touchdown pass in the second quarter that put Denver on top 17-3. The Broncos went on to win, 34-19.

Photo provided by the Atlanta Falcons

"It was a great experience. It was one of the most magical years I have ever spent in coaching," Brooks said. "We had come off a 7-9 season our first year in Atlanta, which was much like my first year in St. Louis. The fact that we finished the regular season 14-2 the next year was one of the biggest turnarounds in NFL history."

Brooks stayed with Falcons for two more seasons, but he came to realize that he just wasn't comfortable as an assistant after 19 years of calling the shots. And if he was going

The Falcons didn't miss a beat when Brooks filled in for ailing head coach Dan Reeves.

to get another head coaching job, Brooks now was sure that he wanted it to be in college, so he resigned his job in Atlanta and returned home to Oregon.

When I first went to Atlanta, I felt like there was not any question that I could be successful in that league, that I still wanted to scratch that itch but I started to change that tune after a couple years there, even after we had gone to the Super Bowl. I felt like if I was going to be a head coach again, I would want to do it at the collegiate level," he explained. "It is just that the process in the NFL about building power bases with different individuals in some organizations wore on me. Whether it is the general manager or the personnel guy or the college personnel guy, trying to get all those people on the same page is sometimes a very difficult thing. At the college level, other than the fan base, athletic director and president you have to please, most college situations allow the coach to be in charge of football from A to Z. In the NFL, that usually never happens."

But after two years of golfing and fishing and hanging out with friends in Eugene, Oregon, Brooks was wondering if that chance to be a head coach again was ever going to come.

Photo provided by Karen Brooks

Karen Brooks shows off Rich's Super Bowl ring.

Chapter Fifteen

Changing the
Culture of
Kentucky Football

WHEN BROOKS WAS IN THE COURTSHIP PHASE WITH UK, he saw facilities that were light years ahead of what he found when he accepted the challenge of building the Oregon program. But he soon discovered one of the liabilities of the Kentucky job was something he couldn't see—a culture of losing that included a variety of heartbreaking defeats seemingly as long as the list of memorable victories for the storied Wildcat basketball program.

Joker Phillips says he sensed it in his playing days, which included successive bowl trips in 1983 and 1984. And during his first stint as a UK assistant, Phillips could still feel that ominous cloud of doubt floating over the team when the outcome of a game was hanging in the balance. That was exactly the mindset Brooks knew had to change.

"I think that the people were used to having things go badly for them and their team. I heard since the day I got here about the 'Commonwealth curse' and it was very evident obviously by the LSU game the year before I got here (2002) and what a tough loss that was," Brooks said of the Tigers' 75-yard pass play on the final play of the game that came to be known as LSU's "Bluegrass Miracle."

"That was the poster child of what Kentucky football was about, and I think that had to be changed," Brooks said. "It is not even acceptable to have those thought processes in your head in my opinion, because when things go wrong, you are more willing to accept it. That trickles down to what your players believe. If they read about it, hear about it enough, do they believe it? I think two things need to happen: one, you need to get better players but

Photo by Victoria Graff

Brooks is a combination of "fire and ice" on the sidelines, says sportswriter Tom Barnhart.

you also need to get new players and keep talking to them about 'hey, what happened here in the past has nothing to do with you and that you can create a new culture. You can be part of the solution and not part of the problem. You can be part of the turnaround at Kentucky football in a more positive note."

That's why Brooks seized on opportunities like the comeback win over Vandy in a disappointing 2004 season.

"Part of that losing games in the fourth quarter is the belief you can't win games in the fourth quarter in either your players or your fan base. If you don't change that attitude then you got real problems. I wish there was a magic button, but there is not. You have to have someone step up and make a play, you have to have players playing like they played in the first quarter and second quarter and not thinking about negative things in the fourth quarter," he said. "That is harder to accomplish than it is to talk about."

No matter what form of adversity befell the Wildcats, Brooks' rejection of the cause being anything outside the control of the coaches and players never wavered. But getting players to believe was going to take some time.

"One thing I noticed when I first came in is that you had guys on the team who were just extremely discouraged because of previous seasons where it was just disappointing, guys that had come in three, four years and not gone to a bowl game," said Jarmon, who joined the Big Blue family in 2005. "Guys that were on that team that were the (veterans) in that '06 season, those guys definitely led the charge because guys like (defensive end) Durrell White (and others), they saw the potential. (Offensive lineman) Mike Aitcheson, he was a great inspiration, those kinds of guys that Coach Brooks and staff went out and got, and those guys just made everything possible. They made a lot of us grow up and understand that, 'yeah, we're here, it's a game of football, but it means a lot more than that to everyone.'"

Russ Porter always admired Brooks' tenacity as they grew up together. And in his legal practice, Porter finds himself reflecting on how he's heard his friend deliver pregame speeches.

"I was in his English class, and he wasn't the greatest speaker when called upon, but when he is in front of young men, he is a tremendous speaker. I have learned a lot from him. As I am a trial lawyer, in my career, there has been more than one thing I have stolen from him in a closing argument," Porter said. "He just uses examples of life in different things. He used to talk about a man in the glass and there is a poem called 'The Man in a Glass' and he uses it every other year. He can speak it so much better than I can tell you but he is very good at it, and it inspired the hell outta me."

When you get what you want in your struggle for self
And the world makes you king for a day,
Just go to the mirror and look at yourself
And see what that man has to say.

For it isn't your father or mother or wife
Whose judgment upon you must pass.
The fellow whose verdict counts most in you life
Is the one staring back from the glass.

You may be like Jack Horner and chisel a plum
And think you're a wonderful guy.
But the man in the glass says you're only a bum
If you can't look him straight in the eye.

He's the fellow to please-never mind all the rest,
For he's with you clear to the end.
And you've passed your most dangerous, difficult test
If the man in the glass is your friend.

You may fool the whole world down the pathway of years
And get pats on the back as you pass.
But your final reward will be heartache and tears
If you've cheated the man in the glass.

— Anonymous
The Man In The Glass

"Sometimes it doesn't work and he will tell you, 'I didn't have them ready to play'. That might be Rich's best quality as a coach. He will accept responsibility and then try to let success go onto other people and stay on the side," Porter said. "When there is failure, he will say 'I didn't get it done, I didn't put in the right scheme, I didn't get them ready to play'. You will never hear him badmouth a coach or a player. He just won't do that, and I think that is a great quality."

Tony Neely says he never thinks of Brooks' age (68 on August 20, 2009) because of the energy level the coach brings to work each and every day. And Phillips believes that consistency is why Brooks has succeeded when so many predicted failure.

"I think he was the perfect guy for this job. I say this because, a young guy, young coach would have come in here and when things got bad, he would start veering off and changing his plan. We as coaches thought we needed to change some things too. But the old man said this was the way we were going to do it and kept on the straight and narrow," reflected Phillips. "We get in our meetings and there is some knock down, drag outs. We don't always agree. He doesn't always agree with us but when we walk out of that room, we walk out on the same page and speak the same language. I think that has helped us. It is not me telling a kid something, then Mitch telling a kid something, or Randy (Sanders) telling him something different. We are all on the same page and as soon as you walk out of that room, (Brooks) says 'this is how it is going to be'. He will say it and we all sell what we came up with. It might not be the way I would have done it or Randy would have done it, but it is the way the head coach wants it and that is what we are going to sell."

Columnist Rick Bozich says Kentucky football is a hard job whether you're "66 or 36." And he has been impressed by Brooks' approach to the job.

"He's at a point in his career where a lot of times guys don't want to invest that much time into that kind of a project. He carries himself like a guy who's 20 years younger," Bozich explained. "He's got a really good perspective on football and on life. I think a lot of younger coaches could learn a lot by watching him. I think it's a great experience for Joker Phillips. He can learn about what it means to be a head coach by watching him."

Ortmayer says the college game is a much different animal for a coach than professional football, but Brooks operated comfortably in both.

"Rich is a head coach to the truest since of the word. Being a head coach in the NFL and being a head coach in college football are vastly different businesses. The NFL is a blue-collar job. Period. You have nothing to do but coach this football team. Being a head coach in college football, you have

Photo by Victoria Graff

Brooks was the "perfect guy" for this job, says future UK head coach Joker Phillips.

a lot of extraneous situations not only dealing with media and administration but student athletes rather than professional players. I think that one of the things Rich does very well is that he has the ability to see the big picture," said Ortmayer. "It is difficult for a football coach because generally, someone has to be in charge of winning today and so someone has to be in charge of winning tomorrow and it doesn't have to be the same person. In the NFL, I don't think it has to be. In college, Rich has to see the big picture and have the ability to see the small picture on game weeks and see how important it is. That is a real strength of his is that he has the ability to do that wherever he has gone."

"Number one, he brings a real toughness to the job," said Terry Donahue, the former UCLA head coach when Brooks was an assistant in 1976. "And he's resilient. Rich was always very positive and very strong in his opinions. He was a guy who knew what he believed in, and if you asked Rich a question, you got a direct answer. I was attracted to that."

In covering the SEC, Tony Barnhart has talked to many Kentucky players over the time Brooks has been at Kentucky. He says it's been clear to him that they are believers in their coach.

"I think the players know how much he cares. And they know that he knows what he's doing. He's like the very, very good coaches that can be successful in any era. That was the thing about Bear Bryant. The players always related to him because they knew how good he was and how much he cared. I think that's what you can say about Coach Brooks," Barnhart said. "I had a pro coach tell me one time 'there are a lot of different ways to win, and I have proven that my way is one of those ways'. I think Coach Brooks falls into that category. (He) had an idea of what he wanted to do there at Kentucky but it was going to take him some time—like it does for any coach at Kentucky, to build enough depth to be competitive. It's hard. That's what he's been able to do over the last (few) years. "

Brooks says he had no magic formula for recharging the football batteries at Kentucky. He says the reversal starts to happen when players refuse to accept that their destiny is beyond their control.

"I wish I were smart enough to tell you why that transition took place and how it took place, but it usually comes with getting new players in a position that won't accept old fallacies and the old parables. They are going to establish something new and they are not going to fold or panic in those types of situations. They are going to look forward to having an opportunity to win a game that has an opportunity to give up a play that will lose the game," he said.

Former players like Tommy Cook think the way Brooks works with his assistant coaches also creates success.

"He lets his assistants do a lot of the coaching but when he needs to put his foot down, he does it. It empowers the position coaches to make decisions and that carries through to meeting rooms. It helps the players from a trust (standpoint)," Cook noted. "You know exactly what your coach is expecting from you."

On the practice field, Brooks constantly moves between the offense, defense and special teams, observing and occasionally offering input— sometimes sternly.

"He's the most knowledgeable coach I've been around as far as the complete football team," said associate AD John Cropp, a longtime assistant coach himself at the major college level. "I don't ever see him where I don't

Photo by Victoria Graff

Brooks is thankful for the Wildcat fans than hung with the team through the tough times.

think he's knowledgeable about what he's working with and he's respected there by the players and the coaches. I think the area that I've seen the most improvement in is us getting the best 22 people on the field all the time. All coaches talk about it, but he does it better than anybody I've ever seen."

For all of the success Kentucky has enjoyed since the middle of the 2006 season, Brooks also knows the turnaround is not complete.

"I think there is always more to be changed. One, we have had some great moments in the last three years to be followed by lost opportunity if you will. We could have been a bigger factor in the SEC East, and we let that slip between our fingers and out of our hands. I think there is work to be done on a consistent basis with our attitude on the field and execution obviously," he said, adding the fans are a part of the mix, too.

"There is still work to be done in the stands where we don't have the highs and lows as much when it is Mississippi State coming to town and we

Photo by Keith Smiley/TeamCoyle

Brooks interacts with fans during the Cat Walk at the 2009 Liberty Bowl in Memphis.

lose the energy in the stadium. Teams feed off the energy, they really do. One of the greatest things that I tell our players that we can do is go into an opponent's stadium that is going crazy and have them become silent and take the enthusiasm out of the crowd," Brooks continued. "That to me is one of the greatest things you can accomplish in football when you go out on the road is have that stadium get really quiet and look up in the fourth quarter and see the stands empty. That is a real incentive for visiting team to accomplish that."

But make no mistake about this—Brooks is forever grateful to those fans, especially the ones who kept supporting the team in its darkest hours. The Monday night after that dreadful loss to Ohio University in 2004, Brooks came into the studio for his radio call-in show thinking it would be very unpleasant. As host, I told him that from my experience, I was confident the Kentucky fans would rally to his side on his show. But I added that he might want to consider a music CD for the ride home because every caller on every other show would verbally rip him to shreds. Of course, there's always one thing worse for a coach than negative callers and that's no callers. And apathy has never been an issue in the Big Blue Nation.

"Our fan base has been, if nothing else, so resilient to come in the numbers they have come to watch their team even when the results on the field haven't warranted that all the time. I think what is changing is that it has gone from a social experience to an SEC football experience now. More people are buying into the SEC football experience because of what has happened the last three years," he said.

"It sure is rewarding to see the success and how the players have been received. That they can walk around town and campus and not worry about wearing a Kentucky football shirt. Fans actually stop them and thank them, myself as well," Brooks continued. "They come up and say they appreciate what you have done. Just to bring pride and respect back not only to the fan base but also to the letterman and people that have been on the field, tried to compete, and played Kentucky football over the years (is rewarding). It is really an outstanding thing to see a transformation to a more positive outlook."

When Mitch Barnhart was looking for a new coach at Kentucky, one of the qualities he was seeking was a man who was a little "ornery." The AD felt that kind of cockiness was what it would take to prevail with a probation-depleted program in the toughest football league in America.

"It is made up of big name, high profile coaches that can absolutely swallow up a coach that is intimidated by them. There are guys that have won things. It is a really difficult league, and you need somebody who is going to stick his nose in it and fight back. And if they get their nose bloodied in the fight, they are not afraid to fight back. Rich isn't afraid of that," Barnhart said. "And he is a little ornery. And you have got to be a little ornery—you can't be afraid of the fight. Coaches will tell you that they are not afraid of getting in the mix, whether it is in recruiting, on the field, with referees during a game but you can't back down for what you think is right for your program and your young people. And Rich will never, ever back down. He will call people out when he thinks they are wrong. I think a younger coach, a less-experienced coach with different personality of a coach would submit to an older and more veteran guy or to a bigger name personality. Rich will never do that. He stood

Joker Phillips and Brooks at the 2008 announcement that Phillips would succeed Brooks as head coach.

up for Kentucky, our kids, and our program and he was ornery in that since, and I think we needed that."

But Brooks can balance toughness with a tender side that he reveals to his players. And for David Jones, a moment at the team hotel before his final home game in 2008 was emblematic of why players at Kentucky believe so fiercely in their leader.

"He'd start talking about each individual senior, and it's amazing what he remembered about each one of us. He remembered little things. It shows you how much he cares for his players. That's why we love him a whole lot and that's why I'd go to war for Coach Brooks—any time, any day," Jones said.

And if Brooks ever needs his own kick-in-the-pants after a tough loss, Karen is ready.

"He is always tough after a loss. He is not fun at all. He rarely talks anyway, but he gets very quiet and mopey. He is just depressed. I am never depressed, so I guess I am a good balance," she said. "Sometimes I just get mad at him. To be truthful, here (at Kentucky), I don't think he ever got sorry for himself, because I would always say, 'you don't have to do this, this was your choice and if you don't want to do it, we are outta here'. So, the whole mindset was different and wasn't as depressing as it was at Oregon. It is always depressing but he has never been so far in the tank because he knew I would get mad."

Brady Brooks, who served as a ball boy as a youngster when Rich was coaching at Oregon, says his dad's legendary intensity has been dialed down a few notches in this second stint as a college head coach.

"He's mellowed out quite a bit. He was really intense in his first go around. I don't think he had as much fun as he's having now. It comes with age I guess," suggested Brady. "When he was younger, he was maybe more desperate to succeed."

So when will Rich Brooks pass the coaching torch to Phillips?

"I ask him that too, and he won't tell me," Karen said with a laugh. "I don't know. He is like the energizer bunny, I don't know. I think it's especially hard for coaches to ever leave coaching because it's who they are."

Wayne Brooks thinks it will be a difficult decision for his brother to make.

"Yes, I do. I think that it is a final thing that he will be doing in his life. He will be leaving behind the success that he has built there, and I think it will be difficult for him," Wayne said. "I don't know what his thoughts will be, but I am sure he will keep thinking, 'maybe I will stay a few more years and take a couple more levels.' But I think he is going to miss it. He is too competitive."

Brooks may not achieve his stated goal of being the longest tenured football coach at UK, but Tony Barnhart says a strong foundation has been laid by this staff.

"They've established now that you can go to Kentucky and be competitive at the highest level in the Southeastern Conference. I thought it was a brilliant stroke to name Joker Phillips as the coach-in-waiting. "Now, you've got the best chance of not having a drop-off. Everybody knows what Joker has done with the offense since he became a coordinator. If you jump from worst to first in a year, chances are you're not going to maintain that. They've established Kentucky as a program where you're going to expect to go to a bowl every now and then, you're going to put together enough athletes where you've got a shot in the (SEC) East," Barnhart stated. "Understand, Georgia, Florida and Tennessee are not going to quit giving scholarships. To win eight games a year, nine games a year in that division, that's a tough thing to do. The fact that Rich Brooks and that staff have got Kentucky to that level is the best compliment I can give them."

As for how Brooks wants to be remembered by Kentucky fans, he says he wants it to be something out of his control—how the Wildcats perform after he leaves the post.

"I am not good at writing epitaphs. I am at the age where some will be written for me. The real one won't be written for a few years. I just hope that when Joker does take over, I hope the same process can take place like when Mike Bellotti took over at Oregon," Brooks said, "and that people five, 10 years down the road can look and say, 'yeah, we went to those bowl games with Brooks but now we are competing for SEC Championships and National Championships.'"

Chapter Sixteen

Quick
Hitters

IN COLLECTING MEMORIES OF, and stories about, Rich Brooks from more than 50 different people, we asked many of them to give us one word or sentence that sums him up:

"Honorable. A man with great courage and tenacity, a guy if you ever needed something, needed help, you could pick up the phone and immediately he would help. As genuine a person as I have ever been around. A guy that I would trust with my child in a heartbeat."

—Mitch Barnhart, University of Kentucky athletics director

"Honesty has always been there. This was someone who built something. He had taken some time but built something that could be sustained. I would much rather build something that could be sustained rather than just a three-year wonder and then back to zero."

—Dr. Lee Todd, University of Kentucky president

"Integrity. He's a man's man. I loved to go out and go fishing with him or play golf with him. I mean, he's just a helluva guy. I just loved being around him."

—Bill Byrne, Texas A&M AD, former Oregon AD 1984-92

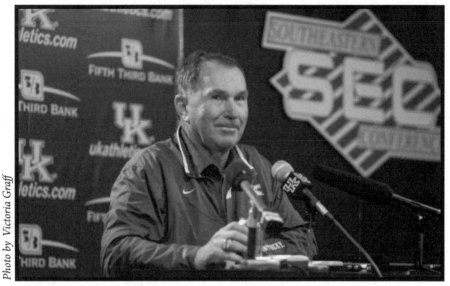

Photo by Victoria Graff

A smiling Brooks greets the media after the 2007 upset of LSU.

"Dead honest. Best I have ever seen in my 50 plus years in dealing with collegiate football coaches."

—Jim Host, Founder
Host Communications

"He's a tough S.O.B."

—Dick Tomey, San Jose State head coach;
fellow assistant with Brooks at UCLA and a rival
when he was head coach at Arizona

"He is made to be the head coach. That is the way he is wound. He thinks globally but also thinks locally. He sees the big picture and the small picture."

—Steve Hellyer, Kentucky's Director of
Football Operations, former media relations director at Oregon

"High integrity. People respect him. They have seen him come up the hard way but success has not gone to his head and is very devoted to his players. It matters to him that people are successful later on."

—Dr. Dave Frohnmayer, president,
University of Oregon 1994-2009

"He is the kind of coach I would like my son to play for."

—Greg Byrne, Mississippi State AD and
former assistant AD at Kentucky

"Just a class act. There are a lot of words to sum him up—sonuvabitch, depending on the day, but he is just a very genuine person and a great family man. I know he loves his job and the sad thing about it is that he knows it is coming to an end."

—Brett Setzer, Brooks' friend

"The guy does a great job at being a leader. He just doesn't demand respect—he earns it by the way he treats people, not only on the team but also in the office and stuff. I just think he does a great job and I really respect him."

—Bill Kollar, Houston Texans' assistant coach;
former coaching colleague with the Atlanta Falcons

"I think he is very straight forward. I think he is honest. I think people know that. I think he stands up from what he believes in and isn't going to veer for what he believes in. He had a plan for how he was going to turn the course for this program, and I don't think he veered at all."

—Dr. Grady Stephens, Brooks' friend
and longtime UK football fan

Tom Leach

"I think the number one thing which makes coaches successful is consistency of communication. Both with the staff and the players. Rich is a head coach to the truest since of the word."

—Steve Ortmayer, University of Kentucky assistant coach

"Our nickname for him at Oregon was 'Daddy Rich'. Because right, wrong, or indifferent, you had to answer to him. And you know through positive or negative experiences with him, that you are going to trust him because he is consistent."

—Steve Brown, University of Kentucky defensive coordinator, former Oregon player under Brooks

"Classy."

—Joker Phillips, University of Kentucky, assistant head coach

"A master coach. Steady, reliable, dependable, courageous."

—John Cropp, University of Kentucky associate AD/administration

"No matter what, he is a players' coach. It is players first. You can see it in his eyes that he loves every single one of his players."

—Andre Woodson, former player (2003-07)

"He is like a father figure. His office door is always open and is someone you can always talk to. That is something that you need as a young guy."

—Wesley Woodyard, former player (2004-07)

"I would have to say compassionate. He cares for every single one of his players, and I think that's what separates him from a lot of coaches."

—Dicky Lyons, Jr., former player (2004-08)

"Driven. Coach Brooks will turn a program around, no matter what he has to do, and he will die doing it."

—Keenan Burton, former player (2003-07)

"Honesty and hard-working are what pop in my head. Sometimes when you are a player, you don't like his honesty when he tells you (that) you aren't good enough or tells you that you need to be better in this area. He is right. He sticks to what he believes in and is not going to change to win a popularity contest. He is a man of character."

—Jacob Tamme, former player (2003-07)

"He is so straight forward. He tells you what he is going to do and has never lied to anyone on the team. He is a man that isn't going to lie. He will put it out there and you can take it or not take it."

—Matt McCutchan, former player (2004-06)

"Patience, perseverance and integrity. That characterizes him very well."

—Tim Mastay, former player (2005-08)

"I'll say a father figure. That's the only thing I can really think of right now to basically explain all of the roles within my two years there."

—Stevie Johnson, former player (2006-07)

"Competitive. A lot of people don't see how competitive he is, whether you're playing him in ping-pong, on the golf course or out at practice. He's one of the most competitive people I've ever met."

—Tommy Cook, former player (2001-05)

"The thing is about Coach Brooks, the reason why you want to go to war for him and all of the coaches is he's a father figure for some of us who are far from home or don't have that touch with a father. You can always count on him, and he cares about his players 100 percent."

—David Jones, former player (2004-08)

"I can't just say one thing about him. The list goes on and on about him. He's a confident man, he's strong man, he's a great friend. I mean he really is. He can be a coach on the field, and he can be your friend off the field, which says a lot."

—Jared Lorenzen, former player (2000-03)

"*Respect. If I walked into his office and he told me the sky was bleeding red, I'd have to see for myself that it was doing anything but (what he said).*"

—Oscar Combs, founder of The Cats Pause

"*I think one thing that is telling of my Dad is his favorite song. His favorite song is 'The Gambler', that Kenny Rodgers song. I think that says a lot about my Dad. He likes the challenge, the gamble. He is very tenacious, doesn't give in and is just a fighter. It is one of the things that comes to mind when I think of him and how much we all admire him and how much he has taught us.*"

—Kasey Brooks Holwerda, daughter

"*One word would be 'integrity'. He has always been that way. I could tell you stories from players that blew me away. I know that he does things the right way and he is a good man.*"

—Kerri Brooks Robinson, daughter

"*I think he is a builder of character and commitment. I think that is the best way to put it. He likes to build the character of young men and see the commitments through.*"

—Denny Boom, son

"*Perseverance. He is a stubborn guy. Honestly, he is just a no-nonsense type of guy. He is a hard worker and doesn't know anything but just to stick to it. If you see where he has come from, it is pretty amazing. He is a special guy.*"

—Brady Brooks, son

"*Honest. And trustworthy.*"

—Karen Brooks, wife

"*A good man. Honest and good. And a hard worker.*"

—Wayne Brooks, brother

Chapter Seventeen

Game
By
Game

Louisville 40 | Kentucky 24

August 31, 2003

Scoring Summary

Louisville	14	7	5	14	—	40
Kentucky	3	7	14	0	—	24

UL - Shelton 6 run (Smith kick)...9:42 1st qtr.
UL - Kamer 2 pass from LeFors (Smith kick)...6:48 1st qtr.
UK - Begley 44 field goal...0:33 1st qtr.
UL - Jackerson 0 block punt return (Smith kick)...12:51 2nd qtr.
UK - Holt 13 pass from Lorenzen (Begley kick)...0:45 2nd qtr.
UL - Team safety...13:59 3rd qtr.
UL - Smith 25 field goal...11:51 3rd qtr.
UK - Davis 1 run (Begley kick)...7:31 3rd qtr.
UK - Burton 31 pass from Lorenzen (Begley kick)...2:41 3rd qtr.
UL - Shelton 22 run (Smith kick)...11:47 4th qtr.
UL - Gates 2 run (Smith kick)...0:06 4th qtr.

Team Statistics	Kentucky	Louisville
First Downs	21	22
Rush Attempts/Net Rushing Yards	36/108	44/240
Passing C/A/I	18/32/2	14/23/1
Net Passing Yards	236	180
Offensive Plays	68	67
Total Offense	344	420
Fumbles/Lost	1/0	0/0
Penalties/Yards	4/20	4/35
Punts/Average	2/17.0	3/36.0
Third Down Conversion	8 of 14	6 of 13
Time of Possession	29:54	30:06

Individual Statistics

Rushing
Kentucky - Davis 15-45-1 TD, Bwenge 5-43, Beach 4-24, Lorenzen 8-8, Johnson 2-7, Boyd 1-(-2), Sucurovic 1-(-17)
Louisville - Shelton 25-151-2 TD, Gates 13-75-1 TD, LeFors 4-19, Bush 2-(-5)

Passing
Kentucky - Lorenzen 18-31-1-236-2 TD, Boyd 0-1-1-0
Louisville - LeFors 14-23-1-180-1 TD

Receiving
Kentucky - Abney 3-51, Davis 3-38, Holt 3-33, Bwenge 3-25, Burton 1-31-1 TD, Marchman 1-25, Bernard 1-18, Drobney 1-7, Beach 1-4, Johnson 1-4
Louisville - Clark 6-94, Russell 3-45, Tinch 2-15, Ghent 1-14, Owens 1-10, Kamer 1-2-1 TD

Tackles
Kentucky - Haydock 10, D. Williams 8, Moore 7, Burns 7, M. Williams 7

Kentucky 37 | Murray State 6

September 6, 2003

Scoring Summary

Murray State	0	6	0	0	—	6
Kentucky	7	16	7	7	—	37

UK - Abney 11 pass from Lorenzen (Begley kick)...0:22 1st qtr.
UK - Bernard 60 pass from Lorenzen (Begley kick)...13:10 2nd qtr.
UK - Team safety...13:00 2nd qtr.
UK - Holt 12 pass from Lorenzen (Begley kick)...9:21 2nd qtr.
MS - Cook 5 run (kick failed)...3:13 2nd qtr.
UK - Bwenge 15 pass from Lorenzen (Begley kick)...12:13 3rd qtr.
UK - Boyd 27 run (Begley kick)...3:48 4th qtr.

Team Statistics	Kentucky	Murray St.
First Downs	16	20
Rush Attempts/Net Rushing Yards	29/103	40/85
Passing C/A/I	15/24/1	14/30/1
Net Passing Yards	205	104
Offensive Plays	53	70
Total Offense	308	189
Fumbles/Lost	2/0	3/1
Penalties/Yards	13/119	6/43
Punts/Average	5/39.2	7/37.3
Third Down Conversion	3 of 11	7 of 16
Time of Possession	28:03	31:57

Individual Statistics

Rushing
Kentucky -Boyd 5-57-1 TD, Bwenge 7-22, Davis 10-18, Abney 1-14, Beach 3-6, Lorenzen 3-(-14)
Murray St. - Lane 16-67, Odoms 3-16, Walker 3-15, Cook 4-11-1 TD, Gallishaw 1-2, Hatchell 1-(-1), Childress 12-(-25)

Passing
Kentucky - Lorenzen 14-21-1-197-4 TD, Boyd 1-3-0-8
Murray St. - Childress 13-27-1-100, Hatchell 1-2-0-4

Receiving
Kentucky - Abney 3-32-1 TD, Drobney 3-29, Bernard 2-64-1 TD, Holt 2-32-1 TD, Boyd 2-9, Johnson 1-18, Bwenge 1-15-1 TD, Cook 1-6
Murray St. - Green 5-36, Nowacki 2-20, Baxter 2-12, Roddy 2-12, Nutter 1-11, Lane 1-9, Arnold 1-4

Tackles
Kentucky - Haydock 11, D. Williams 7, Smith 7

Alabama 27 | Kentucky 17

September 13, 2003

Scoring Summary

Kentucky	0	7	3	7	—	17
Alabama	7	3	3	14	—	27

UA - Williams 15 run (Bostick kick)...3:52 1st qtr.
UA - Bostick 43 field goal...10:13 2nd qtr.
UK - Davis 1 run (Begley kick)...6:33 2nd qtr.
UA - Bostick 30 field goal...7:59 3rd qtr.
UK - Begley 27 field goal...2:22 3rd qtr.
UA - Williams 2 run (Bostick kick)...14:56 4th qtr.
UK - Williams 7 run (Bostick kick)...5:11 4th qtr.
UK - Abney 24 pass from Lorenzen (Begley kick)...4:03 4th qtr.

Team Statistics	Kentucky	Alabama
First Downs	11	29
Rush Attempts/Net Rushing Yards	23/26	53/266
Passing C/A/I	15/24/0	14/27/1
Net Passing Yards	169	198
Offensive Plays	47	80
Total Offense	195	464
Fumbles/Lost	0/0	0/0
Penalties/Yards	6/42	6/60
Punts/Average	6/39.8	3/38.3
Third Down Conversion	4 of 12	4 of 13
Time of Possession	23:34	36:26

Individual Statistics

Rushing
Kentucky - Davis 10-28-1 TD, Bernard 1-6, Lorenzen 8-2, Bwenge 1-0, team 1-(-1), Abney 1-(-2), Cook 1-(-7)
Alabama - Williams 30-174-3 TD, Darby 8-62, Hudson 6-18, Croyle 7-13, McClain 1-1, team 1-(-2)

Passing
Kentucky - Lorenzen 15-24-0-169-1 TD
Alabama - Croyle 14-27-1-198

Receiving
Kentucky - Abney 5-64-1 TD, Holt 3-30, Davis 3-21, Gaffron 1-33, Burton 1-13, Bernard 1-9, Bwenge 1-(-1)
Alabama - Luke 3-50, Fulgham 3-32, Fletcher 2-35, McClain 2-35, Greer 2-26, Johnston 1-17, Williams 1-3

Tackles
Kentucky - M. Williams 11, Haydock 10, D. Williams 10

Kentucky 34 | Indiana 17

September 20, 2003

Scoring Summary

Kentucky	7	6	14	7	—	34
Indiana	0	10	0	7	—	17

UK - Abney 29 pass from Lorenzen (Begley kick)...0:47 1st qtr.
IU - Robertson 21 field goal...11:12 2nd qtr.
IU - Green-Ellis 63 pass from LoVecchio (Robertson kick)...2:51 2nd qtr.
UK - Bernard 51 pass from Lorenzen (team rush fumbled)...2:30 2nd qtr.
UK - Lorenzen 1 run (Begley kick)...7:32 3rd qtr.
UK - Davis 1 run (Begley kick)...2:08 3rd qtr.
IU - Lewis 1 run (Robertson kick)...4:21 4th qtr.
UK - Beach 2 run (Begley kick)...1:02 4th qtr.

Team Statistics	Kentucky	Indiana
First Downs	15	20
Rush Attempts/Net Rushing Yards	41/167	46/183
Passing C/A/I	12/21/0	17/33/1
Net Passing Yards	187	266
Offensive Plays	62	79
Total Offense	354	449
Fumbles/Lost	1/1	0/0
Penalties/Yards	9/88	6/50
Punts/Average	7/46.3	7/37.6
Third Down Conversion	4 of 13	4 of 16
Time of Possession	29:06	30:54

Individual Statistics

Rushing
Kentucky - Beach 10-46-1 TD, Abney 2-45, Davis 16-43-1 TD, Bwenge 6-32, Lorenzen 6-4-1 TD, Boyd 1-(-3)
Indiana - Lewis 17-116-1 TD, Taylor 10-36, Green-Ellis 5-16, Roby 2-12, LoVecchio 12-3

Passing
Kentucky - Lorenzen 11-20-0-147-2 TD, Boyd 1-1-0-40
Indiana - LoVecchio 17-32-1-266-1 TD

Receiving
Kentucky - Bernard 3-100-1 TD, Davis 3-24, Abney 2-37-1 TD, Burton 2-19, Bwenge 1-4, Boyd 1-3
Indiana - Halterman 5-71, Roby 3-32, Johnson 2-33, Taylor 2-8, Green-Ellis 1-63-1 TD, Haney 1-22, Rudanovic 1-21, Lewis 1-9, Spencer 1-7

Tackles
Kentucky - D. Williams 20, Haydock 12, Holts 8, M. Williams 8

Florida 24 | Kentucky 21

September 27, 2003

Scoring Summary

Florida	0	3	0	21	—	24
Kentucky	7	7	7	0	—	21

UK - Beach 1 run (Begley kick)...8:08 1st qtr.
UK - Beach 1 run (Begley kick)...6:38 2nd qtr.
UF - Leach 42 FG...5:49 2nd qtr.
UK - Beach 2 run (Begley kick)...3:23 3rd qtr.
UF - Perez 3 pass from Leak (team pass failed)...14:55 4th qtr.
UF - Perez 10 pass from Leak (Leach kick)...4:46 4th qtr.
UF - Carthon 1 run (Kight pass from Leak)...3:15 4th qtr.

Team Statistics	Kentucky	Florida
First Downs	18	16
Rush Attempts/Net Rushing Yards	44/175	29/93
Passing C/A/I	18/29/2	20/35/2
Net Passing Yards	179	268
Offensive Plays	73	64
Total Offense	354	361
Fumbles/Lost	0/0	2/1
Penalties/Yards	5/45	7/40
Punts/Average	5/38.8	4/44.5
Third Down Conversion	9 of 18	5 of 14
Time of Possession	36:32	23:28

Individual Statistics

Rushing
Kentucky - Beach 18-47-3 TD, Abney 1-42, Bwenge 9-40, Lorenzen 12-36, Boyd 2-9, Davis 1-1, Team 1-0
Florida - Carthon 9-43-1 TD, Wynn 10-40, Perez 1-10, Leak 8-0, Team 1-0

Passing
Kentucky - Lorenzen 18-27-2-179, Boyd 0-1-0-0, Cook 0-1-0-0
Florida - Leak 20-35-2-268-2 TD

Receiving
Kentucky - Gaffron 4-46, Bernard 3-22, Abney 2-25, Burton 2-23, Davis 2-16, Beach 2-10, Fowler 1-20, Holt 1-14, Bwenge 1-3
Florida - Perez 5-102-2 TD, Carthon 4-47, Kight 2-46, Baker 2-20, Small 2-14, Troupe 2-13, Caldwell 2-10, Latsko 1-16

Tackles
Kentucky - D. Williams 11, Anderson 11, M. Williams 9, Burns 9

South Carolina 27 | Kentucky 21

October 9, 2003

Scoring Summary

Kentucky	0	7	0	14	—	21
South Carolina	0	13	14	0	—	27

SC - Turman 1 run (Weaver kick)...13:35 2nd qtr.
SC - Weaver 20 FG...5:43 2nd qtr.
UK - Burton 11 pass from Lorenzen (Begley kick)...2:55 2nd qtr.
SC - Weaver 31 FG...0:00 2nd qtr.
SC - Turman 2 run (Weaver kick)...8:09 3rd qtr.
SC - Turman 1 run (Weaver kick)...1:30 3rd qtr.
UK - Bernard 7 pass from Boyd (Begley kick)...10:16 4th qtr.
UK - Boyd 15 run (Begley kick)...6:05 4th qtr.

Team Statistics	Kentucky	South Carolina
First Downs	18	20
Rush Attempts/Net Rushing Yards	30/117	47/182
Passing C/A/I	17/32/0	17/29/0
Net Passing Yards	210	184
Offensive Plays	62	76
Total Offense	327	366
Fumbles/Lost	2/1	1/0
Penalties/Yards	10/66	8/51
Punts/Average	7/45.0	6/40.7
Third Down Conversion	3 of 13	8 of 16
Time of Possession	26:34	33:26

Individual Statistics

Rushing
Kentucky - Boyd 9-73-1 TD, Bwenge 8-29, Burton 2-20, Beach 4-15, Gaffron 1-0, Davis 1-(-4), Lorenzen 5-(-16)
South Carolina - Summers 16-66, Turman 16-44-3 TD, Boyd 5-33, Pinkins 7-27, Williamson 1-16, team 1-(-1), Thomas 1-(-3)

Passing
Kentucky - Lorenzen 10-18-0-129-1 TD, Boyd 7-14-0-81-1 TD
South Carolina - Pinkins 17-29-0-184

Receiving
Kentucky - Abney 5-94, Bernard 3-45-1 TD, Davis 3-15, Burton 2-20-1 TD, Fowler 2-16, Gaffron 1-18, Holt 1-2
South Carolina - Newton 3-68, Summers 3-33, Turner 2-33, Brownlee 2-20, Williamson 2-6, Whiteside 1-9, Clark 1-8, Thomas 1-4, Turman 1-2, Muhammad 1-1

Tackles
Kentucky - Anderson 19, D. Williams 9, Abdullah 9

Kentucky 35 | Ohio 14

October 18, 2003

Scoring Summary

Ohio	7	0	0	7	—	14
Kentucky	0	7	14	14	—	35

OU - Young 7 run (DiMarino kick)...10:28 1st qtr.
UK - Boyd 8 run (Begley kick)...8:18 2nd qtr.
UK - Boyd 12 run (Begley kick)...12:52 3rd qtr.
UK - Cook 42 pass from Boyd (Begley kick)...9:29 3rd qtr.
OU - Huston 58 pass from Everson (DiMarino kick)...11:54 4th qtr.
UK - Boyd 30 pass from Lorenzen (Begley kick)...10:07 4th qtr.
UK - Abney 16 pass from Lorenzen (Begley kick)...3:00 4th qtr.

Team Statistics	Kentucky	Ohio
First Downs	18	16
Rush Attempts/Net Rushing Yards	42/177	49/148
Passing C/A/I	11/23/0	10/18/1
Net Passing Yards	144	147
Offensive Plays	65	67
Total Offense	321	295
Fumbles/Lost	2/2	3/2
Penalties/Yards	5/37	4/30
Punts/Average	5/36.8	6/36.7
Third Down Conversion	9 of 16	5 of 16
Time of Possession	25:08	34:52

Individual Statistics

Rushing
Kentucky - Boyd 10-85-2 TD, Abney 4-26, Beach 8-21, Johnson 4-19, Davis 6-13, Bwenge 4-12, Lorenzen 3-1, Gibson 1-1, team 2-(-1)
Ohio - Young 10-38-1 TD, Huston 6-37, Miller 1-30, Everson 21-28, Fountain 2-13, Taylor 5-4, team 1-0, Jackson 2-(-1), Mayle 1-(-1)

Passing
Kentucky - Lorenzen 8-14-0-90-2 TD, Boyd 3-9-0-54-1 TD
Ohio - Everson 10-18-1-147-1 TD

Receiving
Kentucky - Abney 6-63-1 TD, Cook 2-50-1 TD, Bernard 2-1, Boyd 1-30-1 TD
Ohio - Porter 2-41, Mayle 2-19, Hackett 2-4, Huston 1-58-1 TD, Ingram 1-12, Young 1-7, Fountain 1-6

Tackles
Kentucky - Anderson 14, Abdullah 12, D. Williams 12

Kentucky 42 | Mississippi State 17

October 25, 2003

Scoring Summary

Mississippi State	10	7	0	0	—	17
Kentucky	0	7	14	21	—	42

MS - Smith 22 FG...6:35 1st qtr.
MS - Norwood 58 run (Smith kick)...0:35 1st qtr.
MS - Bivines 11 pass from Fant (Smith kick)...12:10 2nd qtr.
UK - Johnson 7 run (Begley kick)...0:38 2nd qtr.
UK - Beach 1 run (Begley kick)...11:02 3rd qtr.
UK - Abney 80 punt return (Begley kick)...9:17 3rd qtr.
UK - Abney 53 pass from Lorenzen (Begley kick)...12:47 4th qtr.
UK - Beach 1 run (Begley kick)...10:22 4th qtr.
UK - Gibson 3 run (Begley kick)...2:45 4th qtr.

Team Statistics	Kentucky	Mississippi State
First Downs	20	12
Rush Attempts/Net Rushing Yards	47/154	32/150
Passing C/A/I	16/28/0	14/25/3
Net Passing Yards	256	155
Offensive Plays	75	57
Total Offense	410	305
Fumbles/Lost	3/2	0/0
Penalties/Yards	4/25	12/75
Punts/Average	6/35.7	7/45.3
Third Down Conversion	8 of 14	5 of 14
Time of Possession	32:49	27:11

Individual Statistics

Rushing
Kentucky - Bwenge 7-39, Beach 13-28-2 TD, Johnson 4-22, Abney 1-21, Lorenzen 7-16, Boyd 7-11, Gibson 5-11-1 TD, Sprowles 1-3, Davis 1-3
Mississippi State - Norwood 11-133-1 TD, Turner 12-15, Conner 1-5, York 1-5, Reid 1-2, Fant 6-(-10)

Passing
Kentucky - Lorenzen 16-24-0-256-1 TD, Boyd 0-4-0-0
Mississippi State - Fant 12-21-2-130-1 TD, York 2-4-1-25

Receiving
Kentucky- Abney 4-80-1 TD, Cook 4-43, Bernard 2-44, Boyd 2-28, Burton 1-30, Beach 1-17, Drobney 1-7, Bwenge 1-7
Mississippi State - Jenkins 3-30, Turner 3-13, Conner 2-44, Bivines 2-28-1 TD, Scott 2-25, Ferrill 2-15

Tackles
Kentucky - Smith 11, Anderson 8, M. Williams 8

Arkansas 71 | Kentucky 63

November 1, 2003

Scoring Summary

Arkansas	7	14	0	3	47	—	71
Kentucky	7	0	7	10	39	—	63

AR - Birmingham 10 run (Balseiro kick)...7:57 1st qtr.
UK - A. Hopewell 6 blocked punt return (Begley kick)...0:10 1st qtr.
AR - Smith 26 pass from Jones (Balseiro kick)...8:54 2nd qtr.
AR - Crowder 0 blocked punt return (Balseiro kick)...6:45 2nd qtr.
UK - Bwenge 51 pass from Lorenzen (Begley kick)...3:44 3rd qtr.
UK - Begley 34 FG...7:11 4th qtr.
AR - Balseiro 37 FG...3:22 4th qtr.
UK - Bernard 13 pass from Lorenzen (Begley kick)...1:38 4th qtr.
AR - Pierce 1 run (Balseiro kick)...1 OT
UK - Bwenge 2 run (Begley kick)...1 OT
UK - Bwenge 7 run (Begley kick)...2 OT
AR - Peters 7 pass from Jones (Balseiro kick)...2 OT
AR - Balseiro 25 FG...3 OT
UK - Begley 24 FG...3 OT
UK - Lorenzen 1 run (Abney pass from Lorenzen)...4 OT
AR - Jones 3 run (Pierce pass from Jones)...4 OT
AR - Wilson 15 pass from Jones (pass failed)...5 OT
UK - Lorenzen 2 run (pass failed)...5 OT
UK - Lorenzen 1 run (Cook pass from Lorenzen)...6 OT
AR - Pierce 2 run (Wilson pass from Jones)...6 OT
AR - Birmingham 25 run (Peters pass from Jones)...7 OT

Team Statistics	Kentucky	Arkansas
First Downs	29	29
Rush Attempts/Net Rushing Yards	52/180	71/334
Passing C/A/I	28/51/1	17/28/0
Net Passing Yards	326	271
Offensive Plays	103	99
Total Offense	506	605
Fumbles/Lost	2-1	5-2
Penalties/Yards	8/60	12/87
Punts/Average	7/40.0	6/34.3
Third Down Conversion	10 of 22	13 of 22
Time of Possession	27:07	32:53

Individual Statistics

Rushing
Kentucky - Bwenge 22-89-2 TD, Lorenzen 15-39-3 TD, Davis 5-35,
 Boyd 4-17, Abney 1-2, Johnson 1-1, team 1-0, Burton 3-(-3)
Arkansas - Birmingham 40-196-2 TD, Jones 15-112-1 TD, Cobbs 9-46,
Ousley 1-9, Pierce 2-3-2 TD, Harris 1-(-15), Sorahan 3-(-17)

Passing
Kentucky - Lorenzen 28-49-1-326-2 TD, Boyd 0-2-0-0
Arkansas - Jones 16-25-0-260-3 TD, Sorahan 1-3-0-11

Receiving
Kentucky - Abney 10-91, Bernard 4-82-1 TD, Cook 4-39, Davis 4-13,
Drobney 2-25, Bwenge 1-51-1 TD, Holt 1-17, Burton 1-7, Boyd 1-1
Arkansas - Wilson 9-172-1 TD, Smith 5-69-1 TD, Ousley 1-12, Hicks 1-11,
Peters 1-7-1 TD

Tackles
Kentucky - Anderson 20, D. Williams 18, Smith 13

Vanderbilt 28 | Kentucky 17

November 15, 2003

Scoring Summary

Kentucky	3	0	7	7	—	17
Vanderbilt	0	14	14	0	—	28

UK - Begley 36 FG...2:05 1st qtr.
VU - Davis 24 pass from Cutler (Johnson kick)...11:48 2nd qtr.
VU - Tant 17 pass from Cutler (Johnson kick)...1:44 2nd qtr.
VU - White 43 pass from Cutler (Johnson kick)...11:59 3rd qtr.
UK - Beach 4 run (Begley kick)...7:03 3rd qtr.
VU - Davis 10 pass from Cutler (Johnson kick)...4:40 3rd qtr.
UK - Bernard 11 pass from Lorenzen (Begley kick)...0:28 4th qtr.

Team Statistics	Kentucky	Vanderbilt
First Downs	25	22
Rush Attempts/Net Rushing Yards	37/168	41/246
Passing C/A/I	16/38/1	14/17/0
Net Passing Yards	241	175
Offensive Plays	75	58
Total Offense	409	421
Fumbles/Lost	0-0	2-0
Penalties/Yards	4/40	6/40
Punts/Average	5/45.4	6/38.7
Third Down Conversion	6 of 15	4 of 10
Time of Possession	28:16	31:44

Individual Statistics

Rushing
Kentucky - Beach 18-109-1 TD, Johnson 4-24, Boyd 4-18, Lorenzen 10-14, Bwenge 1-3
Vanderbilt - Cutler 11-129, McKenzie 16-59, Tant 11-55, Smith 1-5, team 2-(-2)

Passing
Kentucky - Lorenzen 15-35-1-234-1 TD, Boyd 1-3-0-7
Vanderbilt - Cutler 14-17-0-175-4 TD

Receiving
Kentucky - Bernard 5-87-1 TD, Abney 4-56, Burton 3-49, Beach 3-41, Holt 1-8
Vanderbilt - Davis 3-39-2 TD, White 2-53-1 TD, Tant 2-18-1 TD, McKenzie 2-10, Smith 1-22, Dunning 1-10, Young 1-9, Loyte 1-7, Getter 1-7

Tackles
Kentucky - D. Williams 8, Anderson 8, Burns 7

Georgia 30 | Kentucky 14

November 22, 2003

Scoring Summary

Kentucky	7	0	3	0	—	10
Georgia	7	10	3	10	—	30

UG - Cooper 10 run (Bennett kick)...13:45 1st qtr.
UK - Lorenzen 1 run (Begley kick)...7:34 1st qtr.
UG - Thomas 1 run (Bennett kick)...13:03 2nd qtr.
UG - Bennett 29 FG...0:00 2nd qtr.
UK - Begley 48 FG...10:34 3rd qtr.
UG - Bennett 29 FG...3:50 3rd qtr.
UG - Bennett 33 FG...13:30 4th qtr.
UG - Powell 8 run (Bennett kick)...3:55 4th qtr.

Team Statistics	Kentucky	Georgia
First Downs	12	26
Rush Attempts/Net Rushing Yards	28/75	46/153
Passing C/A/I	21/36/1	24/38/0
Net Passing Yards	137	289
Offensive Plays	64	84
Total Offense	212	442
Fumbles/Lost	2-0	0-0
Penalties/Yards	7/65	7/52
Punts/Average	7/39.9	5/36.8
Third Down Conversion	4 of 15	9 of 17
Time of Possession	29:59	30:01

Individual Statistics

Rushing
Kentucky- Beach 11-37, Cook 1-14, Bwenge 1-9, Burton 1-7, Thornton 1-7, Johnson 3-6, Boyd 1-4, Davis 1-1, Lorenzen 8-(-10)-1 TD
Georgia - Powell 10-66-1 TD, Lumpkin 7-34, Cooper 9-32-1 TD, Browning 7-27, Thomas 5-10-1 TD, Williams 1-3, Lyons 1-1, Greene 6-(-20)

Passing
Kentucky - Lorenzen 21-34-1-137, Boyd 0-2-0-0
Georgia - Greene 24-38-0-289

Receiving
Kentucky- Abney 7-23, Cook 5-47, Burton 4-26, Davis 3-24, Bernard 2-17
Georgia - Gibson 6-99, Gary 5-32, Brown 4-31, Browning 3-39, Johnson 2-35, Lumpkin 2-30, Cooper 2-23

Tackles
Kentucky - Anderson 21, M. Williams 11, D. Williams 7

Tennessee 20 | Kentucky 7

November 29, 2003

Scoring Summary

Tennessee	0	3	7	10	—	20
Kentucky	7	0	0	0	—	7

UK - Beach 1 run (Begley kick)...2:24 1st qtr.
UT - Wilhoit 33 FG...1:24 2nd qtr.
UT - Jones 18 pass from Clausen (Wilhoit kick)...13:30 3rd qtr.
UT - Wilhoit 47 FG...10:51 4th qtr.
UT - Houston 10 run (Wilhoit kick)...1:27 4th qtr.

Team Statistics	Kentucky	Tennessee
First Downs	14	16
Rush Attempts/Net Rushing Yards	25/51	38/160
Passing C/A/I	19/43/2	11/27/1
Net Passing Yards	136	110
Offensive Plays	68	65
Total Offense	187	270
Fumbles/Lost	2-1	0-0
Penalties/Yards	6/65	6/53
Punts/Average	8/38.4	6/45.0
Third Down Conversion	5 of 17	5 of 15
Time of Possession	26:16	33:44

Individual Statistics

Rushing
Kentucky - Beach 14-33-1 TD, Davis 2-11, Bernard 1-8, Johnson 2-5, Bwenge 1-0, Boyd 1-(-1), Lorenzen 4-(-5)
Tennessee - Houston 12-87-1 TD, Davis 14-56, Riggs 4-13, Tinsley 1-8, Fleming 2-3, Jones 1-2, Clausen 4-(-9)

Passing
Kentucky - Lorenzen 17-39-1-121, Boyd 2-3-1-15
Tennessee - Clausen 11-27-1-110-1 TD

Receiving
Kentucky - Bernard 5-43, Cook 5-37, Burton 3-3, Holt 2-28, Drobney 2-20, Boyd 1-16, Lorenzen 1-(-11)
Tennessee - Fleming 4-30, Jones 3-36-1 TD, Banks 2-28, Houston 1-10, Revill 1-6

Tackles
Kentucky - Anderson 14, M. Williams 8, Caudill 7, D. Williams 7

Louisville 28 | Kentucky 0

September 5, 2003

SCORING SUMMARY

Kentucky	0	0	0	0	—	0
Louisville	0	7	14	7	—	28

UL–Gates 6 run (Carmody kick)...9:43 2nd qtr.
UL–Rhodes 56 interception return (Carmody kick)...13:45 3rd qtr.
UL–Clark 16 pass from LeFors (Carmody kick)...0:54 3rd qtr.
UL–Gates 1 run (Carmody kick)...7:24 4th qtr.

TEAM STATISTICS

	Kentucky	Louisville
First Downs	13	20
Rush Attempts/Net Rushing Yds.	26/66	49/261
Passing C/A/I	14/34/2	14/21/1
Net Passing Yards	172	178
Offensive Plays	60	70
Total Offense	238	439
Fumbles/Lost	1/1	1/0
Penalties/Yards	7/62	8/85
Punts/Average	6/40.8	3/51.0
Third Down Conversions	4-of-15	5-of-15
Time of Possession	25:32	34:28

INDIVIDUAL STATISTICS

RUSHING
Kentucky–Beach 10-24, Boyd 9-17, Bwenge 2-10, McClinton 1-5, Dixon 2-4, Holt 1-3, Davis 1-3
Louisville–Gates 14-112-2 TD, Bush 14-73, Shelton 10-39, LeFors 5-21, Smith 2-19, team 1-(-1), Brohm 3-(-2).

PASSING
Kentucky–Boyd 14-34-2-172
Louisville–LeFors 8-14-1-139-1 TD, Brohm 6-7-0-39

RECEIVING
Kentucky–Parker 3-31, Holt 2-41, Scott 2-22, Burton 2-13, Beach 2-8, Mitchell 1-33, Dewalt 1-24, Davis 1-0.
Louisville–Clark 3-40, Bush 2-41, Tinch 2-37, Jones 2-17, Russell 2-17, Gates 2-10, McCauley 1-16

TACKLES
Kentucky–Anderson 9, Moore 9, Abdullah 8

Kentucky 51 | Indiana 32

September 18, 2004

SCORING SUMMARY

Indiana	9	8	15	0	—	32
Kentucky	3	24	21	3	—	51

IU–Robertson 27 FG...7:45 1st qtr.
UK–Begley 44 FG...3:41 1st qtr.
IU–Taylor 2 run (Braucher kick blocked)...0:46 1st qtr.
UK–Boyd 13 run (Begley kick)...13:27 2nd qtr.
UK–Dixon 67 run (Begley kick)...12:08 2nd qtr.
IU–Roby 44 pass from LoVecchipo (Halterman pass from LoVecchio)...10:11 2nd qtr.
UK–Boyd 9 run (Begley kick)...6:30 2nd qtr.
UK –Begley 23 FG...0:00 2nd qtr.
IU–Adeyanju 4 fumble return...13:59 3rd qtr
UK–Mitchell 19 pass from Boyd (Begley kick)...12:32 3rd qtr.
UK–Bwenge 1 run (Begley kick)...10:25 3rd qtr.
UK–Holt 12 pass from Boyd (Begley kick)...2:59 3rd qtr.
IU–Roby 64 pass from LoVecchio (Green-Ellis pass from LoVecchio)...1:39 3rd qtr.
UK–Begley 28 field goal ...1:28 4th qtr.

TEAM STATISTICS

	Indiana	Kentucky
First Downs	17	28
Rush Att./Net Rushing Yards	38/167	43/355
Passing C/A/I	13/27/1	21/30/0
Net Passing Yards	245	205
Offensive Plays	65	73
Total Offense	412	560
Fumbles/Lost	2/1	3/1
Penalties/Yards	7/55	9/65
Punts/Average	5/40.6	4/35.8
Third Down Conversion	4-of-14	6-of-13
Time of Possession	30:29	29:31

INDIVIDUAL STATISTICS

RUSHING
Kentucky–Boyd 17-130-2 TD; Dixon 9-105-1 TD; Beach 7-44; Little 4-33; Holt 2-30; Bwenge 4-13-1 TD
Indiana–23-115; Powers 3-17; Taylor 5-17-1 TD; Roby 1-10; LoVecchio 6-8

PASSING
Kentucky–Boyd 21-30-0-205-2 TD
Indiana–LoVecchio 12-24-1-236-2 TD; Powers 1-3-0-9

RECEIVING
Kentucky–Holt 6-53-1 TD; Mitchell 3-48-1 TD; Dixon 3-34; Dewalt 3-33; Tamme 3-18; Drobney 2-17; Bwenge 1-2
Indiana–Roby 7-184-2 TD; Green-Ellis 2-28; Gilmore 1-15; Taylor 1-9; Halterman 1-5; Lewis 1-4

TACKLES
Kentucky–Anderson 9, Flowers 6, Wilson 6, Sumrall 5, White 5, Moore 5

Florida 20 | Kentucky 3

September 25, 2004

SCORING SUMMARY

Kentucky	3	0	0	0	—	3
Florida	3	7	3	7	—	20

UK–Begley 51 FG...6:06 1st qtr.
UF–Leach 40 FG...0:00 1st qtr.
UF–Fason 46 run (Leach kick)...9:09 2nd qtr.
UF–Leach 21 FG...11:49 3rd qtr.
UF– Fason 7 pass from Leak (Leach kick)...4:08 4th qtr.

TEAM STATISTICS

	Kentucky	Florida
First Downs	10	26
Rush Attempts/Net Rushing Yards	27/73	40/262
Passing C/A/I	17/35/1	25/43/3
Net Passing Yards	134	261
Offensive Plays	62	83
Total Offense	207	523
Fumbles/Lost	1/1	1/0
Penalties/Yards	6/54	11/91
Punts/Average	7/36.3	2/30.0
Third Down Conversions	4-of-16	10-of-18
Time of Possession	26:16	33:44

INDIVIDUAL STATISTICS

RUSHING
Kentucky–Boyd 14-28, Little 3-18, Bwenge 5-16, Dixon 3-10, Beach 1-3, McClinton 1-(-2)
Florida–Fason 31-210-1 TD, Thornton 6-31, Leak 3-21

PASSING
Kentucky–Boyd 17-35-1-134
Florida–Leak 25-43-3-261-1 TD

RECEIVING
Kentucky–Holt 7-52, Mitchell 2-35, Dixon 2-1, Scott 1-15, Marchman 1-11, Drobney 1-7, Tamme 1-7, Dewalt 1-4, Little 1-2
Florida–Caldwell 8-84, Fason 5-43-1 TD, Small 4-29, Baker 4-22, Jackson 2-67, Latsko 2-16

TACKLES
Kentucky–Sumrall 8, Anderson 7, Williams 7, Abdullah 6

Ohio 28 | Kentucky 16

October 28, 2004

SCORING SUMMARY

Ohio	7	7	0	14	—	28
Kentucky	7	3	0	6	—	16

UK–Bwenge 1 run (Begley kick)...5:19 1st qtr.
Ohio–Hawk 9 run (Rossman kick)...0:04 1st qtr.
Ohio–Mayle 44 pass from Hawk (Rossman kick)...10:24 2nd qtr.
UK–Begley 29 FG...0:36 2nd qtr.
Ohio–Mayle 89 pass from Everson (Rossman kick)...9:38 4th qtr.
Ohio–McRae 12 run (Rossman kick)...7:17 4th qtr.
UK–Dewalt 2 pass from Woodson (Woodson rush failed)...1:10 4th qtr.

TEAM STATISTICS

	Ohio	Kentucky
First Downs	14	19
Rush Att./Net Rushing Yards	40/90	38/90
Passing C/A/I	10/18/0	18/36/3
Net Passing Yards	218	190
Offensive Plays	58	74
Total Offense	308	280
Fumbles/Lost	3/1	3/2
Penalties/Yards	7/50	5/25
Punts/Average	4/39.0	3/46.3
Third Down Conversion	4-of-12	5-of-15
Time of Possession	29:28	30:35

INDIVIDUAL STATISTICS

RUSHING
Kentucky–Dixon 17-90, Davis 1-5, Bwenge 4-5-1 TD, Woodson 3-4, Little 1-2, Holt 2-0, Beach 1-(-1), Boyd 9-(-15)
Ohio–Mayle 5-52-0, McRae 18-34-1 TD, Hawk 8-15-1 TD, Abrams 1-5-0, Jackson 1-2-0, Graham 1-0-0

PASSING
Kentucky–Boyd 12-25-2-118-0, Woodson 6-11-1-72-1 TD
Ohio–Hawk 7-15-0-114-1 TD, Everson 3-3-0-104-1 TD

RECEIVING
Kentucky–Mitchell 4-45, Tamme 3-40, Dewalt 2-30-1 TD, Holt 2-24, Drobney 2-14, Scott 2-13, Parker 1-15, Dixon 1-7, Beach 1-2
Ohio–Jackson 5-55, Mayle 4-157-2 TD, McRae 1-6

TACKLES
Kentucky–Sumrall 8, Anderson 7, Abren 6, Fontaine 6, White 6

Alabama 45 | Kentucky 17

October 9, 2004

SCORING SUMMARY

Alabama	7	10	14	14	—	45
Kentucky	0	7	7	3	—	17

ALA–Castille 1 run (Bostick kick)...1:37 1st qtr.
ALA–Hudson 20 run (Bostick kick)...7:17 2nd qtr.
UK–Boyd 1 run (Begley kick)...2:22 2nd qtr.
ALA–Bostick 36 FG...0:09 2nd qtr.
UK–Drobney 38 pass from Boyd (Begley kick)...12:17 3rd qtr.
ALA–Darby 2 run (Bostick kick)...4:24 3rd qtr.
ALA–Darby 9 run (Bostick kick)...2:33 3rd qtr.
UK–Begley 52 FG...11:48 4th qtr.
ALA–Prothro 100 kickoff return (Bostick kick)...11:34 4th qtr.
ALA–Castille 2 run (Bostick kick)...10:31 4th qtr.

TEAM STATISTICS	Alabama	Kentucky
First Downs	23	12
Rush Att./Net Rushing Yards	63/304	28/77
Passing C/A/I	7-11-0	7-18-0
Net Passing Yards	83	100
Offensive Plays	74	46
Total Offense	387	177
Fumbles/Lost	0/0	5/3
Penalties/Yards	5/35	6/51
Punts/Average	2/43.0	5-42.0
Third Down Conversion	8-of-16	1-of-8
Time of Possession	41:05	18:55

INDIVIDUAL STATISTICS

RUSHING
Kentucky–Boyd 2-23-1 TD, Little 3-20, Holt 1-18, Davis 1-10, Woodson 9-3, Bwenge 1-0, Dixon 1-(-1), Scott 0-4
Alabama–Darby 20-99-2 TD, Hudson 18-99-1 TD, Castille 8-33-2 TD, Johns 12-30, Freeland 1-24, Prothro 1-13, McClain 1-3, Smith 1-2, Pennington 1-1

PASSING
Kentucky–Boyd 4-13-0-65-1 TD, Woodson 3-5-0-35-0
Alabama–Pennington 7-11-0-83-0

RECEIVING
Kentucky–Parker 2-32, Holt 2-19, Drobney 1-38-1 TD, Mitchell 1-7, Beach 1-4
Alabama–Caddell 2-37, Prothro 2-10, Hall 1-18, Darby 1-12, Hudson 1-6

TACKLES
Kentucky–B. Booker 8, Williams 7, Sumrall 7, Schuler 7, Flowers 6, Abdullah 6, Woodyard 6

South Carolina 12 | Kentucky 7

October 16, 2004

SCORING SUMMARY

South Carolina	0	6	0	6	—	12
Kentucky	0	0	0	7	—	7

SC–Brown 43 FG...14:23 2nd qtr.
SC–Brown 20 FG...6:32 2nd qtr.
UK–Bwenge 2 run (Begley kick)...9:52 4th qtr.
SC–Williamson 19 pass from Rathe (Rathe rush failed)...1:28 4th qtr.

TEAM STATISTICS

	Kentucky	South Carolina
First Downs	18	16
Rush Att./Net Rushing Yards	35/80	43/213
Passing C/A/I	22-35-1	9-16-2
Net Passing Yards	171	105
Offensive Plays	70	59
Total Offense	251	318
Fumbles/Lost	4/3	4/3
Penalties/Yards	4/33	4/31
Punts/Average	3/36.3	1/56.0
Third Down Conversions	11-of-18	7-of-14
Time of Possession	30:06	29:54

INDIVIDUAL STATISTICS

RUSHING
Kentucky–Dixon 16-29, Beach 6-28, Boyd 6-15, Bwenge 3-6-1 TD, Holt 1-5, Davis 1-1, Woodson 2-(-4).
South Carolina–Summers 8-60, Turman 8-54, Boyd 10-51, Mitchell 5-28, Gray 2-15, Newton 5-7, Gause 1-0, Rathe 3-(-2).

PASSING
Kentucky–Boyd 18-29-0-149-0, Woodson 4-5-0-22-0, Tamme 0-1-1-0-0
South Carolina–Mitchell 2-7-2-10-0, Rathe 5-7-0-57-1 TD, Newton 2-2-0-38-0

RECEIVING
Kentucky–Holt 10-59, Tamme 3-30, Parker 3-23, Dewalt 2-25, Dixon 2-19, Drobney 1-13, Mitchell 1-2
South Carolina–Boyd 4-54, Williamson 3-31-1 TD, Whiteside 1-16, Turman 1-4

TACKLES
Kentucky–Burns 8, Flowers 7, Schuler 5, Moore 5, Sumrall 5

Auburn 42 | Kentucky 10

October 23, 2004

SCORING SUMMARY

Kentucky	0	7	3	0	-	10
Auburn	21	0	14	7	-	42

AU–Williams 1 run (Vaughn kick)...11:25 1st qtr.
AU–Williams 9 run (Vaughn kick)...7:48 1st qtr.
AU–Brown 12 run (Vaughn kick)...4:31 1st qtr.
UK–Little 4 run (Begley kick)...11:30 2nd qtr.
UK–Begley 37 FG...13:16 3rd qtr.
AU–Brown 17 run (Vaughn kick)...9:34 3rd qtr.
AU–Stewart 1 run (Vaughn kick)...2:46 3rd qtr.
AU–Burnam 15 fumble recovery (Vaughn kick)...5:01 4th qtr.

TEAM STATISTICS

TEAM STATISTICS	Kentucky	Auburn
First Downs	9	17
Rush Att./Net Rushing Yards	36/37	49/210
Passing C/A/I	14-26-0	11-18-1
Net Passing Yards	73	127
Offensive Plays	62	67
Total Offense	110	337
Fumbles/Lost	2/2	2/1
Penalties/Yards	10/57	10/90
Punts/Average	9/37.0	5/38.8
Third Down Conversion	2-of-17	4-of-13
Time of Possession	30:35	29:5

INDIVIDUAL STATISTICS

RUSHING

Kentucky–Little 13-51-1 TD, Holt 3-13, Lyons 1-7, Beach 1-2, Bwenge 1-2, Parker 1-0, Sprowles 1-(-1), Dixon 2-(-6), Davis 1-(-5), Woodson 12-(-26)
Auburn–Williams 17-149-2 TD, Brown 10-53-2 TD, Watson 8-18, Stewart 8-6-1 TD, Cox 1-2, Campbell 5-(-18)

PASSING

Kentucky–Woodson 14-26-0-73-0
Auburn–Campbell 11-15-0-127-0, Cox 0-2-1-0-0, team 0-1-0-0-0

RECEIVING

Kentucky–Holt 4-30, Davis 3-1, Scott 2-15, Mitchell 2-10, Dewalt 2-6, Drobney 1-11
Auburn–Aromashodu 4-49, Brown 2-30, Taylor 2-17, Guess 1-19, Stewart 1-6, Bennett 1-6

TACKLES

Kentucky–Williams 5, Anderson 5, White 5, Abdullah 5, B. Booker 5, Fontaine 5

Mississippi State 22 | Kentucky 7

October 30, 2004

SCORING SUMMARY

Kentucky	0	0	0	7	—	7
Miss. St.	7	3	0	12	—	22

MSU–Culbertson 35 interception return (Andrews kick)...13:58 1st qtr.
MSU–Andrews 33 FG...1:03 2nd qtr.
MSU–Andrews 32 FG...11:35 4th qtr.
UK–Boyd 6 run (Begley kick)...7:14 4th qtr.
MSU–Team safety...3:28 4th qtr.
MSU–Reid 32 run (Andrews kick)...3:17 4th qtr.

TEAM STATISTICS

TEAM STATISTICS	Kentucky	Miss. State
First Downs	14	19
Rush Attempts/Net Rushing Yds.	35/84	49/340
Passing C/A/I	17-33-1	7-18-2
Net Passing Yards	167	79
Offensive Plays	68	67
Total Offense	251	419
Fumbles/Lost	4/0	2/1
Penalties/Yards	6/50	7/55
Punts/Average	9/37.2	6/44.5
Third Down Conversion	3-of-16	3-of-13
Time of Possession	30:46	29:14

INDIVIDUAL STATISTICS

RUSHING
Kentucky–Boyd 15-54-1 TD, Bwenge 3-27, Little 9-25, Holt 1-3, Beach 2-1, McClinton 1-0, Woodson 3-(-8), team 1-(-18)
Mississippi State–Norwood 24-165, Reid 11-109-1 TD, Conner 9-57, Ambrose 2-10, Davis 1-4, Horton 1-(-1), team 1-(-4)

PASSING
Kentucky–Boyd 11-24-1-103-0, Woodson 5-8-0-39-0, Thornton 1-1-0-25-0
Mississippi State–Conner 7-17-2-79-0, Norwood 0-1-0-0-0

RECEIVING
Kentucky–Mitchell 3-51, Drobney 3-29, Parker 3-25, Beach 2-15, Lyons 2-11, R. Williams 1-25, Sprowles 1-6, Tamme 1-5, Holt 1-0
Mississippi State–Reid 2-17, Butler 1-21, Jones 1-16, Milons 1-14, Prosser 1-11, Norwood 1-0

TACKLES
Kentucky–M. Williams 13, Leger 8, Woodyard 8, Abdullah 6, B. Booker 5, Mielsch 5

Georgia 62 | Kentucky 17
November 6, 2004

SCORING SUMMARY

Georgia	3	17	14	28	—	62
Kentucky	0	3	14	0	—	17

UGA–A. Bailey 46 FG...2:57 1st qtr.
UGA–Pope 1 pass from Greene (A. Bailey kick)...11:46 2nd qtr.
UGA–A. Bailey 23 FG...5:32 2nd qtr.
UGA–T. Brown 1 run (A. Bailey kick)...1:21 2nd qtr.
UK–Begley 36 FG...0:00 2nd qtr.
UGA–T. Brown 2 run (A. Bailey kick)...13:26 3rd qtr.
UGA–S. Bailey 35 pass from Shockley (A. Bailey kick)...11:24 3rd qtr.
UK–Little 52 pass from Woodson (Begley kick)...10:17 3rd qtr.
UK–R. Johnson 4 run (A. Bailey kick)...2:42 3rd qtr.
UGA–T. Brown 4 run (A. Bailey kick)...13:44 4th qtr.
UGA–S. Bailey 2 pass from Shockley (A. Bailey kick)...6:18 4th qtr.
UGA–Cooper 8 run (A. Bailey kick)...5:18 4th qtr.
UGA–Milton 2 run (A. Bailey kick)...2:00 4th qtr.

TEAM STATISTICS

	Georgia	Kentucky
First Downs	24	18
Rush Att./Net Rushing Yards	45/245	23/54
Passing C/A/I	19/30/0	25/44/2
Net Passing Yards	344	290
Offensive Plays	75	67
Total Offense	589	344
Fumbles/Lost	4/3	2/1
Penalties/Yards	9/69	10/84
Punts/Average	1-41.0	7-45.4
Third Down Conversion	8-of-14	3-of-14
Time of Possession	32:15	27:45

INDIVIDUAL STATISTICS

RUSHING
Kentucky–Little 6-39, Holt 1-11, R. Johnson 2-8-1 TD, Lewis 2-7, Boyd 5-6, Woodson 5-4, Sprowles 1-2, team 1-(-23).
Georgia–Brown 22-130-3 TD, Shockley 4-62, Milton 7-23-1 TD, Cooper 5-16-1 TD, Ware 3-14, Gartrell 1-2, Greene, 2-(-1),Wilson 1-(-1).

PASSING
Kentucky–Woodson 17-26-0-206-1 TD; Boyd 8-18-2-84-0
Georgia–Greene 14-19-0-259-1 TD; Shockley 5-9-0-85-2 TD; Brown 0-1-0-0-0, Wilson 0-1-0-0-0

RECEIVING
Kentucky–Little 6-106-1 TD, Scott 5-42, Holt 4-37, Parker 2-34, Mitchell 2-27, Beach 2-21, Logan 1-10, D. Davis 1-8, J. Davis 1-4, R. Johnson 1-1
Georgia–Gibson 5-129, Pope 5-91-1 TD, R. Brown 3-58, Bailey 2-37-2 TD, Thomas 2-12, Milton 1-12, T. Brown 1-5.

TACKLES
Kentucky–McClinton 5, Sumrall 5, Abdullah 5, Wilson 4, Moore 4, R. Williams 4, White 4

Kentucky 14 | Vanderbilt 13

November 13, 2004

SCORING SUMMARY

Vanderbilt	0	7	6	0	—	13
Kentucky	0	0	0	14	—	14

VU–Jennings 1 run (Johnson kick)...12:29 2nd qtr.
VU–Young 13 pass from Cutler (Johnson kick failed)...11:55 3rd qtr.
UK–Holt 7 pass from Boyd (Begley kick)...12:12 4th qtr.
UK–Holt 25 pass from Boyd (Begley kick)...1:39 4th qtr.

TEAM STATISTICS	Kentucky	Vanderbilt
First Downs	21	15
Rush Att./Net Rushing Yards	43/172	35/164
Passing C/A/I	16/32/0	18/30/0
Net Passing Yards	202	125
Offensive Plays	75	65
Total Offense	374	289
Fumbles/Lost	2/1	0/0
Penalties/Yards	4/35	6/45
Punts/Average	8/29.9	7/42.6
Third Down Conversion	2-of-13	3-of-14
Time of Possession	32:44	27:16

INDIVIDUAL STATISTICS

RUSHING
Kentucky–Beach 9-69, Little 10-68, Boyd 5-21, R. Johnson 4-15, Mitchell 1-4, Dewalt 2-3, Woodson 2-0, team 2-(-16)
Vanderbilt–Doster 12-84, McKenzie 12-56, Cutler 8-25, Jennings 3-10-1 TD, Tant 2-5, Bright 4-1, Smith 1-(-1), team 1-(-8)

PASSING
Kentucky–Boyd 13-23-0-80-2 TD, Woodson 5-7-0-45-0
Vanderbilt–Cutler 16-32-0-202-1 TD

RECEIVING
Kentucky–Holt 9-87-2 TD, Little 3-7, Mitchell 2-14, Beach 2-7, Tamme 1-6, Scott 1-4
Vanderbilt–Davis 5-71, Dunning 3-44, White 2-24, McKenzie 2-14, Smith 1-23, Young 1-13-1 TD, Garrison 1-8, Doster 1-5

TACKLES
Kentucky–Abdullah 10, Sumrall 9, McClinton 8, D. Johnson 7, K. Booker 6

Tennessee 37 | Kentucky 31

November 27, 2004

SCORING SUMMARY

Kentucky	10	14	7	0	-	31
Tennessee	7	15	0	15	-	37

UK–Begley 45 FG...12:11 1st qtr.
UT–Clausen 1 run (Wilhoit kick)...6:55 1st qtr.
UK–Tamme 20 pass from Boyd (Begley kick)...2:04 1st qtr.
UK–Abren 6 interception return (Begley kick)...11:28 2nd qtr.
UT–Anderson 22 run (Wilhoit kick blocked)...7:56 2nd qtr.
UT–Wilhoit 24 FG...3:45 2nd qtr.
UK–Tamme 16 pass from Boyd (Begley kick)...0:46 2nd qtr.
UT–Meachem 20 pass from Clausen (Houston run failed)...0:06 2nd qtr.
UK–Boyd 1 run (Begley kick)...3:30 3rd qtr.
UT–Brown 12 pass from Clausen (Wilhoit kick)...9:39 4th qtr.
UT–Riggs 12 run (Houston rush)...0:38 4th qtr.

TEAM STATISTICS

TEAM STATISTICS	Kentucky	Tennessee
First Downs	20	34
Rush Att./Net Rushing Yards	29/105	40/204
Passing C/A/I	20-32-1	27-43-2
Net Passing Yards	218	402
Offensive Plays	61	83
Total Offense	323	606
Fumbles/Lost	3/0	0/0
Penalties/Yards	11/88	5/48
Punts/Average	4/45.8	1/33.0
Third Down Conversion	3-of-10	9-of-16
Time of Possession	27:06	32:54

INDIVIDUAL STATISTICS

RUSHING
Kentucky–Holt 1-34, Boyd 10-18-1 TD, Beach 6-16, Dixon 4-13, Davis 2-13, Little 4-9, R. Johnson 1-3, Thornton 1-(-1).
Tennessee–Houston 24-127, Riggs 10-52-1 TD, Anderson 1-22-1 TD, Clausen 2-5-1 TD, Hannon 1-0, Davis 1-0, team 1-(-2).

PASSING
Kentucky–Boyd 20-32-1-218-2
Tennessee–Clausen 26-41-2-349-2, Fayton 1-1-0-53-0, team 0-1-0-0-0

RECEIVING
Kentucky–Mitchell 9-111, Tamme 4-55-2 TD, Little 2-21, Holt 2-13, Johnson 2-10, Parker 1-8.
Tennessee–Meachem 5-145-1 TD, Brown 4-51-1 TD, Fayton 4-45, Houston 3-35, Smith 2-40, Swain 2-26, Brown 2-19, Anderson 2-11, Riggs 1-15, Hannon 1-10, Holbert 1-5.

TACKLES
Kentucky–Sumrall 11, White 9, McClinton 8, Burns 8, Flowers 7, B. Booker 6

Louisville 31 | Kentucky 24

September 4, 2005

SCORING SUMMARY

Louisville	7	21	0	3	—	31
Kentucky	7	0	10	7	—	24

UL–Brohm 1 run (Carmody kick)...8:22 1st qtr.
UK–Beach 6 run (Begley kick)...4:08 1st qtr.
UL–Brohm 1 run (Carmody kick)...14:54 2nd qtr.
UL–Bush 11 run (Carmody kick)...6:32 2nd qtr.
UL–Bush 1 run (Carmody kick)...1:13 2nd qtr.
UK–Begley 37 field goal...11:14 3rd qtr.
UK–Mitchell 21 pass from Woodson (Begley kick)...6:01 3rd qtr.
UL–Carmody 19 field goal...14:17 4th qtr.
UK–Tamme 15 pass from Woodson (Begley kick)...11:52 4th qtr.

TEAM STATISTICS

	Louisville	Kentucky
First Downs	22	17
Rushing Attempts/Net Rushing Yds.	46/209	27/47
Passing C/A/I	19/27/0	17/27/0
Net Passing Yards	179	279
Offensive Plays	73	54
Total Offense	388	325
Fumbles/Lost	4/3	0/0
Penalties/Yards	5/35	3/34
Punts/Average	4/28.8	3/24.7
Third-Down Conversions	9-of-15	5-of-10
Time of Possession	35:20	24:40

INDIVIDUAL STATISTICS

RUSHING (ATT-YARDS-TD)
Kentucky–Little 8-71, Beach 9-32-1, Woodson, 10-(-56)
Louisville–Bush 27-128-2, Smith 12-76, Brohm 7-5-2

PASSING (COMP-ATT-INT-YARDS-TD)
Kentucky–Woodson 17-27-0-278-2
Louisville–Brohm 19-27-0-179-0

RECEIVING (REC-YARDS-TD)
Kentucky–Little 6-49, Burton 4-98, Mitchell 3-33-1, Tamme 2-29-1, Cook 1-53, Beach 1-16
Louisville–Jones 5-32, Clark 4-45, Tinch 4-41, Bush 2-24, Smith 2-19, Barnidge 1-9, Douglas 1-9

TACKLES
Kentucky–Smith 15, Woodyard 9, Abdullah 8, Mills 8

Kentucky 41 | Idaho State 29

September 10, 2005

Scoring Summary

Idaho State	6	10	0	13	—	29
Kentucky	7	7	14	13	—	41

UK–Bwenge 6 run (Begley kick) ... 14:43 1st qtr.
ISU–Johnson 32 FG ... 12:53 1st qtr.
ISU–Johnson 50 FG ... 4:54 1st qtr.
ISU–Johnson 31 FG ... 14:18 1st qtr.
UK–Burton 31 pass from Woodson (Begley kick) ... 5:19 2nd qtr.
ISU–Hagler 1 run (Johnson kick) ... 0:00 2nd qtr.
UK–Drobney 9 pass from Woodson (Begley kick) ... 7:57 3rd qtr.
UK–Beach 2 run (Begley kick) ... 1:42 3rd qtr.
ISU–Hagler 3 run (Johnson kick) ... 6:54 4th qtr.
ISU–Mennear 26 blocked punt return (Hagler pass failed) ... 5:06 4th qtr.
UK–Little 99 kickoff return (Woodson pass failed) ... 4:51 4th qtr.
UK–Beach 2 run (Begley kick) ... 1:18 4th qtr.

Team Statistics

	Idaho State	Kentucky
First Downs	19	16
Rush Attempts/Net Rushing Yds.	36/157	34/143
Passing C/A/I	25/38/4	15/20/0
Net Passing Yards	291	167
Offensive Plays	74	54
Total Offense	448	310
Fumbles/Lost	2/0	1/0
Penalties/Yards	8/51	4/40
Punts/Average	3/32.7	4/26.5
Third-Down Conversions	9-of-17	5-of-11
Time of Possession	33:10	26:50

Individual Statistics

Rushing (att–yards–TD)
Kentucky–Little 19-104, Beach 8-22-2, Holt 1-20, Bwenge 2-16-1, Woodson 2-(-16)
Idaho State–Cornist 18-87 Barnett 11-47, Hagler 7-23-2
Passing (comp–att–int–yards–TD)
Kentucky–Woodson 15-20-0-167-2
Idaho State–Hagler 25-37-4-291-0, Lacey 0-1-0-0-0
Receiving (rec–yards–TD)
Kentucky–Cook 4-42, Little 3-30, Burton 2-46-1, Tamme 2-12, Mitchell 1-18, Drobney 1-9-1, Holt 1-5, Beach 1-5
Idaho State–Thompson 7-69, Okoebor 6-55, Cornist 4-44, Blue 4-29, Simmons 2-80, Lacey 1-9, Barnett 1-5
Tackles
Kentucky - Woodyard 9, Fontaine 6, Day 6, Abdullah 6, Smith 5, Leger 5

Indiana 38 | Kentucky 14

September 17, 2005

SCORING SUMMARY

Kentucky	0	0	14	0	—	14
Indiana	10	7	14	7	—	38

IU–Kleinsmith 22 FG ... 10:19 1st qtr.
IU–O'Neal 14 pass from Powers (Kleinsmith kick) ... 4:07 1st qtr.
IU–Sexton 1 pass from Powers (Kleinsmith kick) ... 5:41 2nd qtr.
UK–Little 13 run (Begley kick) ... 9:34 3rd qtr.
IU–Walker-Roby 9 pass from Powers (Kleinsmith kick) ... 8:01 3rd qtr.
IU–Hardy 4 pass from Powers (Kleinsmith kick) ... 1:26 3rd qtr.
UK–Mitchell 79 pass from Woodson (Begley kick) ... 1:08 3rd qtr.
IU–Washington 1 run (Kleinsmith kick) ... 8:23 4th qtr.

TEAM STATISTICS

	Kentucky	Indiana
First Downs	9	22
Rush Attempts/Net Rushing Yds.	25/77	60/305
Passing C/A/I	11/20/0	17/22/0
Net Passing Yards	140	135
Offensive Plays	45	82
Total Offense	217	440
Fumbles/Lost	1/1	0/0
Penalties/Yards	5/30	9/80
Punts/Average	7/38.6	3/41.3
Third-Down Conversions	2-of-10	8-of-16
Time of Possession	18:23	41:37

INDIVIDUAL STATISTICS

RUSHING (ATT-YARDS-TD)
Kentucky–Little 17-88-1, Beach 1-(-2), Pulley 3-(-3), Woodson 4-(-5)
Indiana–Taylor 17-176, Washington 20-67-1, Sears 9-34, Powers 10-29, Burns 1-2

PASSING (COMP-ATT-INT-YARDS-TD)
Kentucky–Woodson 10-18-0-133-1, Pulley 1-2-0-7-0
Indiana–Powers 17-22-0-135-4

RECEIVING (REC-YARDS-TD)
Kentucky–Tamme 4-25, Mitchell 2-95-1, Little 2-6, Bwenge 1-6, Beach 1-4, Ford 1-4
Indiana–Washington 5-27, Hardy 4-37-1, Bailey 2-24, Thigpen 2-15, O'Neal 1-14-1, Walker-Roby 1-9-1, Rudanovic 1-8, Sexton 1-1-1

TACKLES
Kentucky–Abdullah 12, Woodyard 10, White 9, Williams 6, Leger 6

Florida 49 | Kentucky 28

September 24, 2005

SCORING SUMMARY

Florida	14	35	0	0	—	49
Kentucky	7	0	7	14	—	28

UK–Little 1 run (Begley kick) ... 12:14 1st qtr.
UF–Wynn 16 pass from Leak (Hetland kick) ... 8:42 1st qtr.
UF–Jackson 11 pass from Leak (Hetland kick) ... 1:29 1st qtr.
UF–Wynn 3 run (Hetland kick) ... 13:48 2nd qtr.
UF–Wynn 1 run (Hetland kick) ... 11:11 2nd qtr.
UF–Baker 16 pass from Leak (Hetland kick) ... 4:57 2nd qtr.
UF–Jackson 6 pass from Leak (Hetland kick) ... 2:17 2nd qtr.
UF–Wynn 1 run (Hetland kick) ... 1:44 2nd qtr.
UK–Holt 5 run (Begley kick) ... 12:38 3rd qtr.
UK–Pulley 2 run (Begley kick) ... 8:34 4th qtr.
UK–Pulley 18 run (Begley kick) ... 6:49 4th qtr.

TEAM STATISTICS

	Florida	Kentucky
First Downs	27	19
Rushing Attempts/Net Rushing Yds.	42/187	33/133
Passing C/A/I	28/36/0	15/33/3
Net Passing Yards	350	162
Offensive Plays	78	66
Total Offense	537	295
Fumbles/Lost	2/1	2/1
Penalties/Yards	8/75	1/5
Punts/Average	4/29.2	5/39.6
Third-Down Conversions	12-of-16	5-of-12
Time of Possession	34:44	25:16

INDIVIDUAL STATISTICS

RUSHING (ATT-YARDS-TD)
Kentucky–Little 19-77-1, Pulley 7-32-2, Bwenge 2-7, Woodson 2-7
Holt 1-5-1, Beach 2-5
Florida–Portis 8-59, Wynn 10-40-3, Thornton 7-36, Moore 2-21, Jackson 3-16, Leak 7-9, Manson 4-6, team 1-0
PASSING (COMP-ATT-INT-YARDS-TD)
Kentucky–Woodson 11-27-3-124-0, Pulley 4-6-0-38-0
Florida–Leak 25-32-0-319-4, Portis 3-4-0-31-0
RECEIVING (REC-YARDS-TD)
Kentucky–Mitchell 5-41, Little 3-33, Tamme 2-41, Beach 2-22, Holt 1-17, Ford 1-6, Drobney 1-2
Florida–Jackson 9-105-2, Cornelius 8-138-0, Baker 3-19-1, Wynn 2-31-1, Boateng 1-22, Casey 1-12, Thornton 1-8, Moore 1-7, Manson 1-4, Tookes 1-4
TACKLES
Kentucky - Abdullah 12, Kelley 11, Woodyard 10, R. Williams 9, Moore 6

South Carolina 44 | Kentucky 16

October 8, 2005

SCORING SUMMARY

Kentucky	0	10	6	0	—	16
South Carolina	7	3	14	20	—	44

SC–Mitchell 1 run (Brown kick) ... 1:53 1st qtr.
UK–Beach 2 run (Begley kick) ... 8:54 2nd qtr.
UK–Begley 20 FG ... 6:30 2nd qtr.
SC–Brown 45 FG ... 1:07 2nd qtr.
SC–Rice 27 pass from Mitchell (Brown kick) ... 8:55 3rd qtr.
UK–Little 12 run (Begley kick failed) ... 7:45 3rd qtr.
SC–Rice 8 pass from Mitchell (Brown kick) ... 5:35 3rd qtr.
SC–Simpson 19 fumble return (Brown kick blocked) ... 13:54 4th qtr.
SC–Turman 1 run (Brown kick) ... 5:33 4th qtr.
SC–Newton 16 run (Brown kick) ... 2:47 4th qtr.

TEAM STATISTICS

	Kentucky	South Carolina
First Downs	20	24
Rush Attempts/Net Rushing Yds.	53/213	34/139
Passing C/A/I	12/18/1	24/35/1
Net Passing Yards	95	278
Offensive Plays	71	69
Total Offense	308	417
Fumbles/Lost	5/4	3/1
Penalties/Yards	4/50	9/97
Punts/Average	2/43.0	2/40.5
Third-Down Conversions	6-of-13	7-of-11
Time of Possession	30:49	29:11

INDIVIDUAL STATISTICS

RUSHING (ATT-YARDS-TD)
Kentucky–Little 28-120-1, Beach 11-73-1, Pulley 4-37, Bwenge 1-0, Woodson 9-(-17).
South Carolina–Turman 18-81-1, Newton 3-49-1, Thomas 1-13, Wallace 5-12, Davis 2-2, Sims 1-0, Mitchell 4-(-18)-1.

PASSING (COMP-ATT-INT-YARDS-TD)
Kentucky–Woodson 11-17-1-90-0, Beach 1-1-0-5-0
South Carolina–Mitchell 23-34-1-277-2, Newton 1-1-0-1-0

RECEIVING (REC-YARDS-TD)
Kentucky–Mitchell 4-25, Holt 3-39, Pulley 1-13, Bwenge 1-6, Tamme 1-6, Woodson 1-5, Little 1-1
South Carolina–Rice 8-125-2, Newton 5-63, McKinley 4-42, Thomas 4-28, Whiteside 1-11, Clark 1-9, Wallace 1-0

TACKLES
Kentucky–Smith 8, Kelley 7, R. Williams 6, Woodyard 6.

Ole Miss 13 | Kentucky 7

October 22, 2005

SCORING SUMMARY

Kentucky	0	0	0	7	—	7
Ole Miss	0	10	0	3	—	13

UM–Espy 9 pass from Spurlock (Hinkle kick) ... 3:32 2nd qtr.
UM–Hinkle 45 FG ... 0:05 2nd qtr.
UM–Hinkle 18 FG ... 5:04 4th qtr.
UK–Beach 4 run (Begley kick) ... 2:36 4th qtr.

TEAM STATISTICS

	Kentucky	Ole Miss
First Downs	16	18
Rushing Attempts/Net Rushing Yds.	38/149	39/163
Passing C/A/I	12/22/0	19/38/0
Net Passing Yards	107	198
Offensive Plays	60	77
Total Offense	256	361
Fumbles/Lost	4/3	1/0
Penalties/Yards	9/62	3/25
Punts/Average	8/29.8	6/31.2
Third-Down Conversions	3-of-13	8-of-20
Time of Possession	24:52	35:08

INDIVIDUAL STATISTICS

RUSHING (ATT-YARDS-TD)
Kentucky–Little 14-77, Beach 11-73-1, Pulley 4-15, Bwenge 1-1, Woodson 8-(-17)
Ole Miss–McSwain 24-104, Spurlock 5-39, Turner 5-12, Kendrick 1-8, Biddle 2-5, team 2-(-5)
PASSING (COMP-ATT-INT-YARDS-TD)
Kentucky–Woodson 12-20-0-107-0, Pulley 0-2-0-0-0
Ole Miss–Spurlock 19-38-0-198-1
RECEIVING (REC-YARDS-TD)
Kentucky–Holt 4-41, Cook 2-23, Beach 2-15, D. Davis 1-13, Mitchell 1-9, Pulley 1-6, Little 1-0
Ole Miss–Espy 5-39-1, Hill 4-42, Lane 3-38, Biddle 2-49, Hough 1-12, Pittman 1-11, Brooks 1-5, Kendrick 1-4, McSwain 1-(-2).
TACKLES
Kentucky–Woodyard 10, R. Williams 9, Kelley 7, Schuler 7

Kentucky 13 | Mississippi State 7

October 29, 2005

SCORING SUMMARY

Miss. State	0	0	7	0	—	7
Kentucky	3	7	3	0	—	13

UK–Begley 35 FG ... 2:56 1st qtr.
UK–Little 8 run (Begley kick) ... 10:52 2nd qtr.
UK–Begley 33 FG ... 7:53 3rd qtr.
MS–Thornton 19 run (Carlson kick) ... 4:50 3rd qtr.

TEAM STATISTICS

	Miss. State	Kentucky
First Downs	22	22
Rush Attempts/Net Rushing Yds.	37/173	47/183
Passing C/A/I	17/30/0	13/27/0
Net Passing Yards	202	141
Offensive Plays	74	74
Total Offense	375	324
Fumbles/Lost	1/1	3/1
Penalties/Yards	6/70	7/60
Punts/Average	7/39.1	7/36.0
Third-Down Conversions	3-of-15	5-of-15
Time of Possession	29:09	30:51

INDIVIDUAL STATISTICS

RUSHING (ATT-YARDS-TD)
Kentucky–Little 24-114-1, Beach 14-81, Bwenge 2-7, Pulley 1-2, Burton 1-1, Woodson 2-(-5), team 2-(-17)
Mississippi State–Norwood 20-121, Thornton 10-66-1, Davis 2-2, Henig 5-(-16)

PASSING (COMP-ATT-INT-YARDS-TD)
Kentucky–Woodson 13-27-0-141-0
Mississippi State–Henig 16-31-0-200-0, Conner 1-6-0-2-0

RECEIVING (REC-YARDS-TD)
Kentucky–Little 4-44, Burton 3-38, Mitchell 3-19, Tamme 2-18, Holt 1-22
Mississippi State–Prosser 5-78, Milons 4-51, Norwood 3-26, Long 2-12, Butler 1-27, Humphries 1-4, Davis 1-4

TACKLES
Kentucky–Woodyard 11, R. Williams 7, Abdullah 6, Smith 6.

Auburn 49 | Kentucky 27

November 5, 2005

SCORING SUMMARY

Auburn	7	21	7	14	—	49
Kentucky	7	3	7	10	—	27

UK–Little 25 run (Begley kick) ... 12:11 1st qtr.
AU–Irons 9 run (Vaughn kick) ... 7:08 1st qtr.
AU–Irons 1 run (Vaughn kick) ... 13:39 2nd qtr.
UK–Begley 25 FG ... 10:18 2nd qtr.
AU–Rodriguez 31 pass from Cox (Vaughn kick) ... 7:54 2nd qtr.
AU–Irons 2 run (Vaughn kick) ... 0:56 2nd qtr.
AU–Davis 75 run (Vaughn kick) ... 10:04 3rd qtr.
UK–Little 2 run (Begley kick) ... 8:33 3rd qtr.
AU–Rodriguez 5 run (Vaughn kick) ... 10:14 4th qtr.
UK–Burton 11 pass from Woodson (Begley kick) ... 8:03 4th qtr.
UK–Begley 27 FG ... 4:03 4th qtr.
AU–Smith 46 run (Vaughn kick) ... 1:35 4th qtr.

TEAM STATISTICS

	Auburn	Kentucky
First Downs	24	20
Rushing Attempts/Net Rushing Yds.	49/388	27/115
Passing C/A/I	13/21/0	26/43/1
Net Passing Yards	201	335
Offensive Plays	70	70
Total Offense	589	450
Fumbles/Lost	3/2	0/0
Penalties/Yards	8/70	7/72
Punts/Average	3/52.3	5/41.8
Third-Down Conversions	9-of-13	6-of-16
Time of Possession	32:53	27:07

RUSHING (ATT-YARDS-TD)
Kentucky–Little 17-124-2, Woodson 7-(-2), Beach 3-(-7)
Auburn–Davis 8-162-1, Irons 23-103-3, Smith 13-99-1, Rodriguez 2-17-1, Dede 1-8, Cox 2-(-1)
PASSING (COMP-ATT-INT-YARDS-TD)
Kentucky–Woodson 26-43-1-335-1
Auburn–Cox 13-21-0-201-1
RECEIVING (REC-YARDS-TD)
Kentucky–Burton 7-100-1, Little 6-122, Tamme 5-42, Holt 4-32, Mitchell 3-36, Beach 1-3
Auburn–Rodriguez 3-79-1, Obomanu 3-32, Mix 2-28, Irons 1-18, Guess 1-15, Wallace 1-14, Aromashodu 1-12, Bennett 1-3
TACKLES
Kentucky–McGrath 12, Abdullah 12, R. Williams 8, Woodyard 7, Huffman 7

Kentucky 48 | Vanderbilt 43

November 12, 2005

SCORING SUMMARY

Kentucky	21	13	14	0	—	48
Vanderbilt	3	7	14	19	—	43

VU–Hahnfeldt 33 FG ... 9:39 1st qtr.
UK–Beach 1 run (Begley kick) ... 5:56 1st qtr.
UK–Woodson 7 run (Begley kick) ... 3:26
UK–Smith 72 blocked FG return (Begley kick) ... 00:13 1st qtr.
UK–Begley 46 FG ... 8:46 2nd qtr.
UK–Little 3 run (Begley kick) ... 5:28 2nd qtr.
UK–Begley 31 FG ... 2:47 2nd qtr.
VU–Bennett 13 pass from Cutler (Hahnfeldt kick) ... 1:34 2nd qtr.
UK–Little 2 run (Begley kick) ... 10:56 3rd qtr.
VU–Bennett 2 pass from Cutler (Hahnfeldt kick) ... 4:53 3rd qtr.
UK–Little 65 run (Begley kick) ... 4:33 3rd qtr.
VU–Garrison 35 run (Hahnfeldt kick) ... 1:53 3rd qtr.
VU–Bennett 5 pass from Cutler (pass failed) ... 10:16 4th qtr.
VU–Bennett 13 pass from Cutler (Hahnfeldt kick) ... 6:38 4th qtr.
VU–Bennett 7 pass from Cutler (pass failed) ... 2:09 4th qtr.

TEAM STATISTICS

	Kentucky	Vanderbilt
First Downs	16	30
Rush Attempts/Net Rushing Yds.	43/210	27/119
Passing C/A/I	12/20/1	39/67/0
Net Passing Yards	155	395
Offensive Plays	63	94
Total Offense	365	514
Fumbles/Lost	3/1	4/3
Penalties/Yards	5/36	2/20
Punts/Average	4/30.5	3/34.0
Third-Down Conversions	7-of-16	4-of-16
Time of Possession	28:15	31:45

RUSHING (ATT-YARDS-TD)
Kentucky–Little 28-198-3, Beach 5-11-1, Pulley 1-8, Bwenge 3-5, Woodson 6-(-12)-1
Vanderbilt–Garrison 7-48-1, Cutler 13-38, Jennings 7-33

PASSING (COMP-ATT-INT-YARDS-TD)
Kentucky–Woodson 12-20-1-155-0
Vanderbilt–Cutler 39-66-0-395-5

RECEIVING (REC-YARDS-TD)
Kentucky–Little 5-86, Tamme 4-42, Holt 2-16, Burton 1-11
Vanderbilt–Bennett 13-99-5, Smith 7-110, Garrison 4-53, Jennings 4-34, Dunning 4-32, White 4-18, Anderson 3-49

TACKLES
Kentucky–Huffman 11, Smith 10, R. Williams 8, Schuler 7

Georgia 45 | Kentucky 13

November 19, 2005

SCORING SUMMARY

Kentucky	3	0	3	7	—	13
Georgia	0	24	14	7	—	45

UK–Begley 19 FG ... 0:34 1st qtr.
UGA–Pope 10 pass from Shockley (Coutu kick) ... 12:27 2nd qtr.
UGA–Southerland 2 pass from Shockley (Coutu kick) ... 6:07 2nd qtr.
UGA–Ware 52 run (Coutu kick) ... 4:48 2nd qtr.
UGA –Coutu 56 FG ... 0:00 2nd qtr.
UK–Begley 36 FG ... 9:26 3rd qtr.
UGA–McClendon 21 pass from Shockley (Coutu kick) ... 6:02 3rd qtr.
UGA–McClendon 7 pass from Shockley (Coutu kick) ... 1:58 3rd qtr.
UGA–Bryant 27 pass from Tereshinski (Coutu kick) ... 8:32 4th qtr.
UK–Pulley 7 run (Begley kick) ... 1:07 4th qtr.

TEAM STATISTICS

	Kentucky	Georgia
First Downs	13	21
Rush Attempts/Net Rushing Yds.	31/99	31/169
Passing C/A/I	18/33/0	22/38/0
Net Passing Yards	100	226
Offensive Plays	64	69
Total Offense	199	395
Fumbles/Lost	1/1	3/0
Penalties/Yards	5/54	6/60
Punts/Average	8/36.2	3/42.7
Third-Down Conversions	6-of-18	0-of-10
Time of Possession	32:57	27:03

RUSHING (ATT-YARDS-TD)
Kentucky–Pulley 11-61-1, Little 13-29, Bwenge 2-11, Woodson 5-(-2)
Georgia–Ware 8-71-1, Lumpkin 5-38, Ely-Kelso 1-34, Brown 6-25, Burgett 5-7, Tereshinski 1-2, team 1-(-3), Shockley 4-(-5)
PASSING (COMP-ATT-INT-YARDS-TD)
Kentucky–Woodson 15-26-0-92-0, Pulley 3-7-0-8-0
Georgia–Shockley 17-31-0-159-4, Tereshinski 4-5-0-64-1, Barnes 1-2-0-3-0
RECEIVING (REC-YARDS-TD)
Kentucky–Tamme 5-25, Burton 4-44, Little 4-5, Holt 2-11, Cook 1-9, Brown 1-5, Sprowles 1-1
Georgia–McClendon 4-44-2, Milner 3-32, Bailey 3-32, Bryant 2-34-1, Massaquoi 2-29, Raley 2-22, Harris 2-20, Pope 1-10-1, Johnson 1-3, Southerland 1-2-1, Lumpkin 1-(-2)
TACKLES
Kentucky–McGrath 9, Abdullah 8, R. Williams 5

Tennessee 27 | Kentucky 8

November 26, 2005

Scoring Summary

Tennessee	7	10	7	3	—	27
Kentucky	3	3	0	2	—	8

UT–Meacham 50 pass from Ainge (Wilhoit kick) ...12:50 1st qtr.
UK–Begley 31 FG ... 5:01 1st qtr.
UT–Hannon 32 pass from Ainge (Wilhoit kick) ... 11:31 2nd qtr.
UK–Begley 25 FG ... 6:14 2nd qtr.
UT–Wilhoit 31 FG ... 0:58 2nd qtr.
UT–Harrell 7 interception return (Wilhoit kick) ... 1:19 3rd qtr.
UT–Wilhoit 40 FG ... 13:07 4th qtr.
UK–Team safety (E. Scott forces intentional grounding from end zone)... 6:53 4th qtr.

Team Statistics	Tennessee	Kentucky
First Downs	16	16
Rush Attempts/Net Rushing Yds.	38/150	33/46
Passing C/A/I	17/25/0	27/41/3
Net Passing Yards	221	177
Offensive Plays	63	74
Total Offense	371	223
Fumbles/Lost	3/3	5/1
Penalties/Yards	10/92	2/9
Punts/Average	4/44.3	4/41.8
Third-Down Conversions	4-of-13	7-of-18
Time of Possession	28:23	31:37

Rushing (att-yards-td)
Kentucky–Little 10-43, D. Davis 1-9, Bwenge 2-4, Pulley 18-(-2), Woodson 2-(-8)
Tennessee–Foster 26-114, Rogers 1-26, Yancey 4-23, Taylor 1-7, Ainge 6-(-20)

Passing (comp-att-int-yards-td)
Kentucky–Pulley 23-33-3-155-0, Woodson 4-8-0-22-0
Tennessee–Ainge 17-25-0-221-2

Receiving (rec-yards-td)
Kentucky–Little 11-73, Burton 3-28, Cook 3-28, Holt 3-17, Tamme 2-11, Bwenge 2-8, D. Davis 2-0, Mitchell 1-12
Tennessee–Foster 5-44, Meacham 3-70-1, Smith 3-21, Hannon 2-29-1, Brown 2-25, Swain 1-23, Briscoe 1-9

Tackles
Kentucky–Woodyard 18, R. Williams 9, Smith 7

Louisville 59 | Kentucky 28

September 3, 2006

SCORING SUMMARY

Kentucky	0	14	7	7	-	28
Louisville	14	17	14	14	-	59

UL - Bush 48 run (Carmody kick) ... 13:26 1st qtr.
UL - Bush 4 run (Carmody kick) ... 3:36 1st qtr.
UL - Bolen 1 pass from Brohm (Carmody kick) ... 14:13 2nd qtr.
UL - Bush 5 run (Carmody kick) ... 10:57 2nd qtr.
UL - Carmody 38 FG ... 4:13 2nd qtr.
UK - Burton 73 pass from Woodson (Housley kick) ... 3:03 2nd qtr.
UK - Lyons 4 pass from Woodson (Housley kick) ... 0:21 2nd qtr.
UL - Stripling 1 run (Carmody kick) ... 6:04 3rd qtr.
UK - Lyons 80 pass from Woodson (Housley kick) ... 5:31 3rd qtr.
UL - Stripling 38 run (Carmody kick) ... 3:35 3rd qtr.
UL - Anderson 0 fumble recovery (Carmody kick) ... 8:30 4th qtr.
UK - Burton 100 kickoff return (Housley kick) ... 8:11 4th qtr.
UL - Allen 4 run (Carmody kick) ... 3:52 4th qtr.

TEAM STATISTICS

	Kentucky	Louisville
First Downs	8	31
Rush Attempts/Net Rushing Yds.	19/22	55/363
Passing C/A/I	10/26/0	20/32/0
Net Passing Yards	238	268
Offensive Plays	45	87
Total Offense	260	631
Fumbles/Lost	1/1	1/1
Penalties/Yards	5/35	3/40
Punts/Average	9/40.0	3/34.7
Third-Down Conversions	2-of-12	8-of-15
Time of Possession	21:24	38:36

INDIVIDUAL STATISTICS

RUSHING (ATT-YARDS-TD)
Kentucky - Little 7-21, Dixon 2-5, Pulley 5-1, Woodson 4-(-2), Smith 1-(-3)
Louisville - Bush 17-128-3, Stripling 9-90-2, Smith 12-66, Allen 9-48-1, Douglas 2-27, Bolen 2-5, Brohm 2-1, Tronzo 1-(-1)

PASSING (COMP-ATT-INT-YARDS-TD)
Kentucky - Woodson 9-24-0-231-3, Pulley 1-2-0-7-0
Louisville - Brohm 19-31-0-254-1, Cantwell 1-1-0-14-0

RECEIVING (REC-YARDS-TD)
Kentucky - Burton 4-127-1, Lyons 2-84-2, Tamme 2-12, Dixon 1-8, D. Jones 1-7
Louisville - Douglas 5-87, Barnidge 4-53, Carter 3-48, Urrutia 2-51, Smith 2-14, Kuhn 2-11, Bush 1-3, Bolen 1-1-1

TACKLES
Kentucky - Woodyard 13, McClinton 9, R. Williams 8, M. Johnson 7

Kentucky 41 | Texas State 7

September 9, 2006

SCORING SUMMARY

Texas State	0	0	0	7	-	7
Kentucky	6	21	7	7	-	41

UK - Lyons 10 pass from Woodson (Housley kick failed) ... 0:57 1st qtr.
UK - Dixon 8 run (Housley kick) ... 9:14 2nd qtr.
UK - Lyons 35 pass from Woodson (Housley kick) ... 6:36 2nd qtr.
UK - Conner 17 pass from Woodson (Housley kick) ... 2:08 2nd qtr.
UK - Little 24 run (B. Scott kick) ... 5:56 3rd qtr.
UK - Grinter 1 run (B. Scott kick) ... 12:02 4th qtr.
TSU - Luke 4 pass from Wasson (Bronson kick) ... 10:20 4th qtr.

TEAM STATISTICS

	Texas State	Kentucky
First Downs	10	22
Rush Attempts/Net Rushing Yds.	26/55	40/178
Passing C/A/I	13/27/1	18/26/1
Net Passing Yards	155	247
Offensive Plays	53	66
Total Offense	210	425
Fumbles/Lost	2/1	1/1
Penalties/Yards	4/44	9/101
Punts/Average	8/44.9	2/44.5
Third-Down Conversions	2-of-12	8-of-14
Time of Possession	26:28	33:32

INDIVIDUAL STATISTICS

RUSHING (ATT-YARDS-TD)
Kentucky - Little 12-91-1, Pulley 6-47, Dixon 10-34-1, Smith 2-5, Brown 5-4, D. Jones 1-4, Grinter 1-1, Woodson 3-(-8)
Texas State - Wasson 11-44, Jolly 5-8, Zwinggi 6-8, George 4-(-5)

PASSING (COMP-ATT-INT-YARDS-TD)
Kentucky - Woodson 13-20-1-197-3, Pulley 5-6-0-50-0
Texas State - Wasson 9-20-1-85-1, George 3-5-0-23-0, MacDonald 0-1-0-0-0, Crosby 1-1-0-47-0

RECEIVING (REC-YARDS-TD)
Kentucky - Burton 5-80, S. Johnson 4-34, Lyons 3-54-2, Little 3-39, Conner 1-17-1, Ford 1-15, Murphy 1-8
Texas State - Thomas 2-52, Jolly 2-20, Dunk 2-8, Crosby 1-20, Zwinggi 1-19, Scott 1-13, Darley 1-10, Miller 1-6, Luke 1-4-1, Gilley 1-3

TACKLES
Kentucky - Woodyard 7, McGrath 4, Lewis 3

Kentucky 31 | Ole Miss 14

September 16, 2006

SCORING SUMMARY

Ole Miss	7	7	0	0	-	14
Kentucky	7	14	0	10	-	31

UM - Green 47 pass from Schaeffer (Shene kick) ... 4:35 1st qtr.
UK - Lyons 26 pass from Woodson (Seiber kick) ... 2:07 1st qtr.
UK - Lyons 6 pass from Woodson (Seiber kick) ... 12:35 2nd qtr.
UM - Hough 27 pass from Schaeffer (Shene kick) ... 4:08 2nd qtr.
UK - Pulley 22 pass from Woodson (Seiber kick) ... 1:30 2nd qtr.
UK - Dixon 2 run (Seiber kick) ... 5:30 4th qtr.
UK - Seiber 41 FG ... 3:15 4th qtr.

TEAM STATISTICS

	Ole Miss	Kentucky
First Downs	17	21
Rush Attempts/Net Rushing Yds.	39/205	33/87
Passing C/A/I	13/26/1	22/34/0
Net Passing Yards	190	293
Offensive Plays	65	67
Total Offense	395	380
Fumbles/Lost	6/4	3/1
Penalties/Yards	12/79	5/45
Punts/Average	3/38.7	5/38.0
Third-Down Conversions	7-of-15	4-of-11
Time of Possession	29:40	30:20

INDIVIDUAL STATISTICS

RUSHING (ATT-YARDS-TD)
Kentucky - Little 17-54, Dixon 8-35-1, Conner 1-4, Woodson 5-(-3), team 2-(-3)
Ole Miss - Green-Ellis 19-85, Schaeffer 12-61, Hall 7-46, McCluster 1-13

PASSING (COMP-ATT-INT-YARDS-TD)
Kentucky - Woodson 22-34-0-293-3
Ole Miss - Schaeffer 13-26-1-190-2

RECEIVING (REC-YARDS-TD)
Kentucky - Lyons 4-83-2, Dixon 4-31, Little 3-48, Burton 3-35, Ford 3-28, Pulley 2-30-1, Strickland 1-26, Johnson 1-8, Conner 1-4
Ole Miss - Green 3-53-1, Hodge 3-30, Wallace 2-65, Hough 1-27-1, Lane 1-10, Lewis 1-8, Cook 1-4, Hall 1-(-7)

TACKLES
Kentucky - Kelley 8, Woodyard 8, Jn. Williams 5, McClinton 5, Lindley 5

Florida 26 | Kentucky 7

September 23, 2006

SCORING SUMMARY

Kentucky	0	7	0	0	-	7
Florida	6	6	7	7	-	26

UF - Cornelius 33 pass from Leak (Hetland kick blocked) ... 12:16 1st qtr.
UK - Grinter 1 pass from Woodson (Seiber kick) ... 1:59 2nd qtr.
UF - Wynn 13 run (Hetland kick blocked) ... 0:22 2nd qtr.
UF - Moore 4 run (Hetland kick) ... 7:41 3rd qtr.
UF - Ingram 6 pass from Leak (Hetland kick) ... 10:04 4th qtr.

TEAM STATISTICS

	Kentucky	Florida
First Downs	17	24
Rush Attempts/Net Rushing Yds.	22/39	38/235
Passing C/A/I	26/38/0	16/28/1
Net Passing Yards	210	279
Offensive Plays	60	66
Total Offense	249	514
Fumbles/Lost	2/0	3/1
Penalties/Yards	10/66	10/71
Punts/Average	9/37.1	2/52.0
Third-Down Conversions	4-of-13	4-of-9
Time of Possession	33:43	26:17

INDIVIDUAL STATISTICS

RUSHING (ATT-YARDS-TD)
Kentucky - A. Smith 4-29, Dixon 7-27, Jones 1-7, Bankhead 1-3, Woodson 9-(-27)
Florida - Wynn 14-104-1, Tebow 6-73, Moore 8-54-1, Fayson 1-10, Caldwell 1-5, Rowley 1-3, Cornelius 1-3, Harvin 1-2, Leak 5-(-19)

PASSING (COMP-ATT-INT-YARDS-TD)
Kentucky - Woodson 26-37-0-210-1, team 0-1-0-0-0
Florida - Leak 15-26-1-267-2, Tebow 1-2-0-12-0

RECEIVING (REC-YARDS-TD)
Kentucky - Lyons 7-50, Pulley 6-63, Tamme 5-39, Burton 3-33, Dixon 2-19, Grinter 2-7-1, A.Smith 1-(-1)
Florida - Baker 7-148, Cornelius 4-74-1, Tookes 2-37, Ingram 2-13-1, Moore 1-7

TACKLES
Kentucky - Woodyard 10, Kelley 7, K. Booker 6

Kentucky 45 | Central Michigan 36

September 30, 2006

SCORING SUMMARY

Central Michigan	0	17	10	9	-	36
Kentucky	14	14	10	7	-	45

UK - Burton 3 pass from Woodson (Seiber kick) ... 10:03 1st qtr.
UK - Tamme 19 pass from Woodson (Seiber kick) ... 7:00 1st qtr.
UK - Little 24 pass from Woodson (Seiber kick) ... 13:14 2nd qtr.
CMU - Linson 61 pass from LeFevour (Albreski kick) ... 11:48 2nd qtr.
UK - Dixon 6 run (Seiber kick) ... 7:53 2nd qtr.
CMU - Gardner 10 pass from LeFevour (Albreski kick) ... 4:49 2nd qtr.
CMU - Albreski 19 FG ... 0:00 2nd qtr.
CMU - Albreski 37 FG ... 9:45 3rd qtr.
UK - Burton 42 pass from Woodson (Seiber kick) ... 7:12 3rd qtr.
CMU - Linson 15 pass from LeFevour (Albreski kick) ... 5:47 3rd qtr.
UK - Seiber 28 FG ... 1:18 3rd qtr.
CMU - Albreski 29 FG ... 11:34 4th qtr.
CMU - Anderson 23 pass from LeFevour (LeFevour pass failed) ... 6:58 4th qtr.
UK - Little 3 run (Seiber kick) ... 4:30 4th qtr.

TEAM STATISTICS

	Central Michigan	Kentucky
First Downs	27	18
Rush Attempts/Net Rushing Yds.	34/147	31/107
Passing C/A/I	26/47/1	20/32/1
Net Passing Yards	411	266
Offensive Plays	81	63
Total Offense	558	373
Fumbles/Lost	8/3	1/1
Penalties/Yards	6/45	2/15
Punts/Average	1/41.0	4/40.8
Third-Down Conversions	7-of-15	5-of-12
Time of Possession	30:36	29:24

INDIVIDUAL STATISTICS

RUSHING (ATT-YARDS-TD)
Kentucky - Little 12-70-1, Dixon 12-49-1, D. Jones 1-3, Smith 2-(-5), Woodson 4-(-10)
Central Michigan - Archer 16-69, LeFevour 13-47, Mikulec 1-18, Brunner 2-8, Linson 1-5, Anderson 1-0
PASSING (COMP-ATT-INT-YARDS-TD)
Kentucky - Woodson 20-32-1-266-4
Central Michigan - LeFevour 22-38-0-360-4, Brunner 4-8-0-51-0, Jasmin 0-1-1-0-0
RECEIVING (REC-YARDS-TD)
Kentucky - Burton 9-124-2, Tamme 3-49-1, Dixon 3-46, Little 2-23-1, Pulley 2-14, Jones 1-10
Central Michigan - Anderson 8-137-1, Gardner 6-76-1, Linson 5-134-2, Archer 3-28, Cetoute 1-14, Condeni 1-14, Ollenburger 1-7, Williams 1-1
TACKLES
Kentucky - Woodyard 9, McClinton 8, R. Williams 7, Kelley 7

South Carolina 24 | Kentucky 17

October 7, 2006

SCORING SUMMARY

South Carolina	0	10	7	7	-	24
Kentucky	0	0	10	7	-	17

SC - Newton 7 run (Succop kick) ... 12:26 2nd qtr.
SC - Succop 42 FG ... 2:01 2nd qtr.
SC - Boyd 5 run (Succop kick) ... 11:37 3rd qtr.
UK - Woodson 1 run (Seiber kick) ... 6:57 3rd qtr.
UK - Seiber 31 FG ... 1:54 3rd qtr.
SC - Newton 22 pass from McKinley (Succop kick) ... 4:42 4th qtr.
UK - Lyons 9 pass from Woodson (Seiber kick) ... 2:56 4th qtr.

TEAM STATISTICS

	South Carolina	Kentucky
First Downs	21	17
Rush Attempts/Net Rushing Yds.	39/190	27/62
Passing C/A/I	15/23/1	18/32/1
Net Passing Yards	193	289
Offensive Plays	62	59
Total Offense	383	351
Fumbles/Lost	1/0	2/0
Penalties/Yards	10/68	7/50
Punts/Average	2/39.5	3/43.3
Third-Down Conversions	7-of-13	3-of-11
Time of Possession	31:07	28:53

INDIVIDUAL STATISTICS

RUSHING (ATT-YARDS-TD)
Kentucky - Little 13-50, Masthay 1-17. Dixon 5-13, Woodson 6-(-1)-1, Burton 1-(-7), team 1-(-10)
South Carolina - Boyd 25-113-1, Newton 14-77-1

PASSING (COMP-ATT-INT-YARDS-TD)
Kentucky - Woodson 18-31-1-289-1, Strickland 0-1-0-0-0
South Carolina - Newton 14-22-1-171-0, McKinley 1-1-0-22-1

RECEIVING (REC-YARDS-TD)
Kentucky - Tamme 4-48, Lyons 3-79-1, Burton 3-63, Little 3-43, Pulley 3-39, Grinter 1-11, Ford 1-6
South Carolina - Boyd 4-61, Brown 4-19, McKinley 3-63, Newton 1-22-1, Rice 1-15, Murdock 1-8, Cook 1-5

TACKLES
Kentucky - Woodyard 11, Moore 8, R. Williams 7, White 7, Pryor 6, Kelley 6

LSU 49 | Kentucky 0

October 14, 2006

SCORING SUMMARY

Kentucky	0	0	0	0	-	0
LSU	14	14	14	7	-	49

LSU - Hester 7 run (David kick) ... 8:56 1st qtr.
LSU - Bowe 7 pass from Russell (David kick) ... 4:50 1st qtr.
LSU - Hester 4 run (David kick) ... 12:55 2nd qtr.
LSU - Bowe 48 pass from Russell (David kick) ... 8:59 2nd qtr.
LSU - Doucet 12 run (Jackson kick) ... 12:59 3rd qtr.
LSU - Bowe 8 pass from Flynn (Jackson kick) ... 8:28 3rd qtr.
LSU - Jordan 2 pass from Flynn (Jackson kick) ... 13:05 4th qtr.

TEAM STATISTICS

	Kentucky	LSU
First Downs	14	28
Rush Attempts/Net Rushing Yds.	23/61	43/268
Passing C/A/I	16/41/1	19/25/0
Net Passing Yards	166	278
Offensive Plays	64	68
Total Offense	227	546
Fumbles/Lost	2/0	0/0
Penalties/Yards	9/84	8/41
Punts/Average	7/35.1	2/38.5
Third-Down Conversions	5-of-17	4-of-8
Time of Possession	28:31	31:29

INDIVIDUAL STATISTICS

RUSHING (ATT-YARDS-TD)
Kentucky - Pulley 5-32, Smith 8-22, Dixon 7-13, Woodson 3-(-6)
LSU - Scott 9-56, Williams 8-47, Hester 13-44-2, Holliday 2-34, Flynn 3-32, Vincent 4-20, Perrilloux 2-17, Doucet 1-12-1, Russell 1-6
PASSING (COMP-ATT-INT-YARDS-TD)
Kentucky - Woodson 14-37-1-151-0, Pulley 2-4-0-15-0
LSU - Russell 15-18-0-226-2, Flynn 4-7-0-52-2
RECEIVING (REC-YARDS-TD)
Kentucky - Burton 7-62, Lyons 4-57, A. Smith 2-28, Tamme 1-9, Pulley 1-7, Ford 1-3
LSU - Bowe 6-111-3, Davis 4-59, Doucet 4-54, Hester 2-19, Cole 1-18, Dickson 1-15, Jordan 1-2-1
TACKLES
Kentucky - Woodyard 7, Kelley 6, Jenkins 6, Jn. Williams 6, White 5, M. Johnson 5

Kentucky 34 | Mississippi State 31

October 28, 2006

SCORING SUMMARY

Kentucky	14	0	10	10	-	34
Mississippi State	0	14	3	14	-	31

UK - Burton 16 pass from Woodson (Seiber kick) ... 7:38 1st qtr.
UK - Lyons 18 pass from Woodson (Seiber kick) ... 0:46 1st qtr.
MSU - Burks 75 pass from Henig (Carlson kick) ... 10:21 2nd qtr.
MSU - Smith 15 pass from Henig (Carlson kick) ... 8:42 2nd qtr.
UK - Smith 3 run (Seiber kick) ... 12:45 3rd qtr.
MSU - Carlson 45 FG ... 10:42 3rd qtr.
UK - Seiber 41 FG ... 5:55 3rd qtr.
UK - Burton 33 pass from Woodson (Seiber kick) ... 13:24 4th qtr.
MSU - Burks 36 pass from Henig (Carlson kick) ... 11:46 4th qtr.
UK - Seiber 27 FG ... 8:08 4th qtr.
MSU - Dixon 1 run (Carlson kick) ... 2:20 4th qtr.

TEAM STATISTICS

	Kentucky	MSU
First Downs	22	16
Rush Attempts/Net Rushing Yds.	38/106	24/24
Passing C/A/I	19/29/1	22/41/2
Net Passing Yards	284	384
Offensive Plays	67	65
Total Offense	390	408
Fumbles/Lost	1/1	2/1
Penalties/Yards	8/51	4/45
Punts/Average	4/41.5	4/32.2
Third-Down Conversions	4-of-13	7-of-14
Time of Possession	33:47	26:13

RUSHING (ATT-YARDS-TD)
Kentucky - Smith 17-92-1, Dixon 11-32, Pulley 2-17, Bankhead 1-0, Woodson 6-(-34)
MSU - Thornton 9-17, Dixon 10-14-1, Henig 1-7, Stallworth 2-(-3)

PASSING (COMP-ATT-INT-YARDS-TD)
Kentucky - Woodson 19-28-1-284-3, Pulley 0-1-0-0-0
MSU - Henig 22-41-2-384-3

RECEIVING (REC-YARDS-TD)
Kentucky - Lyons 8-117-1, Burton 5-81-2, A. Smith 2-57, Dixon 2-14, Tamme 1-13, Jones 1-2
MSU - Burks 7-192-2, Smith 6-93-1, Thornton 3-1, Husband 2-16, Bell 1-49, Prosser 1-16, Rogers 1-13, Sherrod 1-4

TACKLES
Kentucky -Kelley 12, Woodyard 6, Lindley 4, Warford 4, Pryor 4, R. Williams 4

Kentucky 24 | Georgia 20

November 4, 2006

SCORING SUMMARY

Georgia	7	7	0	6	-	20
Kentucky	3	7	0	14	-	24

UK - Seiber 48 FG ... 5:18 1st qtr.
UGA - Raley 10 pass from Stafford (Bailey kick) ... 0:24 1st qtr.
UGA - Southerland 1 run (Bailey kick) ... 12:30 2nd qtr.
UK - Burton 5 pass from Woodson (Seiber kick) ... 8:03 2nd qtr.
UK - Burton 10 pass from Woodson (Seiber kick) ... 8:29 4th qtr.
UGA - Ware 3 run (Bailey kick blocked) ... 4:37 4th qtr.
UK - Dixon 3 run (Seiber kick) ... 1:21 4th qtr.

TEAM STATISTICS

	Georgia	Kentucky
First Downs	21	20
Rush Attempts/Net Rushing Yds.	32/159	42/147
Passing C/A/I	16/29/3	23/32/2
Net Passing Yards	230	204
Offensive Plays	61	74
Total Offense	389	351
Fumbles/Lost	1/1	2/1
Penalties/Yards	5/33	3/25
Punts/Average	1/43.0	3/38.3
Third-Down Conversions	5-of-9	5-of-13
Time of Possession	27:51	32:09

INDIVIDUAL STATISTICS

RUSHING (ATT-YARDS-TD)
Kentucky - Smith 19-76, Dixon 8-47-1, Pulley 3-15, Woodson 8-7, Bankhead 2-4, team 1-0, Seiber 1-(-2)
Georgia - Lumpkin 13-85, Stafford 5-35, Ware 9-31-1, Southerland 5-8-1

PASSING (COMP-ATT-INT-YARDS-TD)
Kentucky - Woodson 23-32-2-204-2
Georgia - Stafford 16-28-3-230-1, team 0-1-0-0-0

RECEIVING (REC-YARDS-TD)
Kentucky - Burton 7-73-2, Lyons 5-48, Tamme 4-32, Pulley 2-16, Dixon 2-12, Smith 1-12, D.Jones 1-7, S. Johnson 1-4
Georgia - Milner 4-70, Raley 3-38-1, Ware 2-26, Massaquoi 2-16, Durham 2-14, Goodman 1-29, Bryant 1-25, Lumpkin 1-12

TACKLES
Kentucky - Kelley 10, Woodyard 8, Lindley 7, Jn. Williams 6, McClinton 6

Kentucky 38 | Vanderbilt 26

November 11, 2006

SCORING SUMMARY

Vanderbilt	0	7	13	6	-	26
Kentucky	0	10	7	21	-	38

UK - Seiber 28 FG ... 8:30 2nd qtr.
VU - Nickson 1 run (Hahnfeldt kick) ... 6:39 2nd qtr.
UK - Burton 6 pass from Woodson (Seiber kick) ... 4:09 2nd qtr.
UK - Johnson 29 pass from Woodson (Seiber kick) ... 11:28 3rd qtr.
VU - Walker 35 run (Adams pass failed) ... 4:43 3rd qtr.
VU - Nickson 6 run (Hahnfeldt kick) ... 0:57 3rd qtr.
UK - Little 3 run (Seiber kick) ... 13:16 4th qtr.
UK - Ford 27 pass from Woodson (Seiber kick) ... 7:59 4th qtr.
UK - Burton 57 pass from Woodson (Seiber kick) ... 3:31 4th qtr.
VU - Bennett 41 pass from Nickson (no PAT attempted) ... 0:00 4th qtr.

TEAM STATISTICS

TEAM STATISTICS	Vanderbilt	Kentucky
First Downs	27	26
Rush Attempts/Net Rushing Yds.	30/175	37/147
Passing C/A/I	23/37/2	29/43/0
Net Passing Yards	446	450
Offensive Plays	67	80
Total Offense	621	597
Fumbles/Lost	3/2	1/1
Penalties/Yards	1/5	6/58
Punts/Average	3/38.0	4/29.0
Third-Down Conversions	2-of-9	7-of-16
Time of Possession	29:24	30:36

INDIVIDUAL STATISTICS

RUSHING (ATT-YARDS-TD)
Kentucky - Little 20-132-1, A. Smith 2-9, Dixon 4-6, Pulley 1-3, Woodson 10-(-3)
Vanderbilt - Nickson 16-71-2, Walker 2-43-1, Jackson-Garrison 8-41, Bennett 2-17, Hawkins 2-3

PASSING (COMP-ATT-INT-YARDS-TD)
Kentucky - Woodson 29-42-0-450-4, Pulley 0-1-0-0-0
Vanderbilt - Nickson 23-37-2-446-1

RECEIVING (REC-YARDS-TD)
Kentucky - Burton 11-171-2, Little 8-114, Lyons 3-61, D. Jones 2-31, Johnson 1-29-1, Ford 1-27-1, Dixon 1-6, Pulley 1-6, Tamme 1-5
Vanderbilt - Bennett 11-220-1, White 6-121, G. Smith 3-79, Walker 1-9, Allen 1-9, Anderson 1-8

TACKLES
Kentucky - Woodyard 8, Kelley 8, Warford 7

Kentucky 42 | UL-Monroe 40

November 18, 2006

SCORING SUMMARY

UL-Monroe	10	10	14	6	-	40
Kentucky	14	14	5	9	-	42

ULM - James 78 blocked FG return (Wilson kick) ... 10:31 1st qtr.
UK - Smith 8 run (Seiber kick) ... 8:51 1st qtr.
ULM - Wilson 45 FG ... 4:37 1st qtr.
UK - Burton 37 pass from Woodson (Seiber kick) ... 0:04 1st qtr.
UK - Burton 17 pass from Woodson (Seiber kick) ... 12:17 2nd qtr.
UK - Little 84 punt return (Seiber kick) ... 8:58 2nd qtr.
ULM - Dawson 3 run (Wilson kick) ... 3:51 2nd qtr.
ULM - Wilson 41 FG ... 0:04 2nd qtr.
ULM - Dawson 9 run (Wilson kick) ... 12:29 3rd qtr.
UK - Safety, punter ran out of end zone after bad snap ... 8:38 3rd qtr.
UK - Seiber 26 FG ... 6:13 3rd qtr.
ULM - Dawson 1 run (Wilson kick) ... 2:57 3rd qtr.
UK - Seiber 34 FG ... 14:08 4th qtr.
UK - Burton 25 pass from Woodson (team kick failed) ... 8:17 4th qtr.
ULM - Lancaster 1 run (Lancaster rush failed) ... 0:54 4th qtr.

TEAM STATISTICS

	UL-Monroe	Kentucky
First Downs	28	24
Rush Attempts/Net Rushing Yds.	57/351	29/98
Passing C/A/I	10/19/1	25/35/0
Net Passing Yards	150	359
Offensive Plays	76	64
Total Offense	501	457
Fumbles/Lost	2/0	1/1
Penalties/Yards	11/102	5/45
Punts/Average	2/40.5	1/47.0
Third-Down Conversions	9-of-13	2-of-10
Time of Possession	34:07	25:53

INDIVIDUAL STATISTICS

RUSHING (ATT-YARDS-TD)
Kentucky - Little 19-82, A. Smith 5-25-1, Pulley 1-9, Bankhead 1-3, Woodson 3-(-21)
UL-Monroe - Dawson 26-179-3, Lancaster 14-85-1, Hogan 12-82, McNeal 1-7, Payne 2-4, Stringfellow 1-1, team 1-(-7)

PASSING (COMP-ATT-INT-YARDS-TD)
Kentucky - Woodson 25-35-0-359-3
UL-Monroe - Lancaster 8-15-1-128-0, Payne 1-2-0-17-0, McNeal 1-2-0-5-0

RECEIVING (REC-YARDS-TD)
Kentucky - Burton 9-115-3, Lyons 6-79, Little 5-89, D. Jones 1-44, Ford 1-13, S. Johnson 1-10, Pulley 1-5, Bankhead 1-4
UL-Monroe - Sapp 4-104, Dawson 2-18, Zacharie 2-10, Humphrey 1-12, Hogan 1-6

TACKLES
Kentucky - Woodyard 12, Kelley 9, White 8, Peters 8, McClinton 7

Tennessee 17 | Kentucky 12

November 25, 2006

SCORING SUMMARY

Kentucky	0	12	0	0	-	12
Tennessee	10	0	0	7	-	17

UT - Wilhoit 24 FG ... 7:28 1st qtr.
UT - Meachem 15 pass from Ainge (Wilhoit kick) ... 2:46 1st qtr.
UK - Seiber 21 FG ... 10:04 2nd qtr.
UK - Little 5 pass from Woodson (Seiber kick failed) ... 3:22 2nd qtr.
UK - Seiber 20 FG ... 0:18 2nd qtr.
UT - Coker 1 run (Wilhoit kick) ... 14:02 4th qtr.

TEAM STATISTICS

	Kentucky	Tennessee
First Downs	24	23
Rush Attempts/Net Rushing Yds.	30/128	34/96
Passing C/A/I	26/39/0	19/33/0
Net Passing Yards	282	240
Offensive Plays	69	67
Total Offense	410	336
Fumbles/Lost	1/0	3/1
Penalties/Yards	3/28	4/35
Punts/Average	1/48.0	2/44.0
Third-Down Conversions	7-of-14	7-of-14
Time of Possession	30:28	29:32

INDIVIDUAL STATISTICS

RUSHING (ATT-YARDS-TD)
Kentucky - Little 23-119, Dixon 5-13, Jones 1-3, Woodson 1-(-7)
Tennessee - Coker 22-90-1, Hardesty 7-27, Swain 1-6, Foster 1-(-2), Ainge 3-(-25)

PASSING (COMP-ATT-INT-YARDS-TD)
Kentucky - Woodson 26-39-0-282-1
Tennessee - Ainge 19-33-0-240-1

RECEIVING (REC-YARDS-TD)
Kentucky - Tamme 7-120, Burton 6-42, Little 5-21-1, Lyons 3-60, Ford 2-17, Pulley 2-15, S. Johnson 1-7
Tennessee - Meachem 6-116-1, Coker 4-51, Brown 3-25, Smith 2-19, Swain 2-15, Cottam 1-9, Holbert 1-5

TACKLES
Kentucky - Woodyard 11, R. Williams 7, Lindley 6, Mills 5

Kentucky 28 | Clemson 20

2006 Gaylord Hotels Music City Bowl, December 29, 2006

SCORING SUMMARY

Clemson	0	6	0	14	-	20
Kentucky	7	7	7	7	-	28

UK – M. Johnson 1 run (Seiber kick) ... 11:04 1st qtr.
CU – Barry 32 pass from Proctor (Early kick failed) ... 8:14 2nd qtr.
UK – Ford 70 pass from Woodson (Seiber kick) ... 2:14 2nd qtr.
UK – Lyons 24 pass from Woodson (Seiber kick) ... 8:09 3rd qtr.
UK – Tamme 13 pass from Woodson (Seiber kick) ... 11:29 4th qtr.
CU – Grisham 17 pass from Proctor (Proctor rush failed) ... 7:25 4th qtr.
CU – Kelly 17 pass from Proctor (Palmer pass from Proctor) ... 0:44 4th qtr.

TEAM STATISTICS

	Clemson	Kentucky
First Downs	19	21
Rush Attempts/Net Rushing Yds.	25/130	40/100
Passing C/A/I	23/39/1	21/29/0
Net Passing Yards	272	309
Offensive Plays	64	69
Total Offense	402	409
Fumbles/Lost	3/3	2/2
Penalties/Yards	5/50	8/84
Punts/Average	3/43.7	4/25.0
Third-Down Conversions	4-of-11	7-of-14
Time of Possession	26:16	33:44

INDIVIDUAL STATISTICS

RUSHING (ATT-YARDS-TD)
Kentucky - Little 17-57, Bankhead 3-37, Dixon 8-29, Conner 1-1, M. Johnson 2-1-1, team 1-0, Woodson 8-(-22)
Clemson - Davis 8-53, Proctor 9-32, Spiller 5-24, Ford 1-15, Stuckey 1-5, Merriweather 1-1

PASSING (COMP-ATT-INT-YARDS-TD)
Kentucky - Woodson 20-28-0-299-3, Masthay 1-1-0-10-0
Clemson - Proctor 23-39-1-272-3

RECEIVING (REC-YARDS-TD)
Kentucky - Burton 5-30, Tamme 4-59-1, S. Johnson 3-67, Lyons 2-50-1, Little 2-15, Dixon 2-2, Ford 1-70-1, McClinton 1-10, Pulley 1-6
Clemson - Kelly 6-66-1, Stuckey 5-93, Grisham 5-49-1, Davis 2-13, Barry 1-32-1, Ford 1-8, Harris 1-5, Merriweather 1-4, Palmer 1-2

TACKLES
Kentucky - Woodyard 12, McClinton 9, R. Williams 7

Kentucky 50 | Eastern Kentucky 10

September 1, 2007

SCORING SUMMARY

Eastern Kentucky	0	3	7	0	-	10
Kentucky	17	13	20	0	-	50

UK – Lyons 51 pass from Woodson (Seiber kick) ... 13:15 1st qtr.
UK – Seiber 48 FG ... 5:52 1st qtr.
UK – Burton 5 pass from Woodson (Seiber kick) ... 1:52 1st qtr.
UK – Dixon 8 run (Seiber kick) ... 12:38 2nd qtr.
UK – Smith 7 pass from Woodson (Seiber kick blocked) ... 6:00 2nd qtr.
EKU – O'Connor 45 FG ... 1:04 2nd qtr.
UK – Little 38 run (Seiber kick) ... 14:11 3rd qtr.
EKU – Cromer 4 pass from Holland (Long kick) ... 10:47 3rd qtr.
UK – Dixon 1 run (Seiber kick failed) ... 6:45 3rd qtr.
UK – Smith 12 run (Seiber kick) ... 2:57 3rd qtr.

TEAM STATISTICS

	EKU	Kentucky
First Downs	13	31
Rush Attempts/Net Rushing Yds.	30/130	44/288
Passing C/A/I	16/31/2	23/33/1
Net Passing Yards	72	280
Offensive Plays	61	77
Total Offense	202	568
Fumbles/Lost	0/0	2/1
Penalties/Yards	4/39	7/65
Punts/Average	10/34.0	1/44.0
Third-Down Conversions	2-of-14	7-of-12
Time of Possession	28:51	31:09

INDIVIDUAL STATISTICS

RUSHING (ATT-YARDS-TD)
Kentucky - Little 12-135-1, Dixon 9-77-2, A. Smith 7-53-1, Locke 3-13, A. Brown 2-11, Bowland 2-9, Allen 2-5, Hartline 4-(-3), Woodson 3-(-12)
Eastern Kentucky - Dunn 12-70, Washington 6-32, Greco 3-12, Holland 6-9, Watts 1-3, Walker 1-2, Bradley 1-2

PASSING (COMP-ATT-INT-YARDS-TD)
Kentucky - Woodson 20-29-0-250-3, Hartline 3-4-1-30-0
Eastern Kentucky - Holland 16-25-1-72-1, Greco 0-6-1-0-0

RECEIVING (REC-YARDS-TD)
Kentucky - Lyons 6-113-1, Burton 5-49-1, Tamme 2-33, Little 2-16, Connor 2-8, S. Johnson 1-18, Murphy 1-16, Locke 1-8, Smith 1-7-1, Lanxter 1-6, Ford, 1-6
Eastern Kentucky - Sizemore 3-17, Cromer 3-13, Barber 2-21, Phelps 2-9

TACKLES
Kentucky - M. Johnson 7, J. Williams 7, Maxwell 6, Lewis 6

Kentucky 56 | Kent State 20
September 8, 2007

SCORING SUMMARY

Kent State	7	7	6	0	-	20
Kentucky	14	0	21	21	-	56

KSU – Muldrow 6 run (Reed kick) ... 10:25 1st qtr.
UK – Conner 5 run (Seiber kick) ... 8:14 1st qtr.
UK – S. Johnson 32 pass from Woodson (Seiber kick) ... 0:13 1st qtr.
KSU – Jarvis 10 run (Reed kick) ... 3:15 2nd qtr.
UK – Conner 16 run (Seiber kick) ... 11:03 3rd qtr.
UK – Dixon 18 run (Seiber kick) ... 7:38 3rd qtr.
UK – Burton 51 pass from Woodson (Seiber kick) ... 4:22 3rd qtr.
KSU – Jarvis 22 pass from Edelman (Reed kick failed) ... 0:53 3rd qtr.
UK – Woodson 1 run (Seiber kick) ... 14:38 4th qtr.
UK – A. Smith 12 run (Housley kick) ... 8:08 4th qtr.
UK – Locke 67 run (Housley kick) ... 4:01 4th qtr.

TEAM STATISTICS

	Kent State	Kentucky
First Downs	26	24
Rush Attempts/Net Rushing Yds.	59/324	39/266
Passing C/A/I	12/29/2	15/22/0
Net Passing Yards	129	218
Offensive Plays	88	61
Total Offense	453	484
Fumbles/Lost	4/2	0/0
Penalties/Yards	6/55	5/35
Punts/Average	4/40.5	4/36.2
Third-Down Conversions	10-of-17	4-of-9
Time of Possession	34:56	25:04

INDIVIDUAL STATISTICS

RUSHING (ATT-YARDS-TD)
Kentucky - Little 13-102, Locke 5-75-1, A. Smith 6-54-1, Dixon 4-36-1, Conner 2-21-2, Grinter 1-(-1), Woodson 8-(-21)-1
Kent State - Edelman 24-135, Jarvis 20-131-1, Flowers 9-29, Drager 3-12, Keys 2-11, Muldrow 1-6-1

PASSING (COMP-ATT-INT-YARDS-TD)
Kentucky - Woodson 15-22-0-218-2
Kent State - Edelman 12-28-1-129-1, Magazu 0-1-1-0-0

RECEIVING (REC-YARDS-TD)
Kentucky - Burton 7-109-1, S. Johnson 3-71-1, Lyons 3-21, Little 1-13, Tamme 1-4
Kent State - Jarvis 3-63-1, Sitko 3-21, Robinson 2-13, Bayes 2-11, Vanderink 1-16, Garner 1-5

TACKLES
Kentucky - Woodyard 15, Kelley 11, R. Williams 8, Lindley 7, M. Johnson 6, Harrison 5, Peters 5

Kentucky 40 | Louisville 34

September 15, 2007

SCORING SUMMARY

Louisville	7	14	7	6	-	34
Kentucky	13	6	7	14	-	40

UK – Seiber 36 FG ... 13:58 1st qtr.
UK – Johnson 5 pass from Woodson (Seiber kick) ... 12:02 1st qtr.
UK – Seiber 31 FG ... 6:06 1st qtr.
UL – Allen 8 pass from Brohm (Carmody kick) ... 1:11 1st qtr.
UK – Little 10 run (Seiber kick failed) ... 12:43 2nd qtr.
UL – Douglas 3 pass from Brohm (Carmody kick) ... 7:16 2nd qtr.
UL – Allen 10 run (Carmody kick) ... 1:02 2nd qtr.
UK – Conner 7 pass from Woodson (Seiber kick) ... 9:46 3rd qtr.
UL – Guy 100 kickoff return (Carmody kick) ... 9:31 3rd qtr.
UK – Tamme 5 pass from Woodson (Seiber kick) ... 13:47 4th qtr.
UL – Allen 2 run (Brohm pass failed) ... 1:45 4th qtr.
UK – Johnson 57 pass from Woodson (Seiber kick) ... 0:28 4th qtr.

TEAM STATISTICS

	Louisville	Kentucky
First Downs	26	27
Rush Attempts/Net Rushing Yds.	27/101	35/185
Passing C/A/I	28/43/1	30/46/0
Net Passing Yards	366	275
Offensive Plays	70	81
Total Offense	467	460
Fumbles/Lost	1/1	1/0
Penalties/Yards	7/53	5/65
Punts/Average	2/38.5	3/47.3
Third-Down Conversions	8-of-13	9-of-17
Time of Possession	29:37	30:23

INDIVIDUAL STATISTICS

RUSHING (ATT-YARDS-TD)
Kentucky - Little 27-151-1, Dixon 3-27, Conner 2-7, Woodson 3-0
Louisville - Allen 18-96-2, Spillman 1-6, Stripling 2-6, Brohm 6-(-7)

PASSING (COMP-ATT-INT-YARDS-TD)
Kentucky - Woodson 30-44-0-275-4, team 0-2-0-0-0
Louisville - Brohm 28-43-1-366-2

RECEIVING (REC-YARDS-TD)
Kentucky - Burton 9-99, Dixon 5-29, Tamme 5-27-1, Lyons 4-33, S. Johnson 3-65-2, Little 2-11, Conner 1-7-1, Ford 1-4
Louisville - Douglas 13-223-1, Urrutia 5-72, Allen 4-21-1, Barnidge 2-10, Guy 1-23, Stripling 1-21, Spillman 1-3, Brohm 1-(-7).

TACKLES
Kentucky - Woodyard 13, McClinton 7, Jenkins 6, J. Williams 6

Kentucky 42 | Arkansas 27

September 22, 2007

SCORING SUMMARY

Kentucky	7	7	7	21	-	42
Arkansas	10	10	0	9	-	29

ARK – Tejada 40 FG ... 9:35 1st qtr.
ARK – Robinson 16 fumble return (Tejada kick) ... 9:16 1st qtr.
UK – Little 14 run (Seiber kick) ... 7:29 1st qtr.
ARK – Tejada 20 FG ... 11:05 2nd qtr.
ARK – McFadden 56 run (Tejada kick) ... 5:41 2nd qtr.
UK – Lindley 66 fumble return (Seiber kick) ... 0:26 2nd qtr.
UK – Burton 15 pass from Woodson (Seiber kick) ... 11:00 3rd qtr.
ARK – Safety, Bledsoe tackled Woodson in the end zone ... 11:51 4th qtr.
ARK – Jones 82 kickoff return (Tejada kick) ... 11:40 4th qtr.
UK – Locke 2 run (Woodson rush failed) ... 7:59 4th qtr.
UK – Burton 32 pass from Woodson (Burton pass from Woodson) ... 4:02 4th qtr.
UK – Woodson 1 run (Seiber kick) ... 0:59 4th qtr.

TEAM STATISTICS

	Kentucky	Arkansas
First Downs	23	22
Rush Attempts/Net Rushing Yds.	36/170	51/338
Passing C/A/I	21/39/0	13/28/2
Net Passing Yards	265	157
Offensive Plays	75	79
Total Offense	435	495
Fumbles/Lost	3/3	5/1
Penalties/Yards	7/60	7/55
Punts/Average	7/43.1	7/38.9
Third-Down Conversions	5-of-13	7-of-18
Time of Possession	24:47	35:13

INDIVIDUAL STATISTICS

RUSHING (ATT-YARDS-TD)
Kentucky - Dixon 9-78, Locke 9-48-1, Little 10-47-1, A. Smith 4-20, Woodson 4-(-23)-1
Arkansas - McFadden 29-173-1, Jones 12-133, Smith 5-24, Crawford 1-13, Hillis 1-5, team 1-(-2), Dick 2-(-8)

PASSING (COMP-ATT-INT-YARDS-TD)
Kentucky - Woodson 21-39-0-265-2
Arkansas - Dick 13-28-2-157-0

RECEIVING (REC-YARDS-TD)
Kentucky - S. Johnson 7-111, Tamme 4-46, Burton 3-65-2, Little 3-28, Lyons 2-14, Conner 1-5, A. Smith 1-(-4)
Arkansas - Hillis 2-44, Smith 2-10, McFadden 2-10, Williams 1-24, Tuck 1-21, Salters 1-15, Miller 1-14, Baker 1-11, Johnson 1-8, Jones 1-0

TACKLES
Kentucky - Woodyard 17, J. Williams 8, Jarmon 7, Peters 4, Jenkins 4, Pryor 4, Cobb 4

Kentucky 45 | Florida Atlantic 17

September 29, 2007

Scoring Summary

Florida Atlantic	3	7	0	7	-	17
Kentucky	7	21	7	10	-	45

UK – Lyons 14 pass from Woodson (Seiber kick) ... 7:18 1st qtr.
FAU – Leroy 29 FG ... 0:58 1st qtr.
UK – S. Johnson 27 pass from Woodson (Seiber kick) ... 14:24 2nd qtr.
FAU – Gent 20 pass from Smith (Leroy kick) ... 10:18 2nd qtr.
UK – Lyons 22 pass from Woodson (Seiber kick) ... 5:37 2nd qtr.
UK – Burton 34 pass from Woodson (Seiber kick) ... 1:27 2nd qtr.
UK – Conner 9 pass from Woodson (Seiber kick) ... 4:15 3rd qtr.
UK – Seiber 32 FG ... 9:49 4th qtr.
FAU – Pierre 1 run (Leroy kick) ... 7:12 4th qtr.
UK – M. Johnson 21 interception return (Seiber kick) ... 4:27 4th qtr.

Team Statistics

	FAU	Kentucky
First Downs	20	28
Rush Attempts/Net Rushing Yds.	35/123	40/209
Passing C/A/I	15/28/2	27/35/1
Net Passing Yards	184	305
Offensive Plays	63	75
Total Offense	307	514
Fumbles/Lost	1/1	2/1
Penalties/Yards	6/46	6/90
Punts/Average	4/44.5	2/36.5
Third-Down Conversions	5-of-11	11-of-16
Time of Possession	29:21	30:39

Individual Statistics

Rushing (att-yards-TD)
Kentucky - Little 20-112, Locke 7-53, Dixon 4-16, Grinter 3-15, Conner 1-5, Woodson 2-4, Allen 3-4
Florida Atlantic - Pierre 14-56-1, Clayton 5-34, Rose 3-14, Muniz 3-13, Johnson 1-9, Manley 1-6, Watkins 1-0, Edgecomb 3-(-1), Smith 1-(-8)

Passing (comp-att-int-yards-TD)
Kentucky - Woodson 26-33-1-301-5, Hartline 1-2-0-4-0
Florida Atlantic - Smith 15-25-1-184-1, Clayton 0-2-1-0-0, Gent 0-1-0-0-0

Receiving (rec-yards-TD)
Kentucky - Lyons 8-76-2, Burton 6-100-1, Tamme 5-58, Little 3-24, S. Johnson 2-32-1, Conner 1-9-1, Murphy 1-4, Grinter 1-2
Florida Atlantic - Gent 5-53-1, Harmon 4-63, Johnson 2-23, Grant 2-21, Rose 2-11, Edgecomb 0-13

Tackles
Kentucky - M. Johnson 9, Woodyard 7, McClinton 5, Jarmon 4, Kelley 4

South Carolina 38 | Kentucky 23

October 4, 2007

SCORING SUMMARY

Kentucky	3	7	3	10	-	23
South Carolina	10	7	7	14	-	38

SC – Norwood 2 fumble return (Succop kick) ... 10:53 1st qtr.
UK – Seiber 27 FG ... 5:02 1st qtr.
SC – Succop 29 FG ... 0:57 1st qtr.
UK – Tamme 18 pass from Woodson (Seiber kick) ... 12:13 2nd qtr.
SC – Davis 3 run (Succop kick) ... 0:51 2nd qtr.
SC – Norwood 53 fumble return (Succop kick) ... 13:03 3rd qtr.
UK – Seiber 41 FG ... 10:49 3rd qtr.
UK – Seiber 23 FG ... 14:56 4th qtr.
SC – DiMarco 7 pass from Smelley (Succop kick) ... 11:01 4th qtr.
UK – S. Johnson 6 pass from Woodson (Seiber kick) ... 6:59 4th qtr.
SC – Boyd 27 pass from Smelley (Succop kick) ... 3:28 4th qtr.

TEAM STATISTICS

	Kentucky	USC
First Downs	26	18
Rush Attempts/Net Rushing Yds.	38/157	36/86
Passing C/A/I	23/40/1	17/30/0
Net Passing Yards	227	256
Offensive Plays	78	66
Total Offense	384	342
Fumbles/Lost	5/3	1/1
Penalties/Yards	5/49	6/44
Punts/Average	3/46.3	6/42.0
Third-Down Conversions	3-of-11	6-of-13
Time of Possession	30:03	29:57

INDIVIDUAL STATISTICS

RUSHING (ATT-YARDS-TD)
Kentucky - Little 25-135, Dixon 7-49, Locke 2-22, Woodson 4-(-49)
South Carolina - Davis 17-62-1, Boyd 14-57, Smelley 5-(-33)
PASSING (COMP-ATT-INT-YARDS-TD)
Kentucky - Woodson 23-40-1-227-2
South Carolina - Smelley 17-30-0-256-2
RECEIVING (REC-YARDS-TD)
Kentucky - Burton 7-76, S. Johnson 4-38-1, Lyons 3-31, Dixon 3-24, Little 3-23, Tamme 2-35-1, Conner 1-0
South Carolina - McKinley 5-68, Boyd 3-47-1, Cook 2-36, Brown 2-26, Davis 2-(-2), Saunders 1-50, Lecorn 1-24, DiMarco 1-7-1
TACKLES
Kentucky - Woodyard 7, Lindley 6, R. Williams 6

Kentucky 43 | LSU 37

August 31, 2003

SCORING SUMMARY

LSU	0	17	10	0	7	3	0	-	37
Kentucky	7	7	7	6	7	3	6	-	43

UK – Drake 2 pass from Woodson (Seiber kick) … 2:49 1st qtr.
LSU – Scott 1 run (David kick) … 14:55 2nd qtr.
LSU – David 31 FG … 5:42 2nd qtr.
LSU – Scott 13 run (David kick) … 1:48 2nd qtr.
UK – Woodson 12 run (Seiber kick) … 1:04 2nd qtr.
LSU – Dickson 4 pass from Flynn (David kick) … 9:12 3rd qtr.
LSU – David 30 FG … 3:49 3rd qtr.
UK – Tamme 8 pass from Woodson (Seiber kick) … 1:13 3rd qtr.
UK – Seiber 33 FG … 7:57 4th qtr.
UK – Seiber 27 FG … 4:21 4th qtr.
UK – Locke 1 run (Seiber kick) … 1st OT
LSU – Murphy 2 run (David kick) … 1st OT
LSU – David 38 FG … 2nd OT
UK – Seiber 43 FG … 2nd OT
UK – S. Johnson 7 pass from Woodson (Woodson pass failed) … 3rd OT

TEAM STATISTICS

	LSU	Kentucky
First Downs	22	24
Rush Attempts/Net Rushing Yds.	50/261	41/125
Passing C/A/I	18/37/1	21/38/2
Net Passing Yards	142	250
Offensive Plays	87	79
Total Offense	403	375
Fumbles/Lost	0/0	3/0
Penalties/Yards	12/103	7/62
Punts/Average	4/33.8	3/47.3
Third-Down Conversions	8-of-19	9-of-17
Time of Possession	33:21	26:39

INDIVIDUAL STATISTICS

RUSHING (ATT-YARDS-TD)
Kentucky - Locke 20-64-1, Dixon 17-45, Woodson 3-16-1, team 1-0
LSU - Scott 7-94-2, Hester 18-61, Flynn 10-53, Holliday 5-24, Perrilloux 5-15, Murphy 3-10-1, K. Williams 1-5, Tolliver 1-(-1)

PASSING (COMP-ATT-INT-YARDS-TD)
Kentucky - Woodson 21-38-2-250-3
LSU - Flynn 17-35-1-130-1, Perrilloux 1-2-0-12-0

RECEIVING (REC-YARDS-TD)
Kentucky - S. Johnson 7-134-1, Lyons 6-49, Tamme 3-33-1, Burton 2-13, Dixon 1-18, Drake 1-2-1, Grinter 1-1
LSU - LaFell 4-42, Dickson 4-33-1, Murphy 2-22, J. Mitchell 2-9, Scott 2-6, Byrd 1-13, C. Mitchell 1-8, K. Williams 1-5, Hester 1-4

TACKLES
Kentucky - Woodyard 11, Jarmon 10, Lindley 7, Warford 7, Cobb 7

Florida 45 | Kentucky 37

October 20 2007

SCORING SUMMARY

Florida	14	7	10	14	-	45
Kentucky	7	3	14	13	-	37

UK – Lyons 33 pass from Woodson (Seiber kick) ... 10:31 1st qtr.
UF – Ingram 10 pass from Tebow (Ijjas kick) ... 4:41 1st qtr.
UF – Murphy 66 pass from Tebow (Ijjas kick) ... 0:11 1st qtr.
UK – Seiber 27 FG ... 2:38 2nd qtr.
UF – Hernandez 1 pass from Tebow (Ijjas kick) ... 0:14 2nd qtr.
UF – Caldwell 8 pass from Tebow (Ijjas kick) ... 11:38 3rd qtr.
UK – Tamme 28 pass from Woodson (Seiber kick) ... 8:09 3rd qtr.
UF – Ijjas 21 FG ... 5:48 3rd qtr.
UK – Lyons 50 pass from Woodson (Seiber kick) ... 3:05 3rd qtr.
UF – Harvin 24 run (Ijjas kick) ... 11:57 4th qtr.
UK – Lyons 7 pass from Woodson (Seiber kick) ... 3:35 4th qtr.
UF – Tebow 2 run (Ijjas kick) ... 1:33 4th qtr.
UK – Burton 6 pass from Woodson ... 0:00 4th qtr.

TEAM STATISTICS

	Florida	Kentucky
First Downs	21	29
Rush Attempts/Net Rushing Yds.	37/171	35/97
Passing C/A/I	18/26/0	35/50/0
Net Passing Yards	256	415
Offensive Plays	63	85
Total Offense	427	512
Fumbles/Lost	0/0	0/0
Penalties/Yards	4/25	4/26
Punts/Average	3/45.7	2/34.5
Third-Down Conversions	7-of-11	12-of-21
Time of Possession	27:41	32:19

RUSHING (ATT-YARDS-TD)
Kentucky - Locke 14-76, Dixon 13-59, Woodson 8-(-38)
Florida - Tebow 20-78-1, Harvin 6-47-1, Caldwell 2-19, Moore 6-16, Fayson 3-11

PASSING (COMP-ATT-INT-YARDS-TD)
Kentucky - Woodson 35-50-0-415-5
Florida - Tebow 18-26-0-256-4

RECEIVING (REC-YARDS-TD)
Kentucky - Johnson 8-128, Lyons 8-124-3, Tamme 6-68-1, Burton 5-33-1, Locke 2-36, Smith 2-10, Dixon 2-5, Conner 1-8, Ford 1-3
Florida - Caldwell 6-73-1, Murphy 4-91-1, Harvin 2-50, Ingram 2-20-1, Moore 2-16, James 1-5, Hernandez 1-1-1

TACKLES
Kentucky - Kelley 10, Woodyard 8, Lindley 7, M. Johnson 6, Lewis 6, Cobb 6

Mississippi State 31 | Kentucky 14

October 27, 2007

SCORING SUMMARY

Mississippi State	7	7	10	7	-	31
Kentucky	7	0	7	0	-	14

MS – Husband 11 pass from Carroll (Carlson kick) … 9:08 1st qtr.
UK – S. Johnson 18 pass from Woodson (Seiber kick) … 5:17 1st qtr.
MS – Dixon 1 pass from Carroll (Carlson kick) … 13:36 2nd qtr.
MS – Carlson 31 FG … 12:27 3rd qtr.
MS – Dixon 1 run (Carlson kick) … 8:16 3rd qtr.
UK – S. Johnson 37 pass from Woodson (Seiber kick) … 5:15 3rd qtr.
MS – Ducre 34 run (Carlson kick) … 8:15 4th qtr.

TEAM STATISTICS

	MSU	Kentucky
First Downs	22	19
Rush Attempts/Net Rushing Yds.	51/200	27/89
Passing C/A/I	17/28/0	24/42/3
Net Passing Yards	152	230
Offensive Plays	79	69
Total Offense	352	319
Fumbles/Lost	5/1	4/3
Penalties/Yards	2/20	5/21
Punts/Average	6/41.3	2/37.0
Third-Down Conversions	7-of-15	6-of-15
Time of Possession	34:09	25:51

INDIVIDUAL STATISTICS

RUSHING (ATT-YARDS-TD)
Kentucky - Locke 11-46, Allen 6-30, A. Smith 4-22, Woodson 5-0, Masthay 1-(-9)
Mississippi State - Ducre 19-119-1, Dixon 25-75-1, Burks 1-3, Carroll 5-3
PASSING (COMP-ATT-INT-YARDS-TD)
Kentucky - Woodson 24-42-3-230-2
Mississippi State - 17-28-0-152-2
RECEIVING (REC-YARDS-TD)
Kentucky - Tamme 6-46, Ford 4-34, S. Johnson 3-69-2, Lyons 3-48, Locke 3-16, A. Smith 3-9, Allen 2
Mississippi State - Ducre 5-30, Husband 2-33-1, Bell 2-25, Burks, 2-21, Hoskins 2-18, Dixon 2-1-1, Butler 1-15, Long 1-9
TACKLES
Kentucky - Woodyard 8, Lindley 7, Kelley 6, R. Williams 5, Cobb 5

Kentucky 27 | Vanderbilt 20

November 10, 2007

SCORING SUMMARY

Kentucky	3	10	7	7	-	27
Vanderbilt	0	13	0	7	-	20

UK – Seiber 38 FG ... 1:38 1st qtr.
VU – Walker 14 pass from Adams (Hahnfeldt kick) ... 8:46 2nd qtr.
UK – S. Johnson 55 pass from Woodson (Seiber kick) ... 7:12 2nd qtr.
VU – Bradford 30 pass from Adams (Hahnfeldt kick failed) ... 4:39 3nd qtr.
UK – Seiber 48 FG ... 0:04 2nd qtr.
UK – Grinter 1 run (Seiber kick) ... 9:56 3rd qtr.
VU – Adams 7 run (Hahnfeldt kick) ... 7:31 4th qtr.
UK – Locke 4 run (Seiber kick) ... 5:58 4th qtr.

TEAM STATISTICS

	Kentucky	Vanderbilt
First Downs	19	30
Rush Attempts/Net Rushing Yds.	37/129	48/239
Passing C/A/I	17/29/0	20/34/0
Net Passing Yards	222	193
Offensive Plays	66	82
Total Offense	351	432
Fumbles/Lost	3/1	3/1
Penalties/Yards	13/122	8/6
Punts/Average	5/39.6	4/37.8
Third-Down Conversions	7-of-14	7-of-17
Time of Possession	24:08	35:32

INDIVIDUAL STATISTICS

RUSHING (ATT-YARDS-TD)
Kentucky - Little 15-70, Locke 12-50-1, Woodson 8-9, Grinter 1-1, team 1-(-1)
Vanderbilt - Jackson-Garrison 11-83, Jennings 12-70, Hawkins 7-50, Bennett 5-22, Adams 12-15-1, Walker 1-(-1).

PASSING (COMP-ATT-INT-YARDS-TD)
Kentucky - Woodson 17-28-0-222-1, team 0-1-0-0-0
Vanderbilt - Adams 20-31-0-193-2, Bennett 0-2-0-0-0, team 0-1-0-0-0

RECEIVING (REC-YARDS-TD)
Kentucky - Tamme 4-50, Little 4-49, Burton 4-(-5), Johnson 2-88-1, Lyons 2-14, Locke 1-26
Vanderbilt - Bennett 8-69, Smith 5-49, Jackson-Garrison 2-16, Jennings 2-6, Bradford 1-30-1, Walker 1-14-1, Hawkins 1-9

TACKLES
Kentucky - Harrison 10, Woodyard 9, Cobb 7, Warford 6, Lumpkin 6, Lindley 6, M. Johnson 6

Georgia 24 | Kentucky 13

November 17, 2007

SCORING SUMMARY

Kentucky	10	0	3	0	-	13
Georgia	0	7	14	3	-	24

UK – Burton 36 pass from Woodson (Seiber kick) ... 7:11 1st qtr.
UK – Seiber 31 FG ... 0:57 1st qtr.
GA – Moreno 1 run (Coutu kick) ... 0:40 2nd qtr.
GA – Brown 1 run (Coutu kick) ... 10:49 3rd qtr.
GA – Stafford 10 run (Coutu kick) ... 5:40 3rd qtr.
UK – Seiber 44 FG ... 4:27 3rd qtr.
GA – Coutu 46 FG ... 2:09 4th qtr.

TEAM STATISTICS

	Kentucky	Georgia
First Downs	19	22
Rush Attempts/Net Rushing Yds.	29/29	49/184
Passing C/A/I	24/42/1	12/22/2
Net Passing Yards	268	99
Offensive Plays	71	71
Total Offense	297	283
Fumbles/Lost	0/0	2/2
Penalties/Yards	7/37	4/30
Punts/Average	7/30.3	4/39.0
Third-Down Conversions	5-of-16	9-of-15
Time of Possession	25:45	34:15

INDIVIDUAL STATISTICS

RUSHING (ATT-YARDS-TD)
Kentucky - Little 16-32, Locke 5-28, Dixon 1-5, Woodson 7-(-36)
Georgia - Moreno 22-124-1, Brown 22-73-1, Stafford 3-(-11)-1

PASSING (COMP-ATT-INT-YARDS-TD)
Kentucky - Woodson 24-41-1-268-1, team 0-1-0-0-0
Georgia - Stafford 12-22-2-99-0

RECEIVING (REC-YARDS-TD)
Kentucky - S. Johnson 8-88, Tamme 6-80, Little 5-25, Burton 3-63-1, Lyons 2-12
Georgia - Massaquoi 4-49, Bailey 3-25, Wilson 3-15, Henderson 1-8, Figgins 1-2

TACKLES
Kentucky - Woodyard 12, Peters 6, Harrison 5, Jarmon 4

Tennessee 52 | Kentucky 50

November 24, 2007

SCORING SUMMARY

Tennessee	14	10	7	0	7	0	6	8	-	52
Kentucky	0	7	14	10	7	0	6	6	-	50

UT – Foster 65 pass from Ainge (Lincoln kick) ... 14:44 1st qtr.
UT – Taylor 18 pass from Ainge (Lincoln kick) ... 4:18 1st qtr.
UK – S. Johnson 17 pass from Woodson (Seiber kick) ... 12:12 2nd qtr.
UT – Lincoln 45 FG ... 8:57 2nd qtr.
UT – Hancock 15 pass from Ainge (Lincoln kick) ... 0:17 2nd qtr.
UK – Lyons 5 pass from Woodson (Seiber kick) ... 9:34 3rd qtr.
UT – J. Cottam 2 pass from Ainge (Lincoln kick) ... 1:31 3rd qtr.
UK – Tamme 2 pass from Woodson (Seiber kick) ... 0:01 3rd qtr.
UK – S. Johnson 8 pass from Woodson (Seiber kick) ... 6:11 4th qtr.
UK – Seiber 20 FG ... 0:00 4th qtr.
UK – Burton 8 pass from Woodson (Seiber kick) ... 1st OT
UT – Jones 10 pass from Ainge (Lincoln kick) ... 1st OT
UK – Burton 11 pass from Woodson (Woodson pass intercepted) ... 3rd OT
UT – Rogers 13 pass from Ainge (Foster rush failed) ... 3rd OT
UT – Hancock 40 pass from Ainge (Rogers pass from Ainge) ... 4th OT
UK – Locke 2 run (Woodson rush failed) ... 4th OT

TEAM STATISTICS

	Tennessee	Kentucky
First Downs	24	37
Rush Attempts/Net Rushing Yds.	37/123	48/134
Passing C/A/I	28/45/3	39/62/2
Net Passing Yards	397	430
Offensive Plays	82	110
Total Offense	520	564
Fumbles/Lost	1/0	2/1
Penalties/Yards	8/99	5/40
Punts/Average	5/40.0	7/36.1
Third-Down Conversions	6-of-15	10-of-20
Time of Possession	26:28	33:32

INDIVIDUAL STATISTICS

RUSHING (ATT-YARDS-TD)
Kentucky - Little 24-77, Locke 6-46-1, Grinter 4-20, Conner 1-4, Masthay 1-2, Dixon 1-2, Lyons 1-0, Woodson 10-(-17)
Tennessee - Foster 27-118, Hardesty 8-26, Ainge 2-(-21)

PASSING (COMP-ATT-INT-YARDS-TD)
Kentucky - Woodson 39-62-2-430-6
Tennessee - Ainge 28-45-3-397-7

RECEIVING (REC-YARDS-TD)
Kentucky - Little 11-108, Tamme 9-104-1, Burton 8-83-2, S. Johnson 6-86-2, Lyons 4-42-1, Dixon 1-7
Tennessee - Foster 9-98-1, Taylor 6-103-1, B. Cottam 2-66, Hancock 2-55-2, Briscoe 2-25, Jones 2-20-1, Rogers 2-17-1, Brown 2-11, J. Cottam 1-2-1

TACKLES
Kentucky - Woodyard 10, Lindley 8, Harrison 7, Jarmon 6

Kentucky 35 | Florida State 28

2007 Music City Bowl, December 31, 2007

SCORING SUMMARY

Kentucky	7	7	14	7	-	35
Florida State	7	7	0	14	-	28

UK – Tamme 14 pass from Woodson (Seiber kick) ... 10:39 1st qtr.
FSU – Weatherford 6 run (Cismesia kick) ... 1:49 1st qtr.
UK – S. Johnson 13 pass from Woodson (Seiber kick) ... 8:28 2nd qtr.
FSU – Carter 24 interception return (Cismesia kick) ... 3:28 2nd qtr.
UK – Little 2 pass from Woodson (Seiber kick) ... 6:49 3rd qtr.
UK – Dixon 4 run (Seiber kick) ... 0:04 3rd qtr.
FSU – Weatherford 1 run (Cismesia kick) ... 8:02 4th qtr.
UK – S. Johnson 38 pass from Woodson (Seiber kick) ... 5:19 4th qtr.
FSU – Carr 7 pass from Weatherford (Cismesia kick) ... 2:14 4th qtr.

TEAM STATISTICS

	Kentucky	Florida State
First Downs	29	22
Rush Attempts/Net Rushing Yds.	36-143	33-204
Passing C/A/I	32/50/1	22/50/2
Net Passing Yards	358	276
Offensive Plays	86	83
Total Offense	501	480
Fumbles/Lost	5-3	1-0
Penalties/Yards	7/45	10/102
Punts/Average	5/39.8	6/41.7
Third-Down Conversions	6-of-14	6-of-16
Time of Possession	30:25	29:35

INDIVIDUAL STATISTICS

RUSHING (ATT-YARDS-TD)
Kentucky - Little 28-152, Dixon 4-17-1, Woodson 4-(-26)
Florida State - Smith 17-156, Weatherford 12-48-2, Parker 2-1, Holloway 1-0, team 1-(-1)
PASSING (COMP-ATT-INT-YARDS-TD)
Kentucky - Woodson 32-50-1-358-4
Florida State - Weatherford 22-48-2-276-1, Parker 0-1-0-0-0, team 0-1-0-0-0
RECEIVING (REC-YARDS-TD)
Kentucky - Little 8-50-1, S. Johnson 7-124-2, Burton 7-56, Lyons 5-78, Tamme 3-35-1, Dixon 1-8, Grinter 1-7
Florida State - Parker 8-105, Carr 6-99-1, Fagg 5-51, Owens 2-10, Smith 1-11
TACKLES
Kentucky - Woodyard 15, Kelley 6, Moore 6, Warford 5, McClinton 5

Louisville 2 | Kentucky 27

August 31, 2008

SCORING SUMMARY

Kentucky	0	10	0	17	-	27
Louisville	0	0	0	2	-	2

UK – Seiber 21 FG … 9:53 2nd qtr.
UK – A. Cobb 28 fumble return (Seiber kick) … 5:58 2nd qtr.
UL – TEAM safety … 14:17 4th qtr.
UK – Seiber 25 FG … 6:37 3rd qtr.
UK – Dixon 7 run (Seiber kick) … 6:21 4th qtr.
UK – Pryor 72 fumble return (Seiber kick) … 2:46 4th qtr.

TEAM STATISTICS

	KENTUCKY	LOUISVILLE
First Downs	13	16
Rush Attempts/Net Rushing Yds.	33/63	29/53
Passing C/A/I	16/31/0	20/43/3
Net Passing Yards	147	152
Offensive Plays	64	72
Total Offense	210	205
Fumbles/Lost	3/1	3/2
Penalties/Yards	9/67	6/61
Punts/Average	7/42.3	9/39.7
Third-Down Conversions	4-of-16	5-of-16
Time of Possession	32:40	27:20

RUSHING (ATT-YARDS-TD)
Kentucky – Dixon 12-27-1, Locke 10-25, Allen 4-12, A. Smith 2-10, R. Cobb 1-2, Conner 1-2, team 1-(-2), Hartline 2-(-13)
Louisville – Anderson 12-31, Powell 6-16, Bolen 6-13, Beaumont 1-12, Cantwell 4-(-19)

PASSING (COMP-ATT-INT-YARDS-TD)
Kentucky – Hartline 16-31-0-147-0
Louisville – Cantwell 20-43-3-152-0

RECEIVING (REC-YARDS-TD)
Kentucky – R. Cobb 3-31, Lyons 2-25, Lanxter 2-17, Adams 2-17, Drake 2-14, Dixon 2-7, Conner 1-20, McCaskill 1-10, Locke 1-6
Louisville – Beaumont 9-77, Chichester 3-45, Powell 3-(-2), Robinson 2-12, Nochta 2-9, Burns 1-11

TACKLES
Kentucky – Johnson 5, Kelley 5, Peters 4, McClinton 4, McAtee 4

Kentucky 38 | Norfolk State 3

September 6, 2008

SCORING SUMMARY

Norfolk State	0	3	0	0	-	3
Kentucky	7	14	3	14	-	38

UK – R. Cobb 18 run (Seiber kick) ... 3:29 1st qtr.
UK – R. Cobb 1 run (Seiber kick) ... 11:52 2nd qtr.
UK – Lyons 14 pass from R. Cobb (Seiber kick) ... 2:54 2nd qtr.
NSU – Castellat 24 FG ... 0:19 2nd qtr
UK – Seiber 23 FG ... 11:22 3rd qtr.
UK – Locke 68 run (Seiber kick) ... 14:45 4th qtr.
UK – Allen 3 run (Seiber kick) ... 8:35 4th qtr.

TEAM STATISTICS

	NORFOLK STATE	KENTUCKY
First Downs	8	22
Rush Attempts/Net Rushing Yds.	29/67	44/297
Passing C/A/I	9/24/1	15/26/1
Net Passing Yards	97	147
Offensive Plays	53	70
Total Offense	165	445
Fumbles/Lost	1/0	2/1
Penalties/Yards	6/53	3/20
Punts/Average	9/41.0	4/44.8
Third-Down Conversions	1-of-13	4-of-12
Time of Possession	27:38	32:22

RUSHING (ATT-YARDS-TD)
Kentucky – Locke 5-96-1, Allen 7-71-1, R. Cobb 8-49-2, A. Smith 7-38, Dixon 6-16, Bowland 6-16, Conner 2-10, Hartline 3-2
Norfolk State – Branche 14-47, Cameron 3-14, Cotton 3-8, Hedgeman 2-3, Brown 7-(-5)

PASSING (COMP-ATT-INT-YARDS-TD)
Kentucky – R. Cobb 6-11-1-87-1, Hartline 9-15-0-60-0
Norfolk State – Brown 9-24-1-97-0

RECEIVING (REC-YARDS-TD)
Kentucky – Lyons 5-51-1, Lanxter 2-41, McCaskill 2-17, Dixon 3-10, Locke 1-10, Allen 1-10, Adeyemi 1-8
Norfolk State – Wicker 5-69, Johnson 2-19, Dickerson 1-7, Branche 1-2

TACKLES
Kentucky – Lindley 6, Jarmon 4, McAtee 4, Harrison 4, Lumpkin 4

Kentucky 20 | Middle Tennessee 14

September 13, 2008

SCORING SUMMARY

Middle Tennessee	7	0	7	0	-	14
Kentucky	7	3	0	10	-	20

MT – Gee 62 pass from Craddock (Gendreau kick) ... 9:21 1st qtr.
UK – Grinter 1 pass from Hartline (Seiber kick) ... 3:48 1st qtr.
UK – Seiber 40 FG ... 4:11 2nd qtr.
MT – Beyah 22 pass from Craddock (Gendreau kick) ... 7:26 3rd qtr.
UK – Locke 6 pass from Hartline (Seiber kick) ... 12:20 4th qtr.
UK – Seiber 25 FG ... 6:37 4th qtr.

TEAM STATISTICS

	MIDDLE TENNESSEE	KENTUCKY
First Downs	13	21
Rush Attempts/Net Rushing Yds.	23/31	35/102
Passing C/A/I	21/37/1	28/47/0
Net Passing Yards	352	254
Offensive Plays	60	83
Total Offense	383	356
Fumbles/Lost	1/1	1/1
Penalties/Yards	6/51	6/31
Punts/Average	8/43.1	6/44.5
Third-Down Conversions	5-of-15	7-of-19
Time of Possession	24:54	35:06

RUSHING (ATT-YARDS-TD)

Kentucky – A. Smith 9-36, Locke 10-35, Dixon 11-28, Hartline 4-5, Allen 1-(-2)
Middle Tennessee – Tanner 11-26, Craddock 7-9, Gee 4-7, McDonald 1-(-11)

PASSING (COMP-ATT-INT-YARDS-TD)

Kentucky – Hartline 28-47-0-254-2, team 0-1-0-0-0
Middle Tennessee – Craddock 21-37-1-352-2

RECEIVING (REC-YARDS-TD)

Kentucky – Lyons 12-79, Drake 4-82, Lanxter 3-31, Grinter 2-21-1, Locke 2-12-1, Dixon 2- (-3), Roark Adeyemi 1-9, Conner 1-7
Middle Tennessee – King 6-82, Beyah 5-117-1, Gee 3-106-1, Tanner 1-16, McClover 1-9, McDonald 1-7 Honeycutt 1-6, Delle Donne 1-4, Caldwell 1-3, Kyles 1-2

TACKLES

Kentucky – Johnson 9, Kelley 7, McClinton 6, McAtee 4

Kentucky 41 | Western Kentucky 3

September 27, 2008

SCORING SUMMARY

Western Kentucky	0	3	0	0	-	3
Kentucky	3	14	14	10	-	41

UK – Tydlacka 45 FG ... 10:56 1st qtr.
UK – Dixon 1 run (Seiber kick) ... 11:43 2nd qtr.
WKU – Siewert 50 FG ... 3:07 2nd qtr.
UK – Locke 100 kickoff return (Seiber kick) ... 2:52 2nd qtr.
UK – Smith 35 run (Seiber kick) ... 13:21 3rd qtr.
UK – Allen 2 pass from Hartline (Seiber kick) ... 1:49 3rd qtr
UK – Dixon 2 run (Seiber kick) ... 10:16 4th qtr
UK – Tydlacka 33 FG ... 5:35 4th qtr.

TEAM STATISTICS

	WKU	KENTUCKY
First Downs	8	23
Rush Attempts/Net Rushing Yds.	37/142	38/216
Passing C/A/I	6/14/0	21/32/1
Net Passing Yards	15	182
Offensive Plays	51	70
Total Offense	157	398
Fumbles/Lost	2/1	0/0
Penalties/Yards	1/15	5/35
Punts/Average	8/36.8	4/33.8
Third-Down Conversions	3-of-15	7-of-13
Time of Possession	27:34	32:26

RUSHING (ATT-YARDS-TD)
Kentucky – A. Smith 6-67-1, Dixon 13-45-2, Allen 7-41, Locke 8-34, Hartline 2-17, Adeyemi 1-10, Conner
Western Kentucky – Rainey 9-99, Wolke 4-15, Hayden 3-10, Black 15-8, McCloud 2-5, Booker 4-5

PASSING (COMP-ATT-INT-YARDS-TD)
Kentucky – Hartline 19-30-1-172-1, Fidler 2-2-0-10-0
Western Kentucky – Black 3-10-0-8-0, Wolke 3-4-0-7-0

RECEIVING (REC-YARDS-TD)
Kentucky – Lyons 6-34, Conner 3-32, Boyd 3-16, Locke 2-23, Adams 2-22, Allen 2-13-1,
Grinter 1-23, Drake 1-13, A. Smith 1-6
Western Kentucky – Hayden 2-(-1), Jeter 1-8, Graves 1-6, Savko 1-6, Cooper 1-(-4)

TACKLES
Kentucky – Kelley 6, Pryor 6, Peters 5, Jenkins 5

Alabama 17 | Kentucky 14

October 4, 2008

SCORING SUMMARY

Kentucky	0	0	7	7	-	14
Alabama	14	0	0	3	-	17

UA – Coffee 78 run (Tiffin kick) ... 9:48 1st qtr.
UA – McClain 4 fumble return (Tiffin kick) ... 1:02 1st qtr.
UK – Lyons 26 pass from Hartline (Seiber kick) ... 5:49 3rd qtr.
UA – Tiffin 24 FG ... 2:12 4th qtr.
UK – Ford 48 pass from Hartline (Seiber kick) ... 0:40 4th qtr.

TEAM STATISTICS	ALABAMA	KENTUCKY
First Downs	15	12
Rush Attempts/Net Rushing Yds.	49/282	20/35
Passing C/A/I	7/17/1	20/42/1
Net Passing Yards	106	241
Offensive Plays	66	62
Total Offense	388	276
Fumbles/Lost	3/2	1/1
Penalties/Yards	10/92	9/58
Punts/Average	6/43.2	10/43.2
Third-Down Conversions	5-of-16	5-of-17
Time of Possession	35:45	24:15

RUSHING (ATT-YARDS-TD)
Kentucky – Locke 6-28, Smith 7-18, Dixon 3-10, Allen 1-(-2), Hartline 3-(-19)
Alabama – Coffee 25-218-1, Ingram 11-66, Upchurch 5-19, Maze 1-1, team 1-(-2), Wilson 6-(-20)
PASSING (COMP-ATT-INT-YARDS-TD)
Kentucky – Hartline 20-42-1-241-2
Alabama – Wilson 7-17-1-106-0
RECEIVING (REC-YARDS-TD)
Kentucky – Locke 8-81, Lyons 6-63-1, Grinter 3-29, Adams 2-20, Ford 1-48-1
Alabama – Jones 3-52, Walker 2-30, Coffee 1-15, Stover 1-9
TACKLES
Kentucky – Kelley 13, Williams 8, Harrison 7, Maxwell 5, McClinton 5, Schwindel 5

South Carolina 24 | Kentucky 17

October 11, 2008

SCORING SUMMARY

South Carolina	7	7	0	10	-	24
Kentucky	7	10	0	0	-	17

UK – Lindley 28 interception return (Seiber kick)…4:33 1st qtr.
USC – McKinley 16 pass from Smelley (Succop kick)…4:13 1st qtr.
USC – Munnerlyn 81 blocked FG return (Succop kick)…13:36 2nd qtr.
UK – Dixon 2 run (Seiber kick)…6:23 2nd qtr.
UK – Tydlacka 51 FG …0:04 2nd qtr.
USC – Succop 42 FG…11:58 4th qtr.
USC – Saunders 7 pass from Garcia (Succop kick)…7:08 4th qtr.

TEAM STATISTICS

	SOUTH CAROLINA	KENTUCKY
First Downs	16	13
Rush Attempts/Net Rushing Yds.	34/74	22/62
Passing C/A/I	19/37/2	24/44/2
Net Passing Yards	274	156
Offensive Plays	71	66
Total Offense	348	218
Fumbles/Lost	4/2	1/0
Penalties/Yards	5/47	2/20
Punts/Average	2/43.5	8/45.2
Third-Down Conversions	8-of-17	1-of-16
Time of Possession	30:43	29:18

RUSHING (ATT-YARDS-TD)
Kentucky – Locke 15-51, R. Cobb 2-9, A. Smith 2-4, Dixon 1-2-1, Hartline 2-(-4)
South Carolina – Davis 14-27, Garcia 6-22, Smelley 4-16, Wallace 5-10, McKinley 2-2, Baker 1-0, team 2-(-3)

PASSING (COMP-ATT-INT-YARDS-TD)
Kentucky – Hartline 23-43-2-152-0, R. Cobb 1-1-0-4-0
South Carolina – Smelley 9-23-2-105-1, Garcia 10-14-0-169-1

RECEIVING (REC-YARDS-TD)
Kentucky – Locke 8-57, R. Cobb 8-53, Lyons 2-12, Adeyemi 2-7, Boyd 1-14, Drake 1-12, Grinter 1-3, Conner 1-(-2)
USC – McKinley 7-88-1, Barnes 4-88, Cook 4-36, Saunders 2-20-1, Hills 1-24, Davis 1-180

TACKLES
Kentucky – M. Johnson 12, Moore 5, McAtee 4, Pryor 4, Kelley 4, Peters 4, Oninku 4, Lumpkin 4

Kentucky 21 | Arkansas 20

October 18, 2008

SCORING SUMMARY

Arkansas	7	7	3	3	-	20
Kentucky	0	0	7	14	-	21

AR – M. Smith 2 run (Haddock kick)...8:09 1st qtr.
AR – M. Smith 22 pass from Dick (Haddock kick)...1:15 2nd qtr.
AR – Haddock 19 FG...9:45 3rd qtr.
UK – A. Smith 71 pass from Hartline (Seiber kick)...8:50 3rd qtr.
AR – Haddock 23 FG...10:00 4th qtr.
UK – R. Cobb 32 pass from Hartline (Seiber kick)...4:15 4th qtr.
UK – R. Cobb 21 pass from Hartline (Seiber kick)...2:21 4th qtr.

TEAM STATISTICS	ARKANSAS	KENTUCKY
First Downs	21	15
Rush Attempts/Net Rushing Yds.	51/236	28/88
Passing C/A/I	11/29/2	19/35/2
Net Passing Yards	94	284
Offensive Plays	80	63
Total Offense	330	372
Fumbles/Los	2/2	5/2
Penalties/Yards	13/102	5/53
Punts/Average	6/34.3	4/43.2
Third-Down Conversions	6-of-17	5-of-13
Time of Possession	36:01	23:59

RUSHING (ATT-YARDS-TD)
Kentucky – Allen 7-46, Locke 9-34, A. Smith 3-6, Dixon 1-5, Conner 1-1, Hartline 2-1, R. Cobb 3-(-2), team 2-(-3)
Arkansas – M. Smith 35-192-1, Dick 7-28, Curtis 9-16
PASSING (COMP-ATT-INT-YARDS-TD)
Kentucky – Hartline 17-32-2-239-3, R. Cobb 2-3-0-45-0
Arkansas – Dick 11-29-2-94-1
RECEIVING (REC-YARDS-TD)
Kentucky – A. Smith 5-108-1, R. Cobb 5-73-2, McCaskill 3-30, Adeyemi 2-18, Drake 1-37, Allen 1-9, Locke 1-6, Ford 1-3
Arkansas – M. Smith 3-33-1, Adams 2-24, Crawford 2-21, Davie 2-14, Salters 1-5, Dick 1-(-3)
TACKLES
Kentucky – M. Johnson 15, Kelley 15, McClinton 9, Lentz 7, J. Williams 6

Florida 63 | Kentucky 5

October 25, 2008

SCORING SUMMARY

Kentucky	0	3	0	2	-	5
Florida	28	14	14	7	-	63

UF – Tebow 3 run (Phillips kick)...11:01 1st qtr.
UF – James 1 run (Phillips kick)...9:22 1st qtr.
UF – Harvin 16 run (Phillips kick)...6:44 1st qtr.
UF – Harvin 33 pass from Tebow (Phillips kick)...3:15 1st qtr.
UF – Demps 61 pass from Tebow (Phillips kick)...11:26 2nd qtr.
UK – Seiber 27 FG...5:03 2nd qtr.
UF – Tebow 3 run (Phillips kick)...0:26 2nd qtr.
UF – Black 40 interception return (Phillips kick)...14:51 3rd qtr.
UF – K. Moore 1 run (Phillips kick)...2:59 3rd qtr.
UF – Nelson 38 pass from J. Brantley (Phillips kick)...11:45 4th qtr.
UK – Safety, muffed punt snap, ball kicked out of end zone...4:07 4th qtr.

TEAM STATISTICS

	KENTUCKY	FLORIDA
First Downs	17	23
Rush Attempts/Net Rushing Yds.	33/141	41/214
Passing C/A/I	17/36/1	13/18/1
Net Passing Yards	127	232
Offensive Plays	69	59
Total Offense	268	446
Fumbles/Lost	0/0	2/0
Penalties/Yards	3/30	7/62
Punts/Average	7/36.1	1/41.0
Third-Down Conversions	5-of-17	4-of-8
Time of Possession	32:17	27:43

RUSHING (ATT-YARDS-TD)

Kentucky – R. Cobb 9-52, Allen 6-32, Dixon 6-27, Nance 2-16, A. Smith 8-11, Hartline 1-2, Bowland 1-1
Florida – Demps 7-50, Tebow 9-48-2, K. Moore 8-39-1, Rainey 7-36, Harvin 2-22-1, Brantley 2-14, James 2-9-1, Brown 3-9, team 1-(-13)

PASSING (COMP-ATT-INT-YARDS-TD)

Kentucky – R. Cobb 9-18-0-78-0, Hartline 7-16-1-33-0
Florida – Tebow 11-15-1-180-2, Brantley 2-3-0-52-1

RECEIVING (REC-YARDS-TD)

Kentucky – Dixon 5-19, Conner 3-26, McCaskill 2-22, R. Cobb 2-7, Adams 1-16, Boyd 1-16, Bogue 1-8, Adeyemi 1-8, Ford 1-5
Florida – Demps 4-67-1, Murphy 2-21, Nelson 1-38-1, Harvin 1-33-1, C. Moore 1-25, Rainey 1-16, K. Moore 1-14, Thompson 1-9, James 1-9

TACKLES

Kentucky – Kelley 11, Jenkins 6, Maxwell 5, Moore 4, Jones 4

Kentucky 14 | Mississippi State 13

November 1, 2008

SCORING SUMMARY

Kentucky	0	0	14	0	-	14
Mississippi State	7	0	0	6	-	13

MSU – McRae 29 pass from T. Lee (Carlson kick)…7:10 1st qtr.
UK – R. Cobb 5 run (Seiber kick)…11:08 3rd qtr.
UK – Grinter 3 pass from R. Cobb (Seiber kick)…2:42 3rd qtr.
MSU – Stallworth 10 pass from T. Lee (Carlson kick blocked)…13:57 4th qtr.

TEAM STATISTICS

	KENTUCKY	MSU
First Downs	17	18
Rush Attempts/Net Rushing Yds.	36/128	27/43
Passing C/A/I	16/30/1	26/42/1
Net Passing Yards	146	261
Offensive Plays	66	69
Total Offense	274	304
Fumbles/Lost	1/1	0/0
Penalties/Yards	7/64	5/66
Punts/Average	7/42.9	6/46.0
Third-Down Conversions	3-of-14	5-of-16
Time of Possession	28:38	31:22

RUSHING (ATT-YARDS-TD)
Kentucky – T. Dixon 12-66, R. Cobb 12-31-1, A. Smith 5-18, Hartline 2-12, Allen 2-3, Nance 1-2, team 2-(-4)
Mississippi State – A. Dixon 15-48, Clark 1-19, Stallworth 2-7, Ducre 1-5, team 1-(-2), Lee 7-(-34)
PASSING (COMP-ATT-INT-YARDS-TD)
Kentucky – Hartline 9-17-0-90-0, R. Cobb 7-13-1-56-1
Mississippi State – Lee 26-42-1-261-2
RECEIVING (REC-YARDS-TD)
Kentucky – R. Cobb 3-33, Lanxter 3-22, A. Smith 2-24, McCaskill 2-18, Drake 1-13, Adeyemi 1-8, Allen 1-7, Dixon 1-6, Grinter 1-3-1, Conner 1-2
Mississippi State – Stallworth 8-71-1, McRae 6-73-1, Smith 4-25, Bell 3-35, Henderson 2-45, Clark 2-11, Dixon 1-1
TACKLES
Kentucky – M. Johnson 9, McClinton 7, Lindley 6, Jones 6, A. Cobb 5

Georgia 42 | Kentucky 38

November 8, 2008

SCORING SUMMARY

Georgia	14	7	7	14	-	42
Kentucky	7	7	10	14	-	38

UGA – Massaquoi 29 pass from Stafford (Walsh kick)...13:11 1st qtr.
UGA – Moreno 6 run (Walsh kick)...7:38 1st qtr.
UK – Dixon 3 run (Seiber kick)...1:14 1st qtr.
UK – R. Cobb 2 run (Seiber kick)...7:15 2nd qtr.
UGA – Chapas 11 pass from Stafford (Walsh kick)...4:48 2nd qtr.
UK – Seiber 40 FG...9:19 3rd qtr.
UK – R. Cobb 9 run (Seiber kick)...7:31 3rd qtr.
UGA – Moreno 20 run (Walsh kick)...3:21 3rd qtr.
UK – Dixon 14 run (Seiber kick)...14:26 4th qtr.
UGA – Moreno 18 run (Walsh kick)...13:49 4th qtr.
UK – R. Cobb 1 run (Seiber kick)...12:15 4th qtr.
UGA – Green 11 pass from Stafford (Walsh kick)...1:54 4th qtr.

TEAM STATISTICS

	GEORGIA	KENTUCKY
First Downs	17	20
Rush Attempts/Net Rushing Yds.	30/144	56/226
Passing C/A/I	17/27/0	12/20/1
Net Passing Yards	376	105
Offensive Plays	57	76
Total Offense	520	331
Fumbles/Lost	2/2	3/1
Penalties/Yards	5/58	3/40
Punts/Average	4/26.0	4/42.2
Third-Down Conversions	4-of-10	8-of-17
Time of Possession	25:10	34:50

RUSHING (ATT-YARDS-TD)
Kentucky – R. Cobb 18-82-3, T. Dixon 18-61-2, A. Smith 11-60, Conner 7-26, Allen 1-0, Adeyemi 1-(-3)
Georgia – Moreno 22-123-3, Green 1-28, Samuel 1-2, team 2-(-2), Stafford 4-(-7)

PASSING (COMP-ATT-INT-YARDS-TD)
Kentucky – R. Cobb 12-20-1-105-0
Georgia – Stafford 17-27-0-376-3

RECEIVING (REC-YARDS-TD)
Kentucky – Lanxter 4-25, Dixon 2-24, Adeyemi 2-11, Adams 2-9, Grinter 1-29, A. Smith 1-7
Georgia – Massaquoi 8-191-1, Moreno 3-40, Moore 2-68, Green 2-53-1, Durham 1-13, Chapas 1-11-

TACKLES
Kentucky – M. Johnson 8, Kelley 6, A. Cobb 6, Moore 4, Jarmon 4, Jenkins 4

Vanderbilt 31 | Kentucky 24

November 15, 2008

SCORING SUMMARY

Vanderbilt	14	10	0	7	-	31
Kentucky	0	7	10	7	-	24

VU – Moore 25 pass from C. Nickson (Hahnfeldt kick)...9:31 1st qtr.
VU – Moore 18 pass from C. Nickson (Hahnfeldt kick)...2:00 1st qtr.
UK – Jones 57 blocked FG return (Seiber kick)...8:45 2nd qtr.
VU – Barden 11 pass from C. Nickson (Hahnfeldt kick)...2:49 2nd qtr.
VU – Hahnfeldt 39 FG...0:02 2nd qtr.
UK – Dixon 3 run (Seiber kick)...10:00 3rd qtr.
UK – Seiber 25 FG...2:37 3rd qtr.
VU – Hawkins 4 run (Hahnfeldt kick)...14:14 4th qtr.
UK – R. Cobb 10 run (Seiber kick)...8:22 4th qtr.

TEAM STATISTICS	VANDERBILT	KENTUCKY
First Downs	21	12
Rush Attempts/Net Rushing Yds.	43/213	24/97
Passing C/A/I	15/27/0	11/26/2
Net Passing Yards	155	144
Offensive Plays	70	50
Total Offense	368	241
Fumbles/Lost	5/1	1/0
Penalties/Yards	4/41	5/5
Punts/Average	4/42.0	4/41.8
Third-Down Conversions	7-of-15	1-of-10
Time of Possession	39:18	20:4

RUSHING (ATT-YARDS-TD)
Kentucky – R. Cobb 15-72-1, Masthay 1-17, Dixon 6-6-1, Adeyemi 1-5, A. Smith 1-(-3)
Vanderbilt – Nickson 20-118, Hawkins 15-84-1, Jennings 6-15, TEAM 2-(-4)

PASSING (COMP-ATT-INT-YARDS-TD)
Kentucky – R. Cobb 11-26-2-144-0
Vanderbilt – Nickson 15-27-0-155-3

RECEIVING (REC-YARDS-TD)
Kentucky – Adams 4-61, McCaskill 2-20, A. Smith 2-17, Lanxter 2-12, Grinter 1-34
Vanderbilt – Hawkins 4-49, Barden 4-20-1, Moore 3-51-2, Jennings 2-21, Smith 1-12, Walker 1-2

TACKLES

Tennessee 28 | Kentucky 10

November 29, 2008

SCORING SUMMARY

Kentucky	3	0	0	7	-	10
Tennessee	0	7	7	14	-	28

UK – Seiber 40 FG...5:00 1st qtr.
UT – Crompton 1 run (Lincoln kick)...0:00 2nd qtr.
UT – Moore 63 pass from Crompton (Lincoln kick)...13:44 3rd qtr.
UT – Creer 5 run (Lincoln kick)...14:24 4th qtr.
UT – Jones 2 run (Lincoln kick)...5:44 4th qtr.
UK – A. Smith 1 run (Seiber kick)...3:44 4th qtr.

TEAM STATISTICS

	KENTUCKY	TENNESSEE
First Downs	11	16
Rush Attempts/Net Rushing Yds.	38/96	53/210
Passing C/A/I	9/14/0	6/8/0
Net Passing Yards	97	101
Offensive Plays	52	61
Total Offense	193	311
Fumbles/Lost	0/0	0/0
Penalties/Yards	8/52	2/20
Punts/Average	6/38.2	4/44.8
Third-Down Conversions	4-of-13	6-of-14
Time of Possession	25:42	34:18

RUSHING (ATT-YDS-TD)
Kentucky – Dixon 15-48, R. Cobb 11-22, A. Smith 8-20-1, Conner 2-5, Allen 2-1
Tennessee – Jones 5-67-1, Foster 21-59, Berry 3-26, Creer 6-24-1, Hardesty 8-19, Crompton 8-17-1, team 2-(-2)

PASSING (COMP-ATT-INT-YDS-TD)
Kentucky – R. Cobb 4-7-0-23-0, Hartline 5-7-0-74-0
Tennessee – Crompton 6-8-0-101-1

RECEIVING (REC-YDS-TD)
Kentucky – A. Smith 2-21, Lanxter 2-1, Adams 1-35, Drake 1-18, Dixon 1-10, Adeyemi 1-8, Grinter 1-4
Tennessee – Jones 3-15, Moore 1-63-1, Foster 1-17, Warren 1-6

TACKLES
Kentucky – M. Johnson 12, Kelley 8, Harrison 7, Peters 6, A. Cobb 6, J. Williams 6

Kentucky 25 | East Carolina 19

Liberty Bowl, January 2, 2009

Scoring Summary

Kentucky «	0	3	13	9	25
East Carolina	3	13	3	0	19

Team Statistics

Team Statistics	Kentucky	East Carolina
First Downs	16	17
Rushes - Yards	37-106	31-101
Passing Yards	204	296
Return Yards	75	16
Passing (Att-Comp-Int)	31-19-1	38-18-0
Punts - Average	6-41.8	8-47.8
Fumbles - Lost	1-0	2-1
Penalties - Yards	4-35	4-17
Time of Possession	30:43	29:17

Individual Statistics

Passing

Kentucky	Att	Comp	Yards	Int	TD
Mike Hartline	31	19	204	1	1

East Carolina	Att	Comp	Yards	Int	TD
Patrick Pinkney	36	18	296	0	1

Rushing

Kentucky	Att	Yards	Average	TD
Tony Dixon	28	89	3.2	0
Alfonso Smith	5	28	5.6	0
John Conner	1	1	1.0	0
Mike Hartline	3	-12	-4.0	0

East Carolina	Att	Yards	Average	TD
Brandon Simmons	10	44	4.4	1
Norman Whitley	7	31	4.4	0
J.R. Rogers	3	23	7.7	0
Michael Bowman	1	3	3.0	0
Patrick Pinkney	10	0	0.0	0

Chapter Eighteen

Rich Brooks' Timeline, Awards, Records

Rich Brooks/ Coaching Experience

1963	Oregon State Assistant Freshman Coach
1964	Norte Del Rio HS Assistant Coach
1965-69	Oregon State Assistant Coach, Defensive Ends and Defensive Line
1970	UCLA Assistant Coach, Linebackers
1971-72	Los Angeles Rams (NFL) Assistant Coach, Special Teams and Fundamentals
1973	Oregon State Assistant Coach, Defensive Coordinator
1974-75	San Francisco 49ers (NFL) Assistant Coach, Defensive Backs and Special Teams
1976	UCLA Assistant Coach, Linebackers and Special Teams
1977-94	Oregon Head Coach
1995-96	St. Louis Rams (NFL) Head Coach
1997-2000	Atlanta Falcons (NFL) Assistant Head Coach, Defensive Coordinator
2003-present	Kentucky Head Coach

Rich Brooks/ Career Record as Head Coach
OREGON

1977	2-9	
1978	2-9	
1979	6-5	
1980	6-3-2	
1981	2-9	
1982	2-8-1	
1983	4-6-1	
1984	6-5	
1985	5-6	
1986	5-6	
1987	6-5	
1988	6-6	
1989	8-4	Independence Bowl (def. Tulsa 27-24)
1990	8-4	Freedom Bowl (lost to Colorado State 32-31)
1991	3-8	
1992	6-6	Independence Bowl (lost to Wake Forest 39-35)
1993	5-6	
1994	9-4	Rose Bowl (lost to Penn State 38-20)

NFL/ St. Louis Rams

1995	7-9
1996	6-10

KENTUCKY

2003	4-8	
2004	2-9	
2005	3-8	
2006	8-5	Music City Bowl (def. Clemson 28-20)
2007	8-5	Music City Bowl (def. Florida State 35-28)
2008	7-6	Liberty Bowl (def. East Carolina 25-19)

Chapter Nineteen

Signature Achievements of the Rich Brooks Era

Rich Brooks/ Coaching Honors

1979   Pacific-10 Coach of the Year

District IX Coach of the Year by the AFCA

Slats Gill Award as Sportsman of the Year in the state of Oregon

1989   Slats Gill Award as Sportsman of the Year in the state of Oregon

1994   National Coach of the Year (Bear Bryant Award) by the FWAA

National Coach of the Year by The Sporting News

National Coach of the Year by ESPN/Home Depot

Pacific-10 Coach of the Year

Slats Gill Award as Sportsman of the Year in the state of Oregon

1995   Inducted into the Independence Bowl Hall of Fame

2007   Blanton Collier Award from the Kentucky Chapter of NFL Players
          Association Alumni

University of Oregon Sports Hall of Fame

2009   Northern California Sports Hall of Fame

School Records

Season Average Attendance (69,434 fans/gm in 2008)

Single-game Attendance – 71,024 vs. Florida in 2007

Team Records Set During Brooks Era (2003-present)

Most offensive plays in a season - 1,013 in 2007

Most offensive plays in a game - 110 v. Tennessee, 2007 (four OTs)

Most first downs in a season - 335 in 2007

Most first downs in a game - 37 v. Tennessee, 2007

Most first downs in a game via passing - 27 v. Tennessee, 2007

Most points in a season - 475 in 2007

Most points scored in a quarter (tie) - 21 v. Vanderbilt, 2005

Best average yards per punt return in a season - 20.4 in 2006

Most kickoff return yards in a season - 1,394 in 2007

Most kickoff return yards in a game - 287 v. Idaho State, 2005

Best average kickoff return yards for a season - 26.40 in 2005

Most blocked kicks in a season - 9 in 2004

Most blocked PATs in a season (tie) - 2 in 2008, 2006, 2004

Most blocked PATs in a game (tie) - 2 v. Florida, 2006

Most blocked field goals in a game - 2 v. Ole Miss, 2005

Individual Records Set During Brooks Era (2003-present)

Most offensive plays in a career - Jared Lorenzen, 1,793 plays

Most total offensive yards in a career - Jared Lorenzen, 10, 637 yards

Most career passing attempts - Jared Lorenzen, 1,514 attempts

Most career pass completions - Jared Lorenzen, 862 completions

Most career touchdown passes - Andre Woodson, 79

Most TD passes in a season - Andre Woodson, 40 in 2007

Consecutive passes without an interception -
          Andre Woodson, 325 passes (2006-07)

Total net all-purpose yards - Derek Abney, 5,856 yards

Most net all-purpose yards in a season - Rafael Little, 1,982 (2005)

Best yards-per-play average for a career - Derek Abney, 14.83 yards

Most points scored by a kicker in a season - Lones Seiber, 99 (2007)

Most PATs in a season - Lones Seiber, 51, 2007

Most PATs attempted in a season - Lones Seiber, 54, 2007

Best PAT percentage for a season - Taylor Begley, 1,000 (2003-04)

Most consecutive PATs made in a career - Taylor Begley, 92 (2002-05)

Best average yards per punt return for a season -
        Rafael Little, 22.64 yards (2006)

Most punt return touchdowns for a career - Derek Abney, 6 TDs

Most kickoff returns for a career - Derek Abney, 95 (2000-03)

Most kickoff return yards for a career -
        Derek Abney, 2,315 yards (2000-03)

Most kickoff return yards in a game -
        Keenan Burton, 185 yards v. Louisville, 2006

Most pass breakups in a career - Trevard Lindley, 34   (2006-present)

Most blocked kicks in a career - Lonnell Dewalt, 7 (2004)

Most blocked kicks in a season - Lonnell Dewalt, 7 (2004)

Most blocked kicks in a game - 2 by Dewalt (2004) and
        Curtis Pulley (2005)

Most blocked PATs in a career - 2 by Matt Roark (2008-present) and
        Ray Fontaine (2002-05)

Most blocked PATs in a season - 2 by Matt Roark (2008)

Most blocked punts in a career - 2 by Jacob Tamme (2004-07),
        Andrew Hopewell (2002-04) and
        Dustin Williams (2001-04)

Most blocked field goals in a career - 6 by Lonnell Dewalt (2004)

Most blocked field goals in a season - 6 by Lonnell Dewalt (2004)

Most blocked field goals in a game -
        2 by Curtis Pulley (2005 v. Ole Miss)

SEC Statistical Champions in the Brooks Era

Derek Abney led SEC in kickoff return average (24.1) in 2003

Kentucky led SEC in punt return yards per game (17.2) in 2005

Rafael Little led SEC in punt return average (16.9) in 2005

Rafael Little led SEC in all-purpose yards per game (180.2) in 2005

Kentucky led SEC in passing yards per game (276.7) in 2006

Kentucky led SEC in turnover margin (plus 15) in 2006

Kentucky led SEC in punt return yards per game (20.4) in 2006

Andre Woodson led SEC in total offense (3,378 yards) in 2006

Kentucky led SEC in passing yards per game (287.9) in 2007

Kentucky led SEC in first downs per game (25.8) in 2007

Andre Woodson led SEC in passing yards (3,709) in 2007

Wesley Woodyard led the SEC in tackles (139) in 2007

Kentucky led SEC in kickoff return yards per game (26.4) in 2008

Kentucky led SEC in fewest sacks allowed (13) in 2008

Kentucky led SEC in kickoff coverage (47.3 yds/game allowed) in 2008

Tim Mastay led SEC in punting (45.2 yards) in 2008

Trevard Lindley led SEC in pass breakups (1.15/game) in 2008

First-Time Ever:
- Three bowl wins in three consecutive seasons (2006-08)
- First school in SEC history to have African-Americans serving as offensive and defensive coordinator at the same time
- Nine players earned nomination for Academic All-America (2004)
- Ranked in BCS poll (2007) eight-game winning streak in Commonwealth Stadium (2006-07)
- ESPN "College Football GameDay" visits UK campus for Florida game in 2007

First Time Since 1977:
- Back-to-back 8-win seasons (2007)
- Ranked in Associated Press top 10 (2007)

First Time Since 1964:
- Beat #1 ranked team (2007, defeated LSU 43-37 in 3 OT)
- Two wins over top 10 opponents (2007: #1 LSU, #9 Louisville)

First Time Since 1984:

- Won a bowl game (defeated Clemson 28-20 in 2006 Music City Bowl)

First Time Since 1951:

- Three-consecutive seven-win seasons (2008)

Oher Achievements

- Fourth quarterback in school history to pass for more than 3,000 yards (Andre Woodson)
- Sixth running back in school history to rush for more than 1,000 yards (Rafael Little)
- Third and fourth receivers in school history to surpass 1,000 yards (Keenan Burton and Stevie Johnson)
- Led nation with three players named to Academic All-America team (2005)
- Four different players (Rafael Little, Keenan Burton, Derrick Locke, David Jones)
- Have returned a kickoff for a touchdown in the Brooks era; the most in any coaching era at UK is two

Chapter Twenty

The
Rich Brooks
Foundation

THE RICH BROOKS FOUNDATION supports victims of cancer and other life-threatening diseases and their families. Organizations and causes that have received financial contributions from the RBF include:

- UK Childrens' Hospital
- Markey Cancer Center
- Cardinal Hill Hospital
- Prevent Child Abuse KY
- God's Pantry
- Ronald McDonald Charities
- Parkinson Support Center of Kentuckiana
- Big Brothers/Big Sisters of the Bluegrass
- Central Kentucky Riding for Hope
- Kidney Health Alliance
- Lexington Speech & Hearing Center
- Camp Horsin' Around
- Florence Crittendon Home
- KET

RICH TRADITION

There are a variety of levels at which fans can join the foundation. Supporters of the RBF are able to participate in events like: an invitation to a party celebrating the new recruiting class each February, a spring golf outing, a day at the races at historic Keeneland and an annual bourbon-and-cigar night at a local horse farm.

For more information, contact:
Will Southerland
Executive Director
Rich Brooks Foundation
859-987-6807
richbrooksfoundation.net

Portions of your donation may be tax deductible.

Photo provided by Denny Boom

Karen and Rich with Jorgi Boom, their daughter-in-law whose passing due to cancer prompted the formation of the Rich Brooks Foundation.

Chapter Twenty-One

Team Rosters and Photographs

2003 ROSTER

Number/Name	Position	Height	Weight	Class	Home Town
1 Mike Williams	SS	5-11	184	Jr.	Tallahassee, Fla.
2 Johnny Knight II	WR	6-0	176	RFr.	East Cleveland, Ohio
3 Andre Woodson	QB	6-5	225	Fr.	Radcliff, Ky.
4 Glenn Holt Jr.	WR	6-2	182	So.	Opalocka, Fla.
5 Arliss Beach	TB	6-0	200	So.	Ashland, Ky.
6 john Logan	WR	6-0	178	Fr.	Lexington, Ky.
7 Shane Boyd	QB	6-2	220	Jr.	Lexington, Ky.
8 Maurice Marchman	WR	6-0	190	Fr.	Louisville, Ky.
9 Durrell White	LB	6-3	234	Fr.	Middlesboro, Ky.
10 Tim "Tiger" Funderburk	FS	6-2	192	Sr.	Charlotte, N.C.
11 Manny Thurman	CB	5-11	178	Fr	Lexington, Ky.
12 Derek Abney	WR	5-10	175	Sr.	Mosinee, Wis.
13 Gerad Parker	WR	6-3	200	Jr.	Louisa, Ky
14 Dallas Greer	FS	6-1	193	Fr.	Pineville, Ky.
16 B.J. McCaslin	QB	6-2	196	Jr.	Libertyville, Ill.
17 Tommy Cook	WR	6-0	190	Jr.	Victoria, Texas
18 Jacob Tamme	TE	6-5	212	Fr.	Danville, Ky.
19 Keenan Burton	WR	6-2	180	Fr.	Louisville, Ky.
20 Dominic Lewis	FB	6-3	210	Fr.	Radcliff, Ky
21 Warren Wilson	CB	5-11	175	So.	Texas City, Texas
22 Jared Lorenzen	QB	6-4	260	Sr.	Ft. Thomas, Ky.
23 Eric Ogletree	SS	6-0	205	Jr.	Cincinnati, Ohio
24 Bo Smith	CB	6-0	180	So.	Owensboro, Ky.
25 Alexis Bwenge	TB	6-1	215	So.	St. Apollinaire, Quebec
26 Draak Davis	TB	5-7	170	So.	Vallejo, Calif
26 Martin McPherson	SS	6-2	180	Fr.	Somerset, Ky
27 Leonard Burress	CB	5-11	188	Sr.	Memphis, Tenn.
28 Randy Driver	SS	6-1	208	Fr	Glasgow, Ky.
29 J.J. Bennett	TB	5-7	170	Fr.	Cleveland, Ohio
30 Monquantae Gibson	TB	6-1	195	Jr.	Louisville, Ky.
31 Claude Sagaille	FS	5-10	185	Jr.	Evanston, Ill.
32 Earven Flowers	CB	5-10	185	Jr.	Temple, Texas
33 Andrew Hopewell	TB	5-10	196	So.	Harrodsburg, Ky.
34 Dennis Johnson	LB	6-0	230	Jr.	Vicksburg, MISS.
34 Joe Razzano	FB	6-0	235	Fr.	Milford, Ohio
35 Roger Williams	CB	6-0	185	Fr.	Rockmart. Ga.
36 Antoine Huffman	CB	6-0	175	So.	Jonesboro, Ga.
37 Keith Shelton Jr.	LB	6-3	224	Fr.	Memphis, Tenn.
38 Tewayne Willis	CB	5-7	155	Fr.	Hazard. Ky.
39 Andre Jones	CB	6-0	182	Fr.	Ft. Walton Beach. Fla
40 Justin Sprowles	FB	5-10	214	So.	Charlotte, N.C.
41 Cory Craig	LB	6-1	210	Fr.	Suburg, Ohio
41 Ronald "Rock" Johnson	FB	6-0	245	So.	Cleveland, Ohio
42 Muhammad Abdullah	FS	6-0	200	So.	Folkston, Ga.
43 Ryan Schumm	LB	6-7	235	Fr.	Crestwood, Ky.
44 Brandon King	FB	5-10	200	Fr.	Lawrenceville, Ga.
44 Jon Sumrall	LB	6-2	212	Jr.	Huntsville, Ala.
45 Lamar Mills	NT	6-1	275	Fr.	Slidell, La.
46 Joe Schuler	LB	6-3	240	Fr.	Evansville, Ind.
47 Eric Scott	TE	6-5	245	Fr.	Woodstock, Ga.
48 Terry Clayton	LB	6-1	210	Fr.	Olmstead, Ky.
49 Brad Booker	LB	6-2	238	So.	Smiths Grove, KY.

Number/Name	Position	Height	Weight	Class	Home Town
50 Raymond Fontaine	LB	6-4	215	So.	Ottawa, Ontario
51 Kamaal Ahmad	LB	6-2	238	Jr.	Edmonton, Okla.
52 Justin Haydock	LB	6-3	227	Jr.	Louisville, Ky.
53 Richard Gray	NT	6-1	242	So.	Sevierville, Tenn.
54 Jamie Saylor	LB	5-11	223	Sr.	Bremen, Ga.
55 Chad Anderson	LB	6-2	250	So.	Canton, Ohio
56 Kareem Reid	DE	6-5	263	RFr.	Coral Springs, Fla.
57 Hayden Lane	OT	6-6	270	RFr.	Larenceville, Ga.
58 Travis Slaydon	C	6-3	275	So.	Harlingen, Texas
59 Dustin Williams	LB	6-5	245	So.	Channahon, Ill.
60 Trai Williams	OT	6-4	275	RFr.	Franklin, Ky.
61 Matt Huff	OT	6-5	305	Jr.	Louisville, Ky.
62 Matt McCutchan	OG	6-3	280	So.	Lebanon, Ohio.
63 Ricky Abren	DL	6-3	265	Fr.	Hopkinsville, Ky.
63 William Blair	SN	6-0	226	RFr.	Brodhead, Ky.
64 Deion Holts	LB	6-2	248	So.	Bowling Green, Ky.
64 Cody Morehead	OT	6-5	295	Fr.	West Paducah, Ky.
65 Eric Klope	OT	6-8	310	Fr.	West Paducah, Ky.
65 Jose Walker	DE	6-4	242	RFr.	Harrodsburg. Ky.
66 Brandon Lesniewski	OG	6-2	301	Jr.	Highland, Ind.
67 Patrick Daly	OG	6-6	270	Fr.	Marietta, ga.
68 Jeremy Caudill	DE	6-3	295	Fr.	Martin, Ky.
69 Jason Dickerson	SN	6-2	228	RFr.	Elizabethtown, Ky.
70 Jason Rollins	OG	6-5	295	Jr.	Mt. Vernon, Ohio.
71 James Ferguson	OG	6-1	285	Fr.	Richmond, Ky.
72 Michael Aitcheson	OT	6-3	275	RFr.	Miami, Fla.
73 Antonio Hall	OT	6-5	302	Sr.	Canton, Ohio
74 Nate VanSickel	OC	6-2	289	Sr.	Moulton, Iowa.
75 Sylvester "Big Kat" Miller	OG	6-5	308	Sr.	Glennwood, Ill.
76 Joe Brady	OG	6-3	285	RFr.	Ft. Mitchell, Ky.
77 Casey Shurnate	C	6-3	245	Fr.	Louisville, Ky.
78 Nick Seitze	C	6-5	293	Sr.	Converse, Texas
79 Daniel Burnett	C	6-5	276	Jr.	Lexington, Ky.
82 Chris Bernard	WR	6-1	188	Sr.	Mission Viejo, Calif
83 Kurt Jackson	TE	6-5	245	So.	St. George, Utah
84 Jeremiah Drobney	TE	6-4	245	So.	Massillon, Ohio
85 DeMarcus Wood	WR	6-0	189	So.	Chesapeak, Va.
86 Win Gaffron III	TE	6-5	235	Sr.	Nashville, Tenn.
87 Bruce Fowler	TE	6-4	270	RFr.	New Orleans, La.
88 Daniel Hopewell	WR	5-10	187	Jr.	Harrodsburg. Ky.
89 Taylor Begley	K	6-0	202	So.	Danville, Ky.
89 Kurt Myers	TE	6-5	226	RFr.	Bradenburg, Ky.
90 Ronald Steuber	DE	6-5	240	Jr.	Hebron, Ky.
91 Trey Mielsch	DE	6-3	263	So.	El Maton, Texas
92 Anthony Thornton	P	6-1	197	Jr.	Louisville, Ky.
93 Sevin Sucurovic	P	6-2	195	Jr.	Tuzla, Bosnia
94 Travis Day	LB	6-3	250	Fr.	Columbus, Ga.
95 Clint Ruth	K	6-1	205	Jr.	White House, Tenn.
97 Russell Coodwin	LB	6-3	232	RFr.	Louisville, Ky.
98 Vincent "Sweet Pea" Burns	DE	6-2	264	Jr.	Lake Park, Ga
99 Ellery Moore	NT	6-3	290	Jr.	Massillon, Ohio

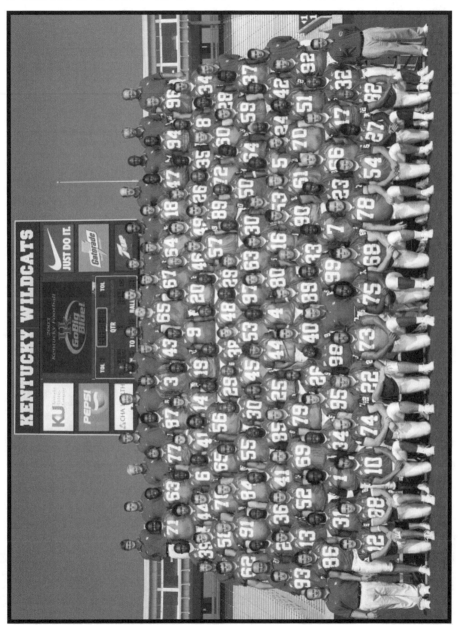

Photo by David Coyle/TeamCoyle

2004 ROSTER

Number/Name	Position	Height	Weight	Class	Home Town
1 Mike Williams	SS	5-11	190	Sr.	Tallahassee, Fla.
2* Marcus McClinton	FS	6-2	200	Fr.	Ft Campbell, Ky.
2* Scott Mitchell	WR	6-3	215	Jr.	League C-tyT, exas
3 Andre Woodson	QB	6-5	230	Fr.-RS	Radcliff, Ky.
4 Glenn Holt Jr.	WR	6-2	195	Jr.	Opalocka, Fla.
5 Alriss Beach	TB	6-0	220	Jr.	Ashland, Ky.
6 John Logan	WR	6-0	195	Fr.-RS	Lexington, Ky.
7 Shane Boyd	QB	6-2	220	Sr.	Lexington, Ky.
8 Lonnell Dewalt	WR	6-6	183	Fr.	Bowling Green, Ky.
9 Durrell White	LB	6-3	245	So.	Middlesboro, Ky.
10 Karl Booker	CB	6-1	180	So.	Chesapeake, W. Va.
11 Joe Joe Brown	QB	6-3	195	Fr.	Cordele, Ga.
12 Dicky Lyons Jr.	WR	5-11	190	Fr.	Neiv Orleans, La.
13 Gerald Parker	WR	6-3	205	Sr.	Louisa, Ky.
14 Dallas Greer	FS	6-1	195	Fr.-RS	Pineville, Ky.
15 Trey Barclay	QB	6-5	240	Sr.	Mayfield, Ky.
16 Wesley Woodyard	SS	6-1	200	Fr.	LaGrange, Ga.
17 Tommy Cook	WR	5-11	203	Sr.	Victoria, Texas
18 Jacob Tamme	TE	6-5	221	Fr.-RS	Dailvllle, Ky.
19 Kennan Burton	WR	6-2	195	So.	Louisville, Ky.
20 Dominic Lewis	TB	6-3	245	Fr.-RS	Radcliff, Ky.
21 Warren Wilson	CB	5-11	175	Jr.	Texas City, Texas
22 Rafael Little	TB	5-11	195	Fr.	Anderson, S C
23 Eric Sears	WR	6-0	180	Fr.-RS	Louisville, Ky.
24 Terrell Bankhead	TB	5-11	210	Jr.	San Diego, Calif.
25 Alexis Bwenge	FB	6-1	229	Jr.	St. Appollinaire, Quebec
26 Draak Davis	TB	5-7	177	Jr	Vallejo, Calif.
27 Gabriel Wallace	FB	6-1	232	Fr.	Ft Campbell, Ky.
28 Tony Dixon	TB	5-10	190	Fr.	Parrish, Ala.
29 Russ Throckmorton	SS	6-0	205	Sr.	Wytheville, Va.
30 Jarrell Williams	CB	5-11	180	Fr.	Cincinnali, Ohio
31 Claude Sagaille	SS	5-10	189	Sr.	Evanston, Ill.
32 Earven Flowers	CB	5-10	193	Sr.	Temple, Texas
33 Andrew Hopewell	TB	5-10	200	Jr.	Harrodsburg, Ky.
34 Dennis Johnson	LB	6-0	233	Jr.	Vicksburg, Miss.
35 Roger Williams	SS	6-0	198	Fr.-RS	Rockmart, Ga.
36 Antoine Huffman	CB	6-0	175	Jr.	Jonesboro, Ga.
37 Keith Shelton Jr.	LB	6-3	240	Jr.	Memphis, Tenn.
38 Clem Fennell	CB	5-8	176	Jr.	Ft Thomas, Ky.
39 Shomari Moore	CB	5-10	180	Fr.	Camden, N.J.
40 Justin Sprowles	FB	5-10	244	Jr.	Charlotte, N.C.
41 Rock Johnson	FB	6-0	245	Jr.	Cleveland, Ohio
42 Muhammed Abdullah	FS	6-0	205	Jr.	Folkston, Ga.
43 Ryan Schumm	LB	6-7	229	Fr.-RS	Crestwood, Ky.
44 Jon Sumrail	LB	6-2	220	Jr.	Hunstville, Ala.
45 Lamar Hillis	NT	6-1	280	So.	Slidell, La.
46 Joe Schuler	LB	6-3	250	Fr.-RS	Evansville, Ind.
47 Eric Mueller	LB	6-3	240	Fr.-RS	Hebron, Ky.
48 Terry Clayton	LB	6-1	232.	Fr.-RS	Olmstead, Ky.

Number/Name	Position	Height	Weight	Class	Home Town
49 Brad Booker	LB	6-2	238	So.	Smith's Grove, Ky.
50 Raymond Fontaine	LB	6-4	220	Jr.	Ottawa, Ontario
51 Kamall Ahmad	LB	6-2	250	Sr.	Edmond, Olda.
52 Justin Haydock	LB	6-3	232	Sr.	Louisville, Ky.
53 Richard Gray	NT	6-1	240	Jr.	Sevierville, Tenn.
54 B. Jay Parsons	DE	6-5	250	Jr.	Irvine, Calif.
55 Chad Anderson	LB	6-2	250	Jr.	Canton. Ohio
56 Tedd Bullock	LB	6-4	230	Fr.	McDermott, Ohio
57 Hayden Lane	OT	6-6	280	So.	Lawrenceville, Ga.
58 Travis Slaydon	C	6-3	270	So.	Harlingen, Texas
59 Dustin Willilams	LB	6-5	250	Jr.	Franklin, Ky.
60 Trai Williams	OG	6-4	275	So.	Louisville, Ky.
61 Matt Huff	OG	6-5	303	Sr.	Louisville, Ky.
62 Matt McCutchan	C	6-3	280	Fr.-RS	Lebanon, Ohio
63 Ricky Abren	NT	6-2	275	Fr.-RS	Hopkinsville, Ky.
64 Cody Morehead	OG	6-5	310	Fr.-RS	West Paducah. Ky.
65 Eric Klope	OT	6-8	315	Fr.-RS	West Paducah. Ky.
66 Jason Leger	NT	6-1	283	Fr.	Brodhead, Ky.
67 Patrick Daly	OT	6-6	290	Fr.-RS	Marietta. Ga.
68 Joe Brady	OG	6-3	300	So.	Ft Mitchell, Ky.
69 Aaron Miller	OT	6-6	295	Fr.	Grayson, Ky.
70 Jason Rollins	OG	6-5	290	So.	Mt. Vernon, Ohio
71 Michael Aitcheson	OT	6-3	285	So.	Miami. Fla.
73 Jason Dickerson	SN	6-1	245	So.	Elizabethtown, Ky.
74 Lee Martin	DE	6-4	235	Fr.	Owensboro, Ky.
75 Micah Jones	OG	6-4	317	Fr.	Mayfield, Ky.
76 Ernie Pelayo	OT	6-5	290	Jr.	Riverside, Calif.
77 Casey Shumate	C	6-3	270	Fr.-RS	Louisville, Ky.
78 Kane Hannaford	OT	6-6	340	Fr.	Palmetto. Fla.
80 Jeff Archer	SN	6-3	225	Jr.	Pittsburgh, Pa.
81 Joe Fischer	TE	6-7	245	Fr.	Latonia, Ky.
82 Kurt Jackson	TE	6-5	245	Jr.	St. George, Utah
84 Jeremiah Drobney	TE	6-4	248	Jr.	Massillon, Ohio
86 Maurice Marchman	WR	6-0	190	So.	Louisville, Ky.
87 Eric Scott	TE	6-5	265	Fr.-RS	Woodstock, Ga.
88 Jamir Davis	TE	6-3	250	Jr.	San Francisco, Calif.
89 Taylor Begley	K	6-0	198	Jr.	Danville, Ky.
90 Cedric Koger	LB	6-4	253	Jr.	Okeechobee. Fla.
91 Trey Mielsch	DE	6-3	280	Jr.	El Maton, Texas
92 Anthony Thornton	P	6-1	202	Sr.	Louisville, Ky.
93 Sevin Sucrovic	P	6-2	190	Sr.	Tulza, Bosnia
94 Travis Day	DE	6-3	264	Fr.-RS	Columbus, Ga.
95 Clint Ruth	K	6-1	205	So.	White House, Tenn.
96 Drew Roberts	LB	6-1	225	Fr.	Lexington, Ky.
97 Nii Adjei Oninku	DE	6-1	240	Fr.	Dayton, Ohio
98 Sweet Pea Burns	DE	6-2	268	Sr.	Lake Park, Ga.
99 Ellery Moore	DE	6-3	290	Sr.	Massillon, Ohio

* indicates duplicate numbers

Photo by David Coyle/TeamCoyle

2005 ROSTER

Number/Name	Position	Height	Weight	Class	Home Town
1 Scott Mitchel	WR	6-3	222	Sr.	League City, Texas
2 Marcus McClinton	FS	6-1	206	So.	Fort Campbell, Ky
3 Andre' Woodson	QB	6-5	230	So.	Radcliff, Ky
4 Glenn Holt, Jr.	WR	6-2	195	Sr.	Miami, Fla
5 Arliss Beach	TB	6-0	220	Sr.	Ashland, Ky
6 John Logan	WR	6-0	189	So.	Lexington, Ky
7 David Jones	CB	5-10	180	Fr.	Huddy, Ky
8 DeMoreo Ford	WR	5-11	175	Fr.	LaGrange, Ga
9 Durrell White	DE	6-3	245	Jr.	Middlesboro, Ky
9* Blake Bowling	QB	6-3	205	Fr.	Middlesboro, Ky
10 Karl Booker	FS	6-1	189	Jr.	Chesapeake, W. Va.
11* Ben McGrath	LB	6-2	240	Fr.	Milford, Ohio
11* Joe Joe Brown	QB	6-3	190	Fr.	Cordelle, Ga
12 Dicky Lyons, Jr.	WR	5-11	190	So.	New Orleans, La
13 Corion Dews-Houston	WR	6-3	232	Fr.	Marietta, Ga
14 Dallas Greer	SS	6-1	195	So.	Pineville Ky
15 Curtis Pulley	QB	6-4	200	Fr.	Hopkinsville, Ky
16* Wesley Woodyard	LB	6-1	200	So.	LaGrange, Ga
16* Divid Hamilton	QB	6-2	198	Jr.	Lexington, Ky
17 Tommy Cook	WR	6-0	206	Sr.	Victoria, Texas
18 Jacob Tamme	TE	6-5	234	So.	Danville, Ky
19 Keenan Burtan	WR	6-2	195	So.	Louisville, Ky
20 Dominic Lewis	DE	6-3	245	So.	Radcliff, Ky
21 Michael Schwindel	FS	6-4	210	Fr.	Hawesville, Ky
22 Rafael Little	TB	5-11	195	So.	Anderson, S.C.
23 Shomari Moore	CB	5-9	180	Fr.-RS	Camden N.J.
24* Terrell Bankhead	TB	5-11	214	Jr.	San Diego, Calif.
24* Bo Smith	CB	6-0	195	Jr.	Owensboro, Ky
25 Alexis Bwenge	FB	6-1	229	Sr.	St. Apollinaire, Quebec
26* Draak Davis	TB	5-7	186	Sr.	Valleio, Calif.
26* Martin McPherson	FS	6-2	200	So.	Sumerset, Ky
27 Thomas Flannery	FB	6-1	240	Fr.-RS	Olive Hill, Ky
29 Alfonso Smith	RB	6-2	190	Fr.	Louisville, Ky
30 Jerrell Williams	CB	5-11	185	Fr.-RS	Cincinnati, Ohio
31 Jordan Nevels	CB	6-0	170	Fr.	Fort Thomas, Ky
32 Trevard Lindley	CB	6-0	175	Fr.	Hiram, Ga
33 Kendall O'Donnell	SS	6-2	185	Fr.-RS	Evansville,Ind
34 Kenny Hawkins	WR	5-9	166	Fr.	Paducah, Ky
35 Roger Williams	SS	6-0	200	So.	Rockmart, Ga
36 Antoine Huffman	CB	6-0	175	Sr.	Jonesboro, Ga
37 Antoine Brown	TB	5-8	198	Fr.	Portge, Ind
38* John Conner	FB	6-0	228	Fr.	West Chester, Ohio
38* Clem Fennell	CB	5-8	180	Sr.	Fort Thomas, Ky
39 Adam Richey	SS	6-0	185	Fr.	Nicholasville, Ky
40 Justin Sprowles	FB	5-10	230	So.	Charlotte, N.C.
41 Ben Bates	LB	6-2	240	Fr.	Plain City, Ohio
42 Muhammad Abdullah	SS	6-0	205	Sr.	Folkston, Ga
43 Mikhail Mabry	LB	6-2	225	Fr.	Mililani, Hawaii
44 Tim Masthay	P/K	6-2	200	Fr.	Murray, Ky
45 Lamar Mills	DT	6-1	285	Jr.	Slidell, La
46 Joe Schuler	LB	6-3	240	So.	Evansville,Ind
47 Eric Mueller	DE	6-3	240	So.	Hebron, Ky

Number/Name	Position	Height	Weight	Class	Home Town
48 Terry Clayton	LB	6-1	232	So.	Olmstead, Ky
49 Zipp Duncan	DE	6-5	250	Fr.	Magnolia, Ky
50 Raymond Fontain	LB	6-4	225	Sr.	Ottawa, Ontario
51 Johnny Williams	LB	6-3	230	Fr.	Neptune Beach, Fla
52 Fatu Turituri	OT	6-3	290	Jr.	Amouli, American Samoa
53 Richard Gray	DT	6-1	240	Sr.	Sevierville, Tenn
54 B. Jay Parsons	DE	6-5	250	Sr.	Irvine, Calif
55 Sefu Mailau Blaylock	OT	6-4	315	Fr.	Salt Lake City, Utah
56 Braxton Kelley	LB	6-2	220	Fr.	LaGrange, Ga
57 Hayden Lane	OT	6-6	280	Jr.	Lawrenceville, Ga
58 Travis Slaydon	C	6-3	270	Jr.	Harlingen Texas
60* Trai Williams	OG	6-4	280	Jr.	Franklin, Ky
60* Johnnie Walker	LB	6-3	215	Fr.	Boswell, Ga
61 Jorge Gonzales	C	6-3	300	Fr.	Tampa, Fla
62 Matt McCutchan	C	6-3	295	Sr.	Lebanon, Ohio
63 Ricky Abren	DT	6-2	285	So.	Hopkinsville, Ky
64 Cody Morehead	OG	6-5	320	So.	West Paducah, Ky
65 Garry Ray Turner	OT	6-6	314	Fr.	Cadiz, Ky
66 Jason Leger	DT	6-1	288	So.	Brodhead, Ky
67 Patrick Daly	OT	6-6	300	So.	Marietta, Ga
68 Michael Williams	OT	6-6	280	Fr.	Richmond, Ky
69 Austin Moss	DE	6-1	235	Fr.	Hopkinsville, Ky
70 Zach Hennis	OT	6-8	325	Fr.	Plain City, Ohio
71 James Alexander	OT	6-5	250	Fr.	Atlanta, Ga
72 Michael Aitcheson	OG	6-3	290	Jr.	Miami, Fla
73 Jason Dickerson	SN	6-1	250	Jr.	Elizabethtown, Ky
74 Joe Fischer	OT	6-6	250	Fr.-RS	Latonia, Ky
75 Micah Jones	OG	6-4	320	So.	Mayfield, Ky
76 Ernie Pelayo	OT	6-6	290	Sr.	Riverside, Calif
77 Casey Shumate	C	6-3	290	So.	Louisville, Ky
78 Christian Johnson	OT	6-4	315	Fr.	Fort Campbell, Ky
79 Garry Williams	OT	6-3	300	Fr.	Louisville, Ky
80 Jeff Archer	SN	6-3	225	Sr.	Pittsburgh, Pa
81 Cody Overby	WR	5-11	192	Fr.	Tampa, Fla
82 Tyler Sexton	TE	6-4	238	Fr.	Somerset, Ky
84 Jeremiah Drobney	TE	6-4	255	Sr.	Massillon, Ohio
85 Anthony Cecil	WR	6-0	187	Fr.	Hodgenville, Ky
86 Ross Bogue	TE	6-5	240	Fr.	Suwanee, Ga
87 Eric Scott	TE	6-5	265	So.	Woodstock, Ga
88 Jamir Davis	TE	6-3	250	Sr.	San Francisco, Calif
89 Taylor Begley	K	6-0	200	Sr.	Danville, Ky
90 Cedric Koger	DE	6-4	266	Sr.	Okeechobee, Fla
91 Trey Mielsch	DT	6-3	280	Sr.	El Maton, Texas
92 Kris Kessler	P/K	6-0	200	Jr.	Lake Mary, Fla
94 Travis Day	DE	6-3	260	So.	Columbus, Ga
95 Ventrell Jenkins	DT	6-2	265	Fr.	Columbia, S.C.
96 Tommy Brummett	P/K	6-2	210	Fr.-RS	St. Louis, Mo
97* J.J. Housley	K	5-10	186	Fr.-RS	Hazard, Ky
97* Nii Adjei Oninku	DE	6-1	245	Fr.-RS	Dayton, Ohio
98 Myron Pryor	DT	6-1	300	Fr.	Louisville, Ky
99 Brian Scott	K	5-11	184	So.	Morehead, Ky

* indicates duplicate numbers

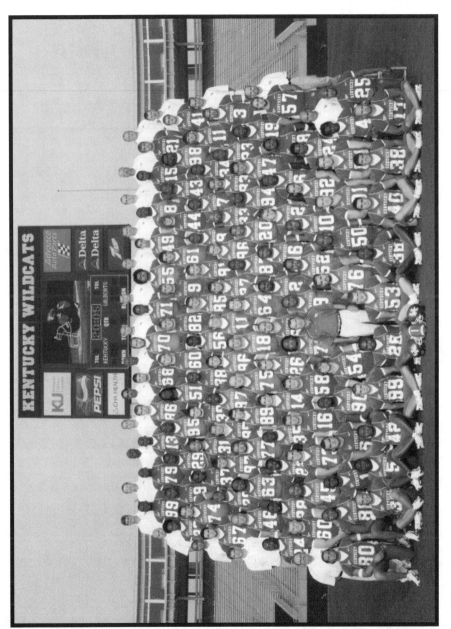

Photo by David Coyle/TeamCoyle

2006 ROSTER

Number/Name	Position	Height	Weight	Class	Home Town
1 Will Fidler	QB	6-4	205	Fr.	Henderson, Ky.
2 Marcus McClinton	FS	6-1	210	So.	Ft. Campbell, Ky.
3 Andre Woodson	QB	6-5	232	Jr.	Radcliff, Ky.
4 Micah Johnson	LB	6-2	255	Fr.	Ft. Campbell, Ky.
5 Mike Hartline	QB	6-6	190	Fr.	Canton, Ohio
6 John Logan	WR	6-0	189	Jr.	Lexington, Ky.
7 David Jones	WR	5-10	185	So.	Red Jacket, W. Va.
8 DeMoreo Ford	WR	5-10	189	So.	LaGrange, Ga.
9 Durrell White	LB	6-3	260	So.	Middlesboro, Ky.
10 Karl Booker	CB	6-1	190	Sr.	Chesapeake, W.Va.
11* Ben McGrath	LB	6-2	230	So.	Milford, Ohio
11* Joe Joe Brown	WR	6-3	195	So.	Cordele, Ga.
12 Dicky Lyons, Jr.	WR	5-11	190	So.	New Orleans, La.
13 Steve Johnson	WR	6-3	198	Jr.	San Francisco, Calif.
14* Rocco Maraoas	QB	6-1	200	Sr.	Canton, Ohio
14* Dallas Greer	QB	6-1	195	Jr.	Pineville, Ky.
15 Curtis Pulley	FS	6-4	200	So.	Hopkinsville, Ky.
16 Wesley Woodyard	LB	6-1	212	Jr.	LaGrange, Ga.
17 E.J. Adams	WR	6-0	194	Fr.	Snellville, Ga
18 Jacob Tamme	TE	6-5	240	Jr.	Danville, Ky.
19 Keenan Burton	WR	6-2	195	Jr.	Louisville, Ky.
20 Dominic Lewis	DE	6-3	258	Jr.	Radcliff, Ky.
21 Michael Schwindel	SS	6-2	210	Fr-RS	Hawesville, Ky.
22 Rafael Little	TB	5-10	188	Jr.	Anderson, S.C.
23 Shomari Moore	CB	5-9	190	So.	Camden, N.J.
24 Terrell Bankhead	FB	5-11	220	Sr.	San Diego, Calif.
25 Ahmad Grigsby Jr.	CB	6-0	195	Sr.	Long Beach, Calif.
26* Terrence Jones	WR	6-2	183	Jr.	Atlanta, Ga.
26* Martin McPherson	FS	6-2	200	Jr.	Somerset, Ky.
27 Ashton Cobb	SS	6-0	205	Fr.	Aliquippa, Pa.
28 Tony Dixon	TB	5-9	203	So.	Parrish, Ala.
29 Alfonso Smith	TB	6-1	190	Fr-RS	Louisville, Ky.
30 Jarrell Williams	CB	5-11	180	So.	Cincinnati, Ohio
31 Jordan Nevels	FS	5-10	175	Fr-RS	Ft. Thomas, Ky.
32 Trevard Lindley	CB	6-0	175	Fr-RS	Hiram, Ga.
33 Antoine Brown	TB	5-9	195	So.	Portage, Ind.
33* Calvin Harrison	FS	6-1	190	Fr.	Columbia, S.C.
34 Paul Warford	CB	5-11	195	Fr.	Richmond, Ky.
35 Roger Williams	SS	6-0	210	Jr.	Rockmart, Ga.
36 Lones Seiber	K	5-8	180	Fr.	Knoxville, Tenn.
37* Patrick Barnette	LB	6-1	206	So.	Eatontown, N.J.
37* Trey Bowland	TB	5-10	190	Fr.	Knoxville, Tenn.
38 John Conner	FB	5-10	233	Fr-RS	West Chester, Ohio
39* Adam Richey	SS	5-11	181	So.	Nicholasville, Ky.
39* Jimmy Chaffin	TB	5-10	175	Fr.	Gray, Ky.
40 Maurice Grinter	FB	5-10	250	Fr.	Louisville, Ky.
41 Ben Bates	FB	6-3	230	Fr-RS	Plain City, Ohio
43 Mikhail Mabry	LB	6-2	235	So.	Mililani, Hawaii
44 Tim Masthav	P/K	6-2	200	So.	Murray, Ky.
45 Lamar Mills	DT	6-1	285	Sr.	Slidell, La.
46 Joe Schuler	LB	6-3	233	Jr.	Evansville, Ind.
47 A.J. Nance	LB	5-11	250	Fr.	Knoxville, Tenn.

Number/Name	Position	Height	Weight	Class	Home Town
48 Terry Clayton	LB	6-1	243	Jr.	Olmstead, Ky.
50 Sam Maxwell	LB	6-3	225	Fr.	Hartwell, Ga.
51 Johnny Williams	LB	6-3	235	So.	Neptune Beach, Fla.
52 Fatu Turituri	OG	6-3	290	Sr.	Amouli, American Samoa
53 Ricky Lumpkin	DE	6-4	260	Fr.	Clarksville, Tenn.
54 Brandon Thurmond	LB	6-2	200	Fr.	Rex, Ga.
55 Sefo Mailau Blaylock	OT	6-4	330	Fr-RS	Salt Lake City, Utah
56 Braxton Kelley	LB	6-0	226	So.	LaGrange, Ga.
57 Hayden Lane	OT	6-6	275	Sr.	Lawrenceville, Ga.
58 Travis Slaydon	SS	6-5	290	Sr.	Harlingen, Texas
59 Eric Scott	C	6-5	275	Jr.	Woodstock, Ga.
60 Trai Williams	OG	6-4	286	Sr.	Franklin, Ky.
61 Jorge Gonzalez	C	6-3	300	Fr-RS	Tampa, Fla.
62 Matt McCutchan	C	6-3	310	Sr.	Lebanon, Ohio
63 Ricky Abren	DT	6-2	285	Jr.	Hopkinsville, Ky.
64 Dustin Luck	OL	6-3	250	Fr.	Poole, Ky.
65 J.J. Helton	SN	6-3	229	Fr.	Franklin, Tenn.
68 Jason Leger	DT	6-1	282	Jr.	Brodhead, Ky.
68 Michael Williams	OG	6-6	290	Fr-RS	Richmond, Ky.
70 Zach Hennis	OT	6-8	310	Fr-RS	Plain City, Ohio
71 James Alexander	OT	6-5	281	So.	Atlanta, Ga.
72 Michael Aitcheson	OG	6-3	300	Sr.	Miami, Fla.
73 Jason Dickerson	SN	6-1	254	So.	Elizabethtown, Ky.
75 Micah Jones	OG	6-4	330	So.	Mayfield, Ky.
76 Justin Jeffries	OT	6-5	300	Fr.	Louisville, Ky.
77 Marcus Davis	OL	6-1	280	Fr.	Union, Ky.
78 Christian Johnson	OG	6-4	325	So.	Ft. Campbell, Ky.
79 Garry Williams	OT	6-3	283	So.	Louisville, Ky.
80 T.C. Drake	TE	6-6	230	Fr.	Bardstown, Ky.
81 Zipp Duncan	TE	6-5	250	Fr-RS	Magnolia, Ky.
82 Tyler Sexton	TE	6-2	254	Fr-RS	Somerset, Ky.
83 Michael Strickland	WR	6-2	190	Fr.	Marietta, Ga.
84 Darrell Stevens	WR	6-0	170	Fr.	Tampa, Fla.
85 Anthony Cecil	WR	6-0	187	Fr-RS	Hodgenville, Ky.
86 Ross Bogue	TE	6-5	235	Fr-RS	Suwanee, Ga.
88 Chris Goode	TE	6-4	220	Fr-RS	Tucker, Ga.
89 Sean Murphy	WR	6-4	195	Jr.	Big Stone Gap, Va.
90 Jammi Paris	DE	6-6	228	Fr.	Gifford, Fla.
91 Corey Peters	DT	6-3	278	Fr.	Louisville, Ky.
92* Josh Minton	DE	6-3	250	Fr.	Somerset, Ky.
92* Kris Kessler	P/K	6-0	186	Sr.	Lake mary, Fla.
93 Austin Moss	DT	6-0	240	Fr-RS	Hopkinsville, Ky.
94 Travis Day	DE	6-3	265	Jr.	Columbia, Ga.
95 Ventrell Jenkins	DT	6-2	280	So.	Columbia, S.C.
96 J.D. Craigman	DT	6-4	250	Jr.	Miami, Fla.
97* Nii Adjei Oninku	DE	6-1	245	So.	Dayton, Ohio
97* J.J. Housely	K	5-10	186	So.	Hazard Ky.
98 Myron Pryor	DT	6-1	300	So.	Louisville, Ky.
99* Jeremy Jarmon	DE	6-3	250	Fr-RS	Collierville, Tenn.
99* Brian Scott	K	5-11	190	Jr.	Morehead, Ky.

* indicates duplicate numbers

Photo by David Coyle/TeamCoyle

2007 ROSTER

Number/Name	Position	Height	Weight	Class	Home Town
1 Will Fidler	QB	6-4	220	Fr-RS	Henderso, Ky
2 Marcus McClinton	FS	6-1	210	Jr.	Fort Campbell, Ky.
3 Andre Woodson	QB	6-5	230	Sr.	Radcliff, Ky.
4 Micah Johnson	LB	6-2	255	So.	Fort Campbell, Ky.
5 Mike Hartline	QB	6-6	201	Fr-RS	Canton, Oh.
6 Taiedo Smith	DB	6-0	175	Fr.	Dunnellon, Fl.
7 David Jones	CB	5-10	185	Jr.	Red Jacket, Va.
8 DeMoreo Ford	WR	5-10	186	Jr.	LaGrange, Ga
9* Brandon Jackson	RB	5-11	202	Fr.	Eugene, Or.
9* Ryan Tydlacka	K/P	6-1	195	Fr.	Louisville, Ky.
10 Matt Lentz	QB	6-3	205	Fr.	Simpsonvile, SC
11 Greg Wilson	DB	6-2	185	Fr.	College Park, Ga.
12 Dicky Lyons Jr.	WR	5-11	190	Jr.	New Orleans, La.
13 Steve Johnson	WR	6-3	198	Sr.	San Francisco, Calif.
14 Anthony Mosley	WR	6-0	170	Fr.	Ellenwood, Ga.
15* Chris Drayton	DB	6-1	196	Fr	Evans, Ga.
15* Curtis Pulley	QB	6-4	200	Jr.	Hopkinsville, Ky
16 Wesley Woodyard	LB	6-1	212	Sr.	LaGrange, Ga.
17* E.J. Adams	CB	6-0	190	So.	Stone Mountain, Ga.
17* Tyler Sargent	QB	6-3	202	Fr.	Waynesville, Oh.
18 Jacob Tamme	TE	6-5	240	Sr	Danville, Ky.
19 Keenan Burton	WR	6-2	203	Sr	Louisville, Ky.
20 Dominic Lewis	DE	6-3	261	Sr.	Radcliff, Ky.
21 Michael Schwindel	LB	6-2	220	So.	Hawesville, Ky.
22 Rafael Little	TB	5-10	200	Sr.	Anderson, S.C.
23 Shomari Moore	CB	5-9	185	Jr.	Camden, N.J.
24 Randall Burden	DB	6-2	170	Fr.	LaGrange, Ga.
25 Ahmad Grigsby Jr.	CB	6-0	188	Jr.	Long Beach, Calif.
26* Terrence Jones	WR	6-2	192	Fr-RS	Atlanta, Ga.
26* Martin McPherson	FS	6-2	215	Sr.	Somerset, Ky.
27 Ashton Cobb	SS	6-0	205	So.	Aliquippa, Pa.
28 Tony Dixon	TB	5-9	203	Jr.	Parrish, Ala.
29 Alfonso Smith	TB	6-1	200	So.	Louisville, Ky.
30 Moncell Allen	RB	5-7	225	Fr.	New Orleans, La.
31 Jordan Nevels	FS	5-10	175	So.	Fort Thomas, Ky.
32 Trevard Lindley	CB	6-0	175	So.	Hiram, Ga.
33 Calvin Harrison	FS	6-1	200	So.	Columbia, S.C.
34 Paul Warford	CB	5-11	200	So.	Richmond, Ky.
35 Roger Williams	SS	6-0	204	Sr.	Rockmart, Ga.
36* Robbie McAtee	CB	5-10	175	Jr.	Louisville, Ky.
36* Lones Seiber	K	5-9	190	So.	Knoxville, Tenn.
37 Trey Bowland	TB	5-10	190	Fr-RS	Knoxville, Tenn.
38 John Conner	FB	5-11	228	So.	West Chester, Ohio
39* Antoine Brown	TB	5-9	196	Fr.	Portage, Ind.
39* Courtney Coffey	DE	5-10	226	Fr.	Spring Hill, Tenn.
40 Maurice Grinter	FB	6-3	250	So.	Louisville, Ky.
41 Derrick Locke	RB	5-10	180	Fr.	Hugo, Okla.
42 Chris Cessna	LB	6-4	220	Fr.	London, Ky.
43 Mikhail Mabry	LB	6-2	235	So.	Murray, Ky
44 Tim Masthay	P/K	6-2	185	Jr.	Pacolet, S.C.
45 Antwane Glenn	DE	6-4	245	Fr.	Tallahassee, Fla.
46 Ronnie Sneed	LB	6-2	235	Fr.	Knoxville, Tenn.
47 A.J. Nance	LB	5-11	250	So.	

Number/Name	Position	Height	Weight	Class	Home Town
48 Terry Clayton	LB	6-1	251	r.	Olmstead, Ky.
49 Antonio Thomas	DB	6-2	212	Fr.	Cowpens, S.C.
50 Sam Maxwell	LB	6-3	235	So.	Hartwell, Ga.
51 Johnny Williams	LB	6-3	240	Jr.	Neptune Beach, Fla.
52 Billy Joe Murphy	OL	6-7	275	Fr.	Gamaliel, Ky.
53 Ricky Lumpkin	DT	6-4	289	Fr-RS	Clarksville, Tenn.
54 Brandon Thurmond	LB	6-2	226	Fr-RS	Rex, Ga.
55 Brad Hart	SN	6-1	219	Fr-RS	Marion, Ky.
56 Braxton Kelley	LB	6-0	226	Jr.	LaGrange, Ga.
57 Jacob Dufrene	LB	6-2	215	Fr.	Cut Off, Ga.
58 Phillip Hibbard	OL	6-7	305	Fr.	Keavy, Ky.
59 Eric Scott	C	6-5	290	Sr.	Woodstock, Ga.
60* Dustin Luck	OG	6-3	250	So.	Poole, Ky.
60* Shane McCord	DL	6-3	271	Fr.	Hartwell, Ga.
61 Jorge Gonzalez	C	6-3	300	So.	Tampa, Fla.
62 Greg Meisner	DE	6-2	240	Fr.	Greensburg, Pa.
63 Jake Lanefski	OL	6-4	265	Fr.	Mobile, Ala.
64 Josh Winchell	OG	6-3	325	Jr.	Southhaven, Miss.
65 J.J. Helton	SN	6-2	230	Fr-RS	Franklin, Tenn.
67 Joe Scott	DL	6-2	250	Fr.	Louisville, Ky.
68 Michael Williams	OG	6-6	294	So.	Richmond, Ky.
69 B.J. Wiedemann	DE	6-1	242	Fr-RS	Rineyville, Ky.
70 Stuart Hines	OL	6-5	275	Fr.	Bowling Green, Ky.
71 James Alexander	OT	6-5	283	So.	Atlanta, Ga.
72 Zipp Duncan	OG	6-2	285	Jr.	Magnolia, Ky.
73 Jess Beets	OT	6-6	285	Jr.	Dove Canyon, Calif.
74 Joe Fischer	OL	6-5	310	Fr.	Latonia, Ky.
75 Brad Durham	OT	6-6	310	Fr.	Mount Vernon, Ky.
76 Justin Jeffries	C	6-1	280	Fr-RS	Louisville, Ky.
77 Marcus Davis	OG	6-4	325	Jr.	Union, Ky.
78 Christian Johnson	OT	6-3	300	So.	Fort Campbell, Ky.
79 Garry Williams	TE	6-6	235	So.	Louisville, Ky.
80 T.C. Drake	WR	6-3	187	Jr.	Bardstown, Ky.
81 Kyrus Lanxter	TE	6-2	242	Sr.	Alcoa, Tenn.
82 Tyler Sexton	WR	6-3	185	Fr.	Somerset, Ky.
83 Jonathan Gholson	DE	6-2	250	Fr	Louisville, Ky.
84 Charles Mustafa	WR	6-3	250	Fr.	College Park, Ga.
85 Anthony Cecil	WR	6-0	191	So.	Hodgenville, Ky.
86 Ross Bogue	TE	6-5	240	So.	Suwanee, Ga.
87 Andre Henderson	WR	6-6	214	Fr-RS	Lexington, Ky.
88 Chris Goode	TE	6-4	240	Fr-RS	Tucker, Ga.
89 Sean Murphy	WR	6-4	190	Sr.	Big Stone Gap, Va.
90 Jamil Paris	DE	6-6	235	So.	Gifford, Fla.
91 Corey Peters	DT	6-3	290	So.	Louisville, Ky.
92 Josh Minton	DE	6-3	250	Fr-RS	Somerset, Ky.
93 Austin Moss	DT	6-0	250	So.	Hopkinsville, Ky.
94 Travis Day	DT	6-3	260	Sr.	Columbus, Ga.
95 Ventrell Jenkins	DT	6-2	285	Jr.	Columbia, S.C.
96 J.D. Craigman	DT	6-4	280	Sr.	Miami, Fla.
97* J.J. Housley	K	5-10	186	Jr.	Hazard, Ky.
97* Nii Adjei Oninku	DE	6-1	248	Jr.	Dayton, Ohio
98 Myron Pryor	DT	6-2	310	Jr.	Louisville, Ky.
99 Jeremy Jarmon	DE	6-3	268	So.	Collierville, Tenn.

* indicates duplicate numbers

Photo by David Coyle/TeamCoyle

2008 ROSTER

Number/Name	Position	Height	Weight	Class	Home Town
1 Will Fidler	QB	6-4	216	So.	Henderson, Ky.
2 Marcus McClinton	FS	6-1	210	Sr.	Fort Campbell, Ky.
3 Matt Roark	WR	6-6	195	Fr.	Acworth, Ga.
4 Micah Johnson	LB	6-2	250	Jr.	Fort Campbell, Ky.
5 Mike Hartline	QB	6-6	204	So.	Canton, Ohio
6 Taiedo Smith	FS	6-0	182	Fr.-RS	Dunnellon, Fla.
7 David Jones	CB	5-10	185	Sr.	Red Jacket, W. Va.
8 DeMoreo Ford	WR	5-10	186	Jr.	LaGrange, Ga.
9 Ryan Tydlacka	K/P	6-1	195	Fr.-RS	Louisville, Ky.
10 Matt Lentz	SS	6-3	209	Fr.-RS	Simpsonville, S.C.
11 Greg Wilson	SS	6-1	195	Fr.-RS	College Park, Ga.
12 Dicky Lyons Jr	WR	5-11	190	Sr.	New Orleans, La.
13 Eric Adeyemi	WR	6-0	170	Fr.	Miami, Fla.
14 Anthony Mosley	CB	6-0	176	Fr.-RS	Ellenwood, Ga.
15 Tyler Sargent	QB	6-4	208	Fr.-RS	Waynesville, Ohio
16 DeAunte Mason	QB	6-3	215	Fr.	Nashville, Tenn.
17 E.J. Adams	WR	6-0	197	Jr.	Stone Mountain, Ga.
18 Randall Cobb	QB	5-11	185	Fr.	Alcoa, Tenn.
19 Winston Guy	FS	6-1	205	Fr.	Lexington, Ky.
20 Derrick Locke	TB	5-9	180	So.	Hugo, Okla.
21 Michael Schwindel	LB	6-2	220	Jr.	Hawesville, Ky.
22 Aaron Boyd	WR	6-3	210	Fr.	Lexington, Ky.
23 Shomari Moore	CB	5-9	185	Sr.	Camden, N.J.
24 Randall Burden	CB	6-0	170	Fr.-RS	LaGrange, Ga.
25 Ahmad Grigsby Jr	CB	6-0	188	Sr.	Long Beach, Calif.
27 Ashton Cobb	SS	6-0	208	Jr.	Aliquippa, Pa.
28 Tony Dixon	TB	5-9	203	Sr.	Parrish, Ala.
29 Alfonso Smith	TB	6-1	204	Jr.	Louisville, Ky.
30 Moncell Allen	FB/TB	5-7	225	So.	New Orleans, La.
32 Trevard Lindley	CB	6-0	175	Jr.	Hirma, Ga.
33 Calvin Harrison	FS	6-1	197	Jr.	Columbia, S.C.
35 Cartier Rice	DB	5-10	180	Fr.	Duncan, S.C.
36* Lones Seiber	K/P	5-9	182	Jr.	Knoxville, Tenn.
36* Robbie McAtee	CB	5-10	175	Sr.	Louisville, Ky.
37 Trey Bowland	TB	5-10	190	So.	Knoxville, Tenn.
38 John Conner	FB	5-11	230	Jr.	West Chester, Ohio
39 William Johnson	LB	6-3	200	Fr.	Nashville, Tenn.
40* Maurice Grinter	TE	6-3	253	Jr.	Louisville, Ky.
40* Daryl Faulkner	CB	5-9	174	So.	Memphis, Tenn.
41 Danny Trevathan	LB	6-1	210	Fr.	Leesburg, Fla.
42 Chris Cessna	LB	6-4	224	Fr.-RS	London, Ky.
43* Mikhail Mabry	LB	6-2	235	Jr.	West Paducah, Ky.
43* Stephen Ball	FB	5-10	224	So.	Cowpens, S.C.
44 Tim Masthay	P/K	6-2	203	Sr.	Murray, Ky.
45 Antwane Glenn	DT	6-3	270	Fr.-RS	Pacolet, S.C.
46 Ronnie Sneed	LB	6-2	235	Fr.-RS	Tallahassee, Fla.
47* A.J. Nance	FB	5-11	241	Jr.	Knoxville, Tenn.
47* Matt Ramsey	CB	6-3	205	So.	Artemus, Ky.
48 Jayce Long	WR	6-0	187	So.	West Paducah, Ky.
49 Antonio Thomas	LB	6-1	224	Fr.-RS	Cowpens, S.C.
50 Sam Maxwell	LB	6-3	228	Jr.	Hartwell, Ga.
51 Johnny Williams	LB	6-3	235	Sr.	Jacksonville, Fla.
52 Billy Joe Murphy	OT	6-6	292	Fr.-RS	Gamaliel, Ky.

Number/Name	Position	Height	Weight	Class	Home Town
53 Ricky Lumpkin	DT	6-4	289	So.	Clarksville, Tenn.
54 Brandon Thurmond	LB	6-2	226	So.	Rex, Ga.
55 Bret Hart	LS	6-1	218	So.	Marion, Ky.
56 Braxton Kelley	LB	6-0	230	Sr.	LaGrange, Ga.
57 Jacob Dufreme	LB	6-2	215	So.	Cut Off, La.
58 Sean Stackhouse	OG	6-4	255	Fr.	Jacksonville, Fla.
59* Dave Ulinksi	OL	6-4	295	Fr.	Louisville, Ky.
59* Jon Thomas	LS	5-10	224	Fr.-RS	Richmond, Ky.
60* Shane McCord	DT	6-2	256	Fr.-RS	Louisville, Ky.
60* Dustin Luck ·	OG	6-3	280	So.	Louisville, Ky.
61 Jorge Gonzalez	C	6-3	300	Jr.	Rineyville, Ky.
62 Greg Meisner	DE	6-1	233	Fr.-RS	Bowling Green, Ky.
63 Jake Lanefski	C	6-4	278	Fr.-RS	Atlanta, Ga.
64 Osaze Idumwonyi	OL	6-1	285	Fr.	Cedar Hill, Texas
65 J.J. Helton	LS	6-3	230	So.	Franklin, Tenn.
66 Chandler Burden	DE	6-5	290	Fr.	Blue Ash, Ohio
67 Joe Scott	DT	6-1	280	Fr.-RS	Louisville, Ky.
68* Michael Williams	OG	6-6	294	Jr.	Richmond, Ky.
68* Luke McDermott	DT	6-1	256	Fr.-RS	Louisville, Ky.
69* Matt Smith	C	6-4	280	Fr.	Louisville, Ky.
69* B.J. Wiedemann	DE	6-4	242	So.	Rineyville, Ky.
70 Stuart Hines	OT	6-4	280	Fr.-RS	Bowling Green, Ky.
71 James Alexander	OT	6-5	295	Jr.	Atlanta, Ga.
72 Zipp Duncan	OG	6-5	290	Jr.	Magnolia, Ky.
73 Jess Beets	OG	6-2	285	Sr.	Dove Canyon, Calif.
74 Trevino Woods	OT	6-5	265	Fr.	Athens, Ga.
75 Brad Durham	OT	6-4	310	So.	Mount Vernon, Ky.
76 Justin Jeffries	OT	6-6	310	Jr.	Louisville, Ky.
77 Marcus Davis	C	6-1	280	So.	Union, Ky.
78 Christian Johnson	OG	6-4	325	Sr.	Fort Campbell, Ky.
79 Garry Williams	OT	6-3	300	Sr.	Louisville, Ky.
80 T.C. Drake	TE	6-6	242	Jr.	Bardstown, Ky.
81 Kyrus Lanxter	WR	6-2	193	So.	Alcoa, Tenn.
82 Tyler Sexton	TE	6-2	242	Jr.	Somerset, Ky.
83* E.J. Fields	WR	6-2	190	Fr.	Frankfort, Ky.
83* Jonathan Gholson	WR	6-2	185	Fr.-RS	Louisville, Ky.
84 Charles Mustafaa	DT	6-3	258	Fr.-RS	College Park, Ga.
85 Gene McCaskill	WR	6-0	175	Fr.	Chester, S.C.
86 Ross Bogue	TE	6-5	245	Jr.	Suwanee, Ga.
87 Andre Henderson	TE	6-6	226	So.	Lexington, Ga.
88 Nik Brazley	WR	5-9	170	Fr.-RS	Louisville, Ky.
89 Brian Murphy	LB	6-0	211	Fr.-RS	Big Stone Gap, Va.
91 Corey Peters	DT	6-3	290	Jr.	Louisville, Ky.
92 Josh Minton	DE	6-3	254	So.	Somerset, Ky.
93 Austin Moss	DE	6-0	250	Jr.	Hopkinsville, Ky.
94 Taylor Wyndham	DE	6-4	210	Fr.	Swansea, S.C.
95 Ventrell Jenkins	DE	6-2	285	Sr.	Columbia, S.C.
96 Collins Ukwu	DE	6-4	220	Fr.	La Vergne, Tenn.
97* Nii Adjei Oninku	DE	6-1	254	Sr.	Dayton, Ohio
97* J.J. Housley	K/P	5-10	186	Jr.	Hazard, Ky.
98 Myron Pryor	DT	6-1	310	Sr.	Louisville, Ky.
99 Jeremy Jarmon	DE	6-3	277	Jr.	Collierville, Tenn.
* indicates duplicate numbers					

TOM LEACH

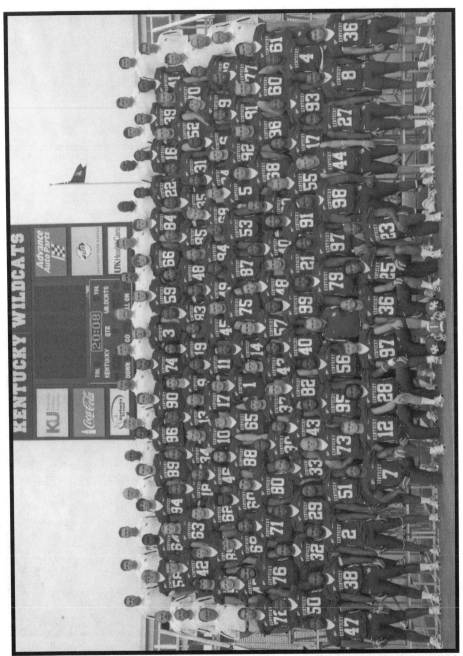

2008 TEAM PHOTOGRAPH

Photo by David Coyle/TeamCoyle

Chapter Twenty-Two

Photos

Photo by Carolyn Towler

Carolyn Towler gave Coach Brooks some bread at the 2008 Kentucky Women's Football Clinic.

The ESPN Gameday bus brought the hosts to the UK campus for the first-time ever in 2007.

UK fans greeted the ESPN Gameday crew with the "We Believe" mantra.

Brooks' attire for the August and September practices usually includes this straw hat.

Brooks works with punter Kris Kessler (92) on his technique during a practice session.

Photo by Tom Leach

Photo by Victoria Graff

Photo by Joshua Yeary

Joshua Yeary (self-described biggest Cat fan in Bell County) with Coach Brooks at Fan Day 2008

New UK men's basketball coach John Calipari talked with Brooks before the 2009 spring Blue-White game.

When he thinks a call has been missed, Brooks won't hesitate to let an official know about it.

Photo by Victoria Graff

Photo by Victoria Graff

Brooks and the Wildcats arrive at the 2006 Music City Bowl.

Photo by Victoria Graff

Photo by Victoria Graff

It took fans a few extra seconds to realize the game was really over and their Cats had upset the nation's number one team.

Photo by Dick Gabriel

Brooks (right) talks with Tom Leach on the postgame radio show on the Big Blue Sports Network after Kentucky's 2006 Music City Bowl win.

Photo provided by Atlanta Falcons

Defensive coordinator Brooks coaches up his unit during the Atlanta Falcons' 1998 Super Bowl season.

Coach Brooks,

I originally planned on getting a card to accompany the Maker's bottle, but I realized no card would provide me with adequate space for writing, so I trust you won't begrudge me for settling for this piece of computer paper! Anyway, as my career at UK has now come to a close I must tell you what a pleasure and honor it has been to play for you and while I know this letter won't do justice to the gratitude I feel, I suppose it will have to suffice.

I remember the summer before my senior season of high school football when I came on campus to kick & punt during a high school passing league. It must have rained the night before because the ground was fairly wet. You were tossing snaps to me from about 8-10 yards away up on field one and after I had punting for a little while some mud had accumulated on the bottom of my cleats. Then it happened; I caught the ball, took my steps to punt, and when my leg came up I spattered mud all over your white UK polo shirt. I thought surely my chances at coming to UK were dashed!!! A little while later, we moved to the old Astroturf field where the parking lot is now. The mud problem should clearly have not been an issue once we moved to that field, but lo and behold I nailed you with a clump of dirt again! I thought maybe I should go ahead and ask Danno just to escort me to my vehicle! Instead, we just kept on punting.

I tell this story because it's somewhat humorous and it's fun to rehash old memories, but also because I feel like it is a parallel to my career under your direction. That is to say, despite the frustrations I caused and mistakes I made, you were not deterred and you stuck with me & continued to believe in me.

When I arrived on campus in the summer of 2005, this time for good, I couldn't have been much more raw as far as being a punter is concerned. On signing day the previous February, I passed up an opportunity to kick at Purdue because first, I wanted to play for UK and help change the face of the program, but also because I trusted you and Coach Ortmayer that I could become an SEC caliber punter and that was something I wanted to do. As that first fall camp unfolded I remember struggling mightily until I finally began to catch on a little bit towards the end camp leading up to the Louisville game. My struggles would continue though and that entire freshman campaign seemed like a roller coaster; as soon as I would bomb a punt I would shank one. I remember being horribly nervous each time I took the field that season and wondering whether or not I could handle four years or if things would ever get better. Sophomore year came around and my first two weeks of fall camp could hardly have been worse... and my attitude wasn't much better. I had basically given up on myself as a punter and I wanted to quit. Although I did try to work hard, I was throwing a pity party in my head and it showed on the practice field. In the midst of that time I remember you approached me on the practice field and asked me if I even liked what I was doing. I answered yes though I knew that was a lie, but I truly appreciated the concern you showed. It was another confirmation to me that I wasn't just an X on a chalkboard, but that there was a human element to the whole deal and at that time nothing could have helped me more. Another inconsistent season followed for me, though perhaps not quite as inconsistent as the first, and my nerves were still unsettled, but the team responded well after the LSU debacle and we found ourselves in Nashville in late December. I worked hard to improve over that month of bowl practice, and I think I did make fundamental strides, but it did not pay off in the Music City Bowl as far as punting goes. Luckily, or rather ingeniously, you took the initiative to call "raider" late in the first half and we executed the fake and scored a touchdown on the next play. I remember being relieved in the timeout huddle when you called the fake, because I was much less sure that I would be able to get the ball off, let alone hit a solid punt, than I was to execute the throw. My first two years had come to a close with that momentous win. Junior year came quickly and I had more confidence and more excitement going into camp than I had the previous two years. Plus I knew I had competition coming in. As I improved in the techniques you had taught me, I found myself having a pretty solid fall camp and drastically improving on kickoffs. But after I punted horribly against Kent State, all the doubts I had about my ability as a punter came crashing down again. The next week leading up to the huge Louisville game, I had a bad week of practice, a bad attitude on the practice field, and quite literally I had given up on myself as a punter. In fact, that Friday night in the hotel, I was strongly considering coming to your office to ask if I could just kickoff and hold because those were what I saw as my strengths and how I could help the team. I didn't punt particularly well against UL, but we won and my average was good (due to a bad decision by UL's returner) so I decided to keep trying (I couldn't stand to let you down). Then things began to click a little bit against Arkansas and I had a few successive games in which I punted fairly well. But I relapsed some at the end of the season again against Vandy and UGA. The season ended well again though with another huge win over FSU! Senior season arrived and though I had some success as a punter you kept me on my toes and trying to improve every single day, and that helped me to keep my focus through every single game. I am exceedingly grateful to have had you as my coach for many reasons, but one of the things I am most grateful is that through the inconsistencies, continual mistakes, and periods of a poor attitude you stuck with me and were always in my corner. Even more so (perhaps what I am most grateful for) you continued to believe in me when I didn't believe in myself.

One of the things I have regretted most about my career and something that has truly bothered me over the past 4 years is to know how much headache and heartache I caused you (in particular those first 2 years). I felt all the same headache and heartache about my poor performances, whether they were in practice or games, and I carried it with me everyday, but the fact that I knew how much time and energy you invested in me and at times you weren't seeing much in the way of returns really amplified the pain I felt. So when I had a fairly solid senior year, and won the 1st Team All-SEC Award, the first thing I thought was this is Coach Brook's award and I wanted to give you the plaque when I received it. If I thought you would accept the plaque I would offer it, but I'll save us the awkward moment! But coach, I would never have gotten to where I am today if it wasn't for you and so I just want you to know how blessed I feel to have played under you. I still know that I need to improve, and that I never quite became the player you thought I could be, but I will continue to try to realize the potential you believe I have, and because of you I am beginning to believe that maybe I can. (If only I can keep the ball outside and swing fully every time!!! It seems so simple, why is it so hard!?) Even if I never get to punt or kick competitively again, your belief in me and your persistence, patience, and integrity have made a mark on me and I hope to emulate those characteristics throughout my life. Thank you for everything you have done for me and every opportunity you have afforded me, I look forward to staying in touch.

Tim Mastay

Index